FALLING INTO FAITH
A JOURNEY TO FREEDOM

Donna Grant Wilcox, MTH, CBT, PhD

Copyright © 2018 Donna Grant Wilcox, MTH, CBT, PhD.

All rights reserved. No part of this book may be used or reproduced by any means, graphic, electronic, or mechanical, including photocopying, recording, taping or by any information storage retrieval system without the written permission of the author except in the case of brief quotations embodied in critical articles and reviews.

WestBow Press books may be ordered through booksellers or by contacting:

WestBow Press
A Division of Thomas Nelson & Zondervan
1663 Liberty Drive
Bloomington, IN 47403
www.westbowpress.com
1 (866) 928-1240

Because of the dynamic nature of the Internet, any web addresses or links contained in this book may have changed since publication and may no longer be valid. The views expressed in this work are solely those of the author and do not necessarily reflect the views of the publisher, and the publisher hereby disclaims any responsibility for them.

Any people depicted in stock imagery provided by Getty Images are models, and such images are being used for illustrative purposes only.
Certain stock imagery © Getty Images.

Scripture quotations marked (NIV) are taken from the Holy Bible, New International Version®, NIV®. Copyright © 1973, 1978, 1984, 2011 by Biblica, Inc.™ Used by permission of Zondervan. All rights reserved worldwide. www.zondervan.com The "NIV" and "New International Version" are trademarks registered in the United States Patent and Trademark Office by Biblica, Inc.™

Scripture taken from the New King James Version®. Copyright © 1982 by Thomas Nelson. Used by permission. All rights reserved.

Scripture quotations marked (AMP) are taken from the Amplified Bible, Copyright © 1954, 1958, 1962, 1964, 1965, 1987 by The Lockman Foundation. Used by permission.

Scripture quotations are taken from the Holy Bible, New Living Translation, copyright ©1996, 2004, 2007, 2013, 2015 by Tyndale House Foundation. Used by permission of Tyndale House Publishers, Inc., Carol Stream, Illinois 60188. All rights reserved.

Scripture quotations taken from the New American Standard Bible® (NASB), Copyright © 1960, 1962, 1963, 1968, 1971, 1972, 1973, 1975, 1977, 1995 by The Lockman Foundation. Used by permission. www.Lockman.org

Scripture taken from the Holy Bible: International Standard Version®. Copyright © 1996-forever by The ISV Foundation. ALL RIGHTS RESERVED INTERNATIONALLY. Used by permission.

Scripture taken from the King James Version of the Bible.

ISBN: 978-1-9736-2253-6 (sc)
ISBN: 978-1-9736-2254-3 (hc)
ISBN: 978-1-9736-2252-9 (e)

Library of Congress Control Number: 2018902897

Print information available on the last page.

WestBow Press rev. date: 4/2/2018

There are very few people who can walk into a room and within seconds have everyone excited and smiling. Donna sheds a light that sparkles, creating a glow that flows from her to all she touches. She speaks through her heart and faith, which touches the soul of all who sees or hears her.

Dr. William Solomon, M.D.
Geriatric Medicine
Medical Director
Namaste Hospice ~ Denver Metro Area

As a part of Donna's family, I've been privileged to witness, and be a part of Donna's miraculous, restorative journey. Her life and story is an encouraging and challenging example to all of us. We overcome by the testimony of our faith! This is an inspiring testimony to that truth, and to the life changing power of Faith in God and His loving kindness to restore life, peace, and hope to our mind, body, and spirit. A must read!

Rev. David Grant
Assemblies of God Minister
Co-founder and Director of Project Rescue

As someone who, for several decades, has ministered to women who are on the journey to healing and health, I find Donna Wilcox's story uniquely inspiring and full of hope. Her honesty with her own brokenness and addictions makes her falling into faith and hope all the more compelling to read. I heartily recommend this book for women looking for hope and healing, whatever their area of struggle.

Dr. Beth Grant
Assemblies of God Minister
Co-founder and Director of Project Rescue

Donna Wilcox embodies the true meaning of character in every sense of the word. She sets a wonderful example for all of us on how to really "live" life. As a person who has sometimes struggled with faith, I can say that Donna has truly shown me its power. If only all of us could be as impervious to opposition and negativity. In whatever form you receive Donna's words of wisdom, heed them as they are truth delivered with true conviction and by a real example.

Julie Gentry
Director of Dispatch (and friend)

Donna's life has caused me to want to have more faith in God. Her story of holding on to God during the hardest of times has challenged me to do the same. As she shares her life, faith and perseverance, you will be inspired to trust God more.

Dan Baumann
Author & International Speaker,
Imprisoned in Iran, A Beautiful Way

Though he may stumble, he will not fall,
for the LORD upholds him with His hand.
—Psalm 37:24 (NIV)

First and foremost, I want to thank Jesus Christ my Lord for salvation, healing, and all the blessings He has brought into our lives. You are so good and faithful toward your children.

To Bob, I love you, baby. Our journey continues to overflow with adventure, growth, and so much joy. It is a privilege to be married to someone I respect and admire immensely. Thanks for hanging in there with me through every battle, every victory, and all the tears and laughter. Every crazy southern blonde should have a Bob.

To my wonderful parents, when you received your promotion, heaven gained two beautiful treasures. Thank you for always being there with love and encouragement. You were friends to so many people scattered around the globe. Your ministry and spirit of giving amazed me through the years. I'm proud to be your daughter.

To our God-given granddaughter, Hannah Grace Yeager. When God handpicked our very first special granddaughter, He gave us so much more than we deserved. You are an amazing young lady and an incredible artist. Thank you for listening to my vision for the book cover and creating something beautiful. God has great plans for your life. We love you, baby, all the way to Jesus and back.

To our Cori Ausenhus, what a gift you are to Bob and me. We love you and Steve with all our hearts. Thank you for choosing to be our family and sticking with us through the years. Because of you (and Steve), we have three precious, God-given grandbabies, Hannah, Caleb, and Jakob. You are a gifted photographer and artist. Thank you for making us look good. We count it a privilege to call you family ... *and our girl.* You truly are my best friend and an amazing prayer warrior.

A special thanks to all our God-given children. To date, we have enjoyed the privilege of being Mama Donna and Papa Bob to 49 amazing human beings. Because of your willingness to be a part of our family, we are now very proud grandparents with many beautiful grandbabies. I pray each one of you knows just how much we love you. Thank you for making our lives richer in ways we never imagined. Continue to grow in God and never stop seeking Him in everything you do.

To all of our family and friends, we love you very much and appreciate your prayers, love, and support. Your generosity allowed us to accomplish many things while on the mission field. Although ministry and geography have changed for us through the years, you have remained true and faithful.

Gloria Grant Bailey and David Grant, what a blessing you are to me. You are more like a sister and brother, not just first cousins. Your love and encouragement have never wavered. Thank you for having eyes that see the good and rejoice in the redemption and restoration God has performed in my life.

Bob and Donna Wilcox

Rev. Edward and Mary Grant

Cover design by Hannah Yeager
Idoni Studio, idonistudio.weebly.com
<u>Idoniartstudio@gmail.com</u>

Cori Ausenhus, photographer, with Dr. Donna Grant Wilcox

CONTENTS

Foreword xiii
Introduction xv

1	Setting the Stage	1
2	Mischief and Miracles	5
3	Devil-Possessed Chickens and Bikinis	11
4	A Childhood Missed	25
5	Persistence Pays Off	37
6	The Difference between Hope and Faith	43
7	Honeysuckle and Vanilla	59
8	Daughter, Where Is Your Faith?	71
9	His Mercies Fail Not	81
10	Challenges, Changes, and God's Amazing Grace	89
11	Friends and Farewells	93
12	Mama Says Hello to Jesus	101
13	It's Time to Get Real	107
14	By Their Fruit You Will Know Them	119
15	Overcoming Depression … It's Time for Some Therapy	127
16	Beauty for Ashes, Joy for Mourning	137
17	Learning What It Means to Be Forgiven	147
18	Marriage According to God … Politically Incorrect	157
19	Guard and Protect Your Mind	171
20	Lessons from Furniture	185
21	It's Time to Get Your Praise On	197
22	How Bad Do You Want It?	205
23	Balance, Boldness, and Discovery	213

24	Watch Out, World ... Here We Come	.225
25	Why We Struggle	.243
26	Baby, I Want a Mountain	.251

Conclusion 263
Suggested Reading 267

FOREWORD

When I read about the life of my friend Dr. Donna Wilcox, I am even more amazed at how she has allowed God to shape and use her days. Donna's books have inspired and enlightened me to trust in God's involvement in our lives. *Falling into Faith: A Journey to Freedom* is just as inspiring and thought-provoking as her other writings.

Several things draw me into Donna's writings: humor, wisdom, the ability to connect, and her unique experiences. She could have easily used some of these experiences to view the world as a harsh and unkind place. Yet she realizes the opportunity to rise above and help others. Enjoy the humor and glean the wisdom.

Reverend James Finch
Senior Pastor
Columbine Hills Church of the Nazarene
Littleton, Colorado

INTRODUCTION

Falling into Faith: A Journey to Freedom is about an imperfect but ever-growing faith that learns the joy of falling into a trust relationship with God, knowing He will not allow the righteous to fall. "Though he may stumble, he will not fall, for the LORD upholds him with His hand. I was young and now I am old, yet I have never seen the righteous forsaken or their children begging bread" (Psalm 37:24–25 NIV). It is also about the power of God in the name of Jesus to heal and restore our lives, even when our faith feels weak and inadequate.

God literally brought me back from the brink of death due to sickness and disease. His patient love and grace remained constant even when I strayed from His will to choose my own path. In this ongoing journey, I have experienced what a loving and faithful Father Jesus Christ, the Son of God, is to all who fall into His loving hands of mercy. He cares for His children without showing favoritism.

As you read the pages of my life, I pray the eyes of your understanding are opened to see God as the loving, forgiving, and faithful Father He is. I pray you come to the full knowledge with certainty and without reservation that He is the one true God of restoration. One who longs to bring hope to the hopeless and replace the ashes and ruins of our lives with beauty and abundance. His only requests are a repentant heart, faithful obedience to His Word, to love Him with all our hearts, and to love one another.

I refer to Jesus Christ, God the Father, and the Holy Spirit throughout my book. God is a single being existing simultaneously as three distinct persons. The Bible clearly speaks of God the Father, God the Son (Jesus

Christ), and God the Holy Spirit. According to scripture, the three are equal and eternal, one in essence, nature, power, action, and will.

Obedience to God and a passion for encouraging others through my testimony is why I write, minister, counsel, provide a little laughter, and sing. Stepping out in faith and out of my comfort zone presented many new challenges. Throughout the process, I discovered an amazing truth about our Creator. When the Lord opens the door to a new opportunity and we choose to step out in faith and say yes, He will equip, encourage, and bring wisdom to our lives in exciting and powerful ways.

Riddled with pain and despair for many years, I faced each day with immense uncertainty from my circumstances and a dim probability of a future. Through perseverance and choosing daily to run into the arms of God, faith began replacing fear. A joy emerged and created the strength to believe I could be an overcomer. Because of Jesus Christ, I am an overcomer. He is merciful, powerful, and faithful, and His Word is truth. What He has done for me He will do for all who seek Him and choose to believe.

God's Word says, "They triumphed over him by the blood of the Lamb and by the word of their testimony; they did not love their lives so much as to shrink from death" (Revelation 12:11 NIV). Because of this, I rejoice in sharing my testimony of healing and restoration. Some things you may find humorous, and other things just down right painful. Above all, I pray you are challenged, strengthened, and encouraged.

> So do not be ashamed to testify about our Lord, or ashamed of me his prisoner; But join with me in suffering for the gospel, by the power of God, *who has saved us and called us to a holy life-Not because of anything we have done, but because of His own purpose and grace.* This grace was given to us in Christ Jesus before the beginning of time. (2 Timothy 1:8–9 NIV; emphasis added)

> I will instruct thee and teach thee in the way which thou shalt go; I will guide thee with Mine eye. (Psalm 32:8 KJV)

With Jesus Christ as the Lord of our lives, we have the greatest source of power. There is none greater. Before beginning this adventure of falling, allow me to leave you with a few important truths:

- The truth is Christ died for every one of us. He alone has the power to save, heal, and restore.
- The truth is there is forgiveness of sin for all who ask in faith and believe.
- The truth is you can break the generational curses of sin and bondage in your life through Christ and His shed blood.
- The truth is God is victorious, and Satan is already defeated.
- The truth is everything we receive from God is by faith. Therefore, by faith we must be willing to believe and receive.

"And everything that does not come from faith is sin."
(Romans 14:23 NIV)

Now, let's get going on this roller coaster I call my life. I pray it gives you the courage to begin falling into your own faith journey of freedom.
Come on along and take the F
                          A
                        L
                           L

CHAPTER 1

SETTING THE STAGE

Setting the stage for the pages of my life to unfold before you brings me to an important task and responsibility, one that demands a light shine brightly on how desperately God longs to mold each of us into an amazing creation—a vessel—that is unique in every aspect and filled with godly wisdom and power.

Our purpose is to bring glory to God as we overflow with blessings, even when life is unpredictable, heartbreaking, and challenging. Through the joy and struggles, our lives should lovingly point others to Christ and create a desire to seek and know Him. The outcome is a powerful, loving relationship with our Savior and one another.

As I begin the journey of sharing my story, we will first seek wisdom from our Refiner and Purifier, and our Master Potter. Understanding what we are reading and studying changes everything. It is the difference between wisdom and simple knowledge. "The entrance of your words give light; it gives understanding to the simple" (Psalm 119:130 NKJV).

Before I share the details of my life, let us examine the reason our earthly journeys are often wrought with pain and discomfort. Our heavenly Father does not cause bad things to happen to His children; however, He most certainly allows things for a greater purpose. There are also instances where we are simply reaping what we have sown. In those moments of difficulty, God is always at work on our behalves with a plan of restoration, healing, and beauty. He will never allow the enemy to overtake and destroy us. If we choose to place our trust in God, blessings and healing replace pain and devastation. I'm living proof of this fact.

Donna Grant Wilcox, MTH, CBT, PhD

We live in a fallen world. Sin, disobedience, and political correctness in today's society are the new norm, even within many of our churches. It appears a growing number of people in our country are embracing the "whatever feels good, do it" philosophy, accompanied by a disrespect toward anything relating to God and morality. As I write this, our nation is in political and moral decay with unprecedented division. I'm so thankful the Bible tells us how it eventually ends. For the believers, when our days on earth are complete, we'll be with our Lord and Savior for eternity. Until then, we can walk in peace knowing God is in control and He will never leave or forsake His children.

As you begin this journey with me, we will explore the meaning of the following scripture: "He will sit as a refiner and purifier of silver" (Malachi 3:3 NIV). This verse is a beautiful illustration of the deep commitment God has toward His children. It truly makes a magnificent statement about the character and nature of God. To understand and catch a glimpse of the Father's loving character, we must investigate the process of refining silver. Through analyzing how it is done, a beautiful picture emerges detailing the patience, love, and skill our heavenly Father puts into molding our lives into something of value and worth.

Silversmiths work with silver to create jewelry, vases, dishes, flatware, candlesticks, handles, knobs, and so on. To do their jobs, they use many tools. Here are a few: a smoldering torch, piercing saw, files, mallets, hammers, pickling acid, and a polishing machine. I don't know about you, but none of these instruments sound very pleasant. However, our focus should be on their purpose. A silversmith grasps a piece of silver with a tool as he or she holds it over fire to heat it. The silversmith is particularly careful to hold the silver in the middle of the fire, where the flames are the hottest, making sure to burn away all the impurities.

Think about this for a moment and reflect on the scripture: "He sits as a refiner and purifier of silver." When life is hard and we feel like we are being held over the fire, never forget God is there and holding us in the palm of His hand. If with patience we allow Him to work in our lives, the impurities that prevent us from experiencing victory will be destroyed.

There is one more critical detail about the process, and it is key to understanding how a silversmith thinks and creates his masterpieces. He carefully keeps his eye on the silver as he sits in front of the fire, securely holding the silver the entire time it is being refined. He is aware of an important fact: if it is left a moment too long in the flames, it will be destroyed.

When we give God permission to work in our lives, we will not be destroyed. He never takes His eyes off us. Our Creator, God the Father, is all-powerful and sovereign. His purposes for His creations will be fulfilled. Like the silversmith who creates something unique and beautiful, the potter also creates each piece to meet a specific objective. And so it is with God, who forms each one of us with beautiful plans for our lives. There is great value in becoming clay in the hands of the Master Potter or silver in the hands of our Refiner and Purifier. "Yet you, LORD, are our Father. We are the clay, you are the potter; we are all the work of your hand" (Isaiah 64:8 NIV).

Just as a potter kneads clay to remove impurities and air bubbles and a silversmith uses fire, God removes impurities through life's challenges and obstacles to make us useful and fruitful for His service. Just as a potter turns the wheel and shapes the clay into a useful vessel, so God uses the turning of events to shape His children—His precious ones. When we are being held in that hot spot or on the Potter's wheel, He never leaves us alone. He knows the outcome will bring forth beauty and an intimacy with Him.

Because of the new covenant God established with us through Jesus Christ, we can trust the Master Potter, our Refiner and Purifier, to meticulously work out our imperfections and gently mold us into the likeness of His Son.

> We are assured and know that [God being a partner in their labor] all things work together and are [fitting into a plan] for good to and for those who love God and are called according to [His] design and purpose. (Romans 8:28 AMP)

We are given free will to choose our responses to the reality of this truth. Due to human nature, we usually fall into these two categories: (1) rebel against God and resent Him because we don't like what we see or feel; (2) by faith, we press into God and take comfort in the fact He is carefully molding us into something beautiful for His glory.

Choosing to trust our Creator opens the door for us to see Him carefully and strategically work out every detail as He brings success and victory in the face of life's challenges. By hanging on and trusting God, we will bring glory to His name and lack no good thing.

> For the LORD God is a sun and shield; The LORD gives grace and glory; *No good thing does He withhold from those who walk uprightly.* (Psalm 84:11 NASB; emphasis added)

> When a potter makes jars out of clay, doesn't he have a right to use the same lump of clay to make one jar for decoration and another to throw garbage into? In the same way, even though God has the right to show his anger and his power, he is very patient with those on whom his anger falls, who are destined for destruction. He does this to make the riches of his glory shine even brighter on those to whom he shows mercy, who were prepared in advance for glory. And we are among those whom he selected, both from the Jews and from the Gentiles. (Romans 9:21–27 NIV)

You are never so messed up or marred beyond repair that Father God cannot create something miraculous out of your life. He longs to safely hold and lovingly mold you while forming a trusting and intimate relationship with you—His precious child.

As you read through the details of my crazy and miraculous life, I pray a newfound hope is renewed and your eyes are enlightened to God's truth. He desires to do amazing things in and through each and every one of us.

You may feel as though you need a seat belt at times, but like I tell my patients, "Don't worry. We'll get through this together."

Let the journey begin as I share the life and times of Donna Grant Wilcox.

CHAPTER 2

MISCHIEF AND MIRACLES

Born in Mobile, Alabama, I am the youngest of three preacher's kids (commonly referred to as PKs), with an older brother and an older sister. Larry is eleven years older than me, and Robbie is three years older.

In the 1960s, discovering the gender of a child before birth wasn't an option. The months of waiting became a time filled with old wives' tales and exciting guessing games. Mother claimed during her pregnancy she just knew I would be a girl—and, as she put it, "a prissy little thing." Anyone who knows me would say without hesitation, "She got that right."

My parents decided my name should be Donna after the actress Donna Reed. For those old enough to remember *The Donna Reed Show*, she often vacuumed and cleaned the house in a dress, high heels, and pearls. She always wore pearls. Some readers may know her as Mary Hatch Bailey, the wife of Mr. George Bailey from the movie *It's a Wonderful Life*.

Donna means "woman" or "lady" in Italian. The original meaning is closer to "lady of the home" and was a title of respect. Although I am not Italian, I appreciate knowing the special meaning of my name. I'm a mixture of Irish and Native American Indian. Quite the combination. My blonde hair and fair skin accents the Irish, but my high cheekbones and facial profile shows off the Native American Indian side of my family. Needless to say, I received a double dose of stubbornness and a temperamental nature.

There is something wonderful about knowing who you are and

where you came from. Not everyone has the privilege of knowing the why, how, and who. Regardless, our heavenly Father can rewrite our stories and give each of us an amazing present and future. Even with the knowledge of where I came from and our rich family history, God still beautifully rewrote my story. He brought meaning and value to years of pain, despair, and hopelessness. I'm so thankful He did.

As a young man, Dad answered the call to preach. Because he was a licensed and ordained minister, our lives revolved around church. A preacher's home is usually the center of attention, and we were no exception to this rule. Too often, it seemed a spotlight shone directly on our house, giving people a lot to observe, judge, gossip, laugh, and pray about.

Early on, I faced numerous health problems. Always labeled "the sick one," I desired more than anything to be happy and healthy. Comments like "Oh, poor Donna, she's always so sick" had a profound and negative effect on my life in every way. I began to understand at a very early age the importance of our words and how they affect others. They can build up or tear down, heal or wound, bring hope or despair. Words are truly powerful.

About a year after I was born, we left Mobile. Dad accepted a pastoral position at a church in Graceville, a small town in Florida located approximately twenty miles from Dothan, Alabama. We lived in the parsonage next to the church, a charming little white house with an old-fashioned front porch and white picket fence. The town embraced a warm Mayberry kind of feeling, with a small, close-knit community. People were welcoming and quickly became family.

Directly across the street was a small park bench facing the road. This bench captivated my attention. Mother kept a watchful eye because she knew her little girl's weakness—socializing. If anyone sat down alone, I wanted to dart across the street with the hope of making a new friend. Mother stated I often begged and pleaded, "Please Mama, let me go. They are all alone with no one to talk to." The ultimate little social bug, I cannot ever remember feeling shy. I truly loved being around people and making friends.

Mother, a talented musician, sang and played the piano, organ, and accordion. She began teaching us to sing as soon as we could talk. God put a song inside my heart at a very early age. By the time I was three, my sister, mother, and I harmonized and sang in church and on the radio. When we sang in church, Mom often stood me on the altar next to the piano so the congregation could see me. Blessed with a good set of lungs (a polite way of saying I sang loud), hearing me was never a problem. Music and people became my passions. I sang anytime, anywhere, and for anyone willing to listen.

Music is a powerful therapeutic and healing tool for the mind, body, and spirit. It causes the brain to release a neurotransmitter called dopamine, a feel-good hormone. Listening to music with someone else can also release prolactin, a hormone that bonds people together. As a child, it brought joy to our home and continues to do so today in my own family. Dad kept old cassette tapes of "his girls" singing and played them often until he passed away in December 2011.

One Sunday morning, my parents were getting ready for church. Robbie and I had measles, so we stayed home with Larry. Giving in to my pitiful pleas, Mama finally agreed that if Larry stayed right with me, I could sit on the bed and cut out paper dolls. Everything seemed to be going along just fine until the phone rang. Larry ran to answer it, and for no apparent reason, I began jumping on the bed with the scissors in my hand. The scary part, they were the long, sharp, stainless steel kind. I knew this was a big no-no, but kids will be kids.

You can guess what happened next. Falling off the bed, I landed on the scissors, stabbing myself in the chest. Hearing the bang, Larry ran back in the room. To his horror, he found me facedown on the floor and motionless. Turning me over, he saw the scissors plunged deep into my chest. Larry yelled for Robbie to run over to the church and get Mom and Dad. Within minutes, they rushed in, finding me on the floor in my brother's arms. Panicking, Larry suddenly grabbed the handle and pulled the scissors out, but no blood came from the wound. Fearing there could be internal bleeding, everyone prayed as Daddy scooped me up in his arms and rushed to the nearest hospital in Dothan, Alabama. The entire congregation and many of our neighbors followed closed behind.

Word quickly spread, and someone called the local radio station. The disc jockey informed listeners about the accident and asked everyone to please pray for three-year-old "little Donna Grant." Our community came together in faith and prayer as they waited to hear news from the hospital.

The emergency room doctor took x-rays to determine the severity of the wound. He soon came out in disbelief, advising my parents the scissors literally missed my heart and lungs by a hair, and there appeared to be no trace of internal bleeding. He exclaimed, "This is nothing less than a miracle." My parents stated throughout the entire ordeal I never cried and appeared strangely calm.

After this incident, people came to our church to see the little girl who had the whole town praying. Mother never wanted us to forget God's hand of protection. The local newspaper wrote an article about the accident and "The little miracle child named Donna." She kept the newspaper article in a drawer at home, often reading it as a reminder of God's never-failing love and mercy.

Through the years, I faced many challenges and hospitalizations. During those times, Mother kept the article close by as a reminder of God's mercy. She often made me look at it as she firmly stated, "Child, you are a miracle. God is going to heal you."

The scar remains today, along with many others. They serve as a reminder of the enemy's failures and God's miracle-working power.

Father God is our Healer and Protector, and nothing is too hard or impossible for Him. The enemy wants to destroy our lives, but God has the ultimate say. He will not only carry us through our trials but will use the things meant to destroy our minds and bodies, creating in us a strength and courage to face the giants with victory and wisdom. However, it is up to us to choose Him and His will. God gave us an incredible gift called free will. If we choose well, our lives will be blessed.

When we commit our hearts to the Lord and walk in obedience, the Bible tells us He will take the curses of our lives and bring forth a blessing. When God performs the miraculous in and through us, it is not solely for our benefit. He longs to use it as a lifeline to salvation, hope, blessing, healing, and wisdom in the hearts and lives of everyone we meet.

Throughout the Bible, there are numerous stories of God's amazing power, turning what was meant for evil into something good. The story of Joseph is an excellent example. This young man went through unimaginable and painful situations, yet his words show a profound wisdom and understanding of God's hand carefully working out "all things for the good."

> His brothers then came and threw themselves down before him. "We are your slaves," they said. But Joseph said to them, *"Don't be afraid. Am I in the place of God? You intended to harm me, but God intended it for good to accomplish what is now being done, the saving of many lives."* (Genesis 50:1–20 NIV; emphasis added)

A minister's life is often like that of a military family. When you feel God is calling you to a new ministry opportunity, you move. Sometimes you move often. Prior to pastoring, Mom and Dad were traveling evangelists. In the early years of their ministry, they held revival services at a small church in Fort Walton Beach, Florida. While there, my parents felt a burden for this church and strong desire to keep the lines of communication open. A pastoral position became available, and although our family loved Graceville, Dad and Mom answered the call God placed in their hearts years earlier and accepted the position. Embarking on a brand-new journey, we packed up and headed further south.

Fort Walton Beach is a small town in northwest Florida located between Pensacola and Panama City, along North Florida's Gulf Coast, often called the Emerald Coast. Miles of beautiful beaches grace the area with sand as white as snow—not a bad place to call home. In fact, Fort Walton Beach became home to our family for over thirty years.

If you are from the South, it is common to refer to my hometown area as Florabama or LA (Lower Alabama). Due to my strong southern accent, people who are not from the South often ask where I am from. I frequently say LA, just to see their expression. Once I explain, they normally look relieved for some reason. It is quite amusing and leads to some interesting conversations about my southern roots.

CHAPTER 3

DEVIL-POSSESSED CHICKENS AND BIKINIS

Some of my fondest memories as a child were Saturday visitations with my father. One particular Saturday, he only had one planned visit, so my parents decided to take us all shopping in Pensacola. Before embarking on the forty-five-minute drive, they planned on making a quick stop to pray for an elderly couple who was sick and unable to get around very well. Pulling in their driveway, Larry requested to stay in the car, but Robbie and I wanted to sit on the front porch. Exiting the car, Mom instructed Larry to keep a close eye on us.

Young, gullible, and barely four at the time, my sister could make me believe anything. She convinced me God spoke directly to her, giving specific instructions on things we were supposed to do for Him. It did not matter how strange the request; with all my heart I believed she heard directly from heaven. Once Robbie received one of these so-called revelations, trouble soon followed. The highlight of Larry's existence seemed to be watching the predicaments his little sisters got into due to these revelations. The fact that I never learned my lesson added to his amusement.

The elderly couple lived in a little white house with a screened-in front porch that ran the full length of the house. An old stove sat by the entrance door, filled with bowls full of eggs. In fact, there were many bowls of eggs all over the porch because this was their source of income. The yard had a large, fenced-in area with chickens running all around. Some of the chickens were very odd looking, with a strange red thing on the top of their heads. Not understanding why, I asked my all-knowing sister, "Robbie, what's the red thing on those chickens' heads?"

She proceeded to tell me about a message she received straight from heaven. "Oh, Donna, the Lord told me they are demon-possessed chickens, and we are supposed to throw eggs at them and make the red thing fall off to cast the demons out."

Certain Robbie heard directly from God, I began hurling eggs toward those poor roosters. A four-year-old cannot throw very far, and all my eggs ended up on the front sidewalk. As this ritual of exorcism played out, Larry peered from the car in amazement, wondering what in the world his little sisters were thinking as he laughed hysterically.

Mom and Dad eventually came out to find us dutifully standing on the porch. They were inside maybe fifteen minutes, but it does not take children long to get into mischief. Parents often have a sixth sense when it comes to their kids, and something sure didn't seem right. They began noticing the empty bowls. Where were the eggs?

The real tell-all awaited them outside. Looking down at all the broken eggs scattered on and around the sidewalk, Mom turned toward us with a glare. In disbelief, she asked, "What have you girls done?" I immediately knew Robbie must have gotten her information from God all messed up. Surely He didn't tell her to do something that would get us in big trouble.

Confused and not wanting a spanking, I pointed to the sky and said, "Mama, you won't believe it, but this huge bird flew over and dropped all these eggs."

Remorse for telling a lie quickly took over, and I blurted out the whole ugly truth. I begged her to understand. We were just trying to cast the devil out of the chickens, but she did not want to hear it. Perplexed, I wondered, *Doesn't Mama care about those poor chickens?* Mom proceeded to expand my education by explaining the difference between chickens and roosters. This left me with a confusing thought. *God made all the animals, so why didn't He tell Robbie about those roosters, and why did He tell her they were demon-possessed chickens?* Somehow, my little brain concluded she did not get the information straight, and I continued to believe Robbie had a direct line to God.

Madder and hotter than a firecracker, Mother yelled for Larry as she dragged us to the car. In tears from laughing so hard, Larry explained to Mom and Dad how hilarious the whole thing had been to watch. Dad went back inside to advise the couple what his sweet, (not so) innocent little girls had done. He used our shopping money and paid for the eggs, stating we would be back later that day to clean their yard and house.

With shopping no longer on the agenda, we went back home, where our parents made us think long and hard about our actions. All three of us had to get down on our knees and repent. When we went back to the elderly couple's home, we apologized and began cleaning. Not being the most experienced cleaners, big brother did a lot of the work. He didn't get the last laugh after all, ha. As time passed, Mom and Dad could barely relay the story to friends and family without a really good chuckle.

When I think about this story, it reminds me of the innocence of children and their willingness to believe anything. Gullible and naïve, it seemed simple and logical to trust Robbie completely. Daddy preached about people in the Bible who heard directly from God; surely He could talk to her too. Not to mention the stories of Jesus and the disciples casting out demons. It made perfect sense to me. Children have such a pure and uncomplicated form of reasoning. It's understandable why Jesus encourages us to become as a child in our thinking.

> He called a little child and had him stand among them. And He said, "I tell you the truth, unless you change and become like little children, you will never enter the kingdom of heaven. Therefore, whoever humbles himself like this child is the greatest in the kingdom of heaven." (Matthew 18:2–4 NIV)

Unlike most adults, children believe what you say. If you tell them Santa Claus comes down chimneys and leaves presents at Christmas, they believe you. Even if they do not have a chimney, they still trust Santa will find a way to get in the house. Mom or Dad said it, and that settles it. This is how our heavenly Father longs for us to be toward Him and His holy Word. If Jesus Christ our Savior said He could and would heal, restore, bless, and prosper us, take Him at His word and believe without doubting.

Even if ... you do not have all the answers.
Even if ... you do not see how in the world it is possible.
Even if ... the entire world says you are crazy and fanatical for believing.

We should rejoice just thinking about God's promises; instead, we make receiving them so difficult. Along life's journey, we learn to use excuses to justify our lack of faith or sheer unwillingness to walk the path of total submission and obedience. Flesh tells us it is too hard, and many times we feel unworthy. We sit and analyze why the God of heaven and earth should or would ever choose to bless our mess. Then comes maturity. This is where we lose many of those childlike qualities that are so important in our relationship with God.

Years of heartache and pain came and went before I rediscovered the child within longing to come out of hiding. I am thankful God is so patient and merciful. Little did I realize the safest, happiest, and most fulfilling place to be is in the Master's hands, continuously falling into a deeper trust relationship with the great I Am.

Through the years, mischief and miracles remained a constant source of laughter, amusement, and encouragement in our home, but, praise God, no more devil-possessed chickens. Pleasing Daddy became my focus in life. In adoration, I followed him around, loving every minute we spent together. He never seemed to mind having a little shadow hanging on his every word and keeping a close eye on him.

Each Saturday, I accompanied Dad as he visited newcomers to the church and anyone in need of prayer. During one of these weekly visitations, another comical event occurred. Our last scheduled stop of the day took us to a young woman's house who attended church for the first time the previous Sunday. Wearing only a bikini bathing suit, she lay on a lawn chair sunning in the front yard for the whole world to see. In the sixties, the church had many rules and regulations. Mixed swimming and bikinis were simply not acceptable. A respectable woman only wore a whole-piece bathing suit, certainly not a two-piece. Seeing a bikini on television was one thing, but seeing one up close shocked and amazed me. To make matters worse, she wore it in front of my daddy.

Instructing me to stay in the car, Dad promised to say a quick hello and

Falling into Faith

leave. Not wanting to miss anything, I rolled down the window and stared intensely as he made his way to this half-naked woman. Greeting her with a handshake, Dad handed her a business card, but before he could turn around, I loudly hollered out the window, "Daddy, why are you holding that naked woman's hand? I'm telling Mama when we get home." Unfortunately, my little eyes did not see him handing her a card. Quite the contrary, they saw my daddy holding a half-naked woman's hand. You can imagine the shock and surprise on his poor face as he bolted back to the car.

All the way home, he tried to calm me down and explain. Refusing to listen, I tearfully exclaimed, "When we get home, Daddy, I'm telling Mama! You are in big trouble!" Pulling into the driveway and before Dad put the car in park, I jumped out and ran inside screaming for Mama. Within minutes, he strolled in the house laughing and shaking his head. Unable to see the humor in the situation, I boldly informed Mama about the half-naked woman, stating Daddy must be punished. She just laughed and gave me a big hug, assuring me Daddy only held hands with his girls. Unwilling to budge, I stood firm, all the while thinking, *Didn't she hear me? That woman was half-naked. What part of "I saw it" didn't she understand?* In total frustration, I decided to run away. Grabbing a loaf of bread and a glass of water, I headed to my playhouse outside, determined to stay there until they came to their senses.

I eventually came inside because water tends to go right through you. I didn't see Daddy, and Mama told me he was being punished and she had sent him to their room. Although Mom's decision to punish Dad pleased me, I quickly came to his defense by advising her it really wasn't his fault. Daddy just wanted the half-naked woman to know about Jesus.

My parents were totally devoted to one another. Mom always said she never had to worry about Dad because I kept such a good eye on him. In my childlike heart, I knew how wonderful Daddy was and he belonged to us and no one else. When it came to Mom, Dad was completely smitten and loved her deeply. They demonstrated loyalty, affection, and unity.

Today's society is much more complicated. Children do not often see true devotion, respect, and love, from their parents or caretakers. Many children grow up with only one parent or not raised by their birth parents at all. There are tragic and sad circumstances all around us. No home is perfect; however, if we will serve and trust God, He can do amazing and miraculous things for us, regardless of our situation. We have this promise: "The LORD will perfect that which concerns me; Your mercy, O LORD, endures forever; Do not forsake the works of Your hands" (Psalm 138:8 KJV).

I briefly mentioned the story of Joseph in the previous chapter. Let's look a little closer at his life. Talk about a rough childhood. Joseph's brothers were very jealous. They felt their father loved him more than he loved any of them. According to scripture, they had good reasons to feel this way: "Jacob loved Joseph more than any of his other children because Joseph had been born to him in his old age" (Genesis 37:3 NLT).

Desiring to express his deep love for Joseph, his father made him a beautiful coat of many colors; however, the other sons did not receive one. This only added to their hatred and jealousy. Joseph seemed to make matters worse by telling them about his dreams. Read the following scripture, and you will understand why this became more than his brothers could take.

> Joseph had a dream, and when he told it to his brothers, they hated him all the more. He said to them, "Listen to this dream I had: We were binding sheaves of grain out in the field when suddenly my sheaf rose and stood upright, while your sheaves gathered around mine and bowed down to it." His brothers said to him, "Do you intend to reign over us? Will you actually rule us?" And they hated him all the more because of his dream and what he had said. (Genesis 37:5–8 NIV)

One day, Jacob sent Joseph to check on his brothers who had been gone for quite a while pasturing the sheep at Shechem. The brothers saw Joseph coming and immediately planned to harm him. Fortunately, Reuben prevented his brothers from killing Joseph. The following scriptures paint a vivid picture of just how deep the resentment and

Falling into Faith

jealousy penetrated the brothers' hearts and how dangerous the situation became for Joseph.

> When Joseph's brothers saw him coming, they recognized him in the distance. As he approached, they made plans to kill him. "Here comes the dreamer!" they said. "Come on, let's kill him and throw him into one of these cisterns. We can tell our father, 'A wild animal has eaten him.' Then we'll see what becomes of his dreams!" But when Reuben heard of their scheme, he came to Joseph's rescue. "Let's not kill him," he said. "Why should we shed any blood? Let's just throw him into this empty cistern here in the wilderness. Then he'll die without our laying a hand on him." Reuben was secretly planning to rescue Joseph and return him to his father. So when Joseph arrived, his brothers ripped off the beautiful robe he was wearing. Then they grabbed him and threw him into the cistern. Now the cistern was empty; there was no water in it. Then, just as they were sitting down to eat, they looked up and saw a caravan of camels in the distance coming toward them. It was a group of Ishmaelite traders taking a load of gum, balm, and aromatic resin from Gilead down to Egypt. Judah said to his brothers, "What will we gain by killing our brother? We'd have to cover up the crime. Instead of hurting him, let's sell him to those Ishmaelite traders. After all, he is our brother—our own flesh and blood!" And his brothers agreed. (Genesis 37:18–27 NLT)

Joseph was sold into slavery and taken to Egypt. Potiphar, an Egyptian officer and captain of the guard for Pharaoh, the king of Egypt, purchased him. The Bible tells us, "The LORD was with Joseph, so he succeeded in everything he did as he served in the home of his Egyptian master" (Genesis 39:2 NIV).

As you continue reading Genesis chapter 39, scriptures reveal something important, something we should pay close attention to.

Throughout the hardships, God blessed Joseph and caused him to succeed, but he still continued to face many difficult and painful times. It did not mean the Lord had forsaken him; it simply meant God's path to fulfilling His ultimate best, in and through Joseph, would take him down a challenging path. Through it all, God remained faithful. He brought blessings, favor, and wisdom into Joseph's life as He prepared him for the arduous days ahead.

Potiphar's wife began lusting after Joseph and shamelessly pursued him, but he refused to give into temptation. She was enraged by his refusal and falsely accused Joseph of raping her. Believing his wife's lie, Potiphar became furious and threw him in prison. Even in prison, God stayed faithful and caused Joseph to succeed. His good plans for Joseph did not change due to difficult and unjust circumstances.

> But the LORD was with Joseph in the prison and showed him his faithful love. And the LORD made Joseph a favorite with the prison warden. Before long, the warden put Joseph in charge of all the other prisoners and over everything that happened in the prison. The warden had no more worries, because Joseph took care of everything. *The LORD was with him and caused everything he did to succeed.* (Genesis 39:21–23 NLT; emphasis added)

Joseph's journey eventually led him to a prominent place and time in history; however, to receive the fulfillment of God's best and ultimate purpose for his life, Joseph walked a long, hard road. During his sojourn into slavery and prison, Joseph diligently and faithfully trusted God. With integrity, he exemplified an amazing work ethic. When it seemed as if he was forgotten, God brought forth a beautiful "suddenly."

Years later, the king of Egypt (Pharaoh) experienced a disturbing dream. Desperate for answers, Pharaoh summoned the magicians and wise men of Egypt to interpret his dream, but they could not understand what it meant. Then it happened; "God's suddenly."

> Finally, the king's chief cup-bearer spoke up. "Today I have been reminded of my failure," he told Pharaoh.

> "Some time ago, you were angry with the chief baker and me, and you imprisoned us in the palace of the captain of the guard. One night the chief baker and I each had a dream, and each dream had its own meaning. There was a young Hebrew man with us in the prison who was a slave of the captain of the guard. We told him our dreams, and he told us what each of our dreams meant. And everything happened just as he had predicted. I was restored to my position as cup-bearer, and the chief baker was executed and impaled on a pole." Pharaoh sent for Joseph at once, and he was quickly brought from the prison. After he shaved and changed his clothes, he went in and stood before Pharaoh. Then Pharaoh said to Joseph, "I had a dream last night, and no one here can tell me what it means. But I have heard that when you hear about a dream you can interpret it." "It is beyond my power to do this," Joseph replied. "But God can tell you what it means and set you at ease." (Genesis 41:9–16 NLT)

Joseph interpreted the dream, telling Pharaoh there would be seven years of prosperity and seven years of famine. Joseph advised the king to put someone in charge of gathering the food produced during the good years, so there would be food to eat during the years of famine. This pleased Pharaoh, and something extraordinary happened.

> So Pharaoh asked his officials, "Can we find anyone else like this man so obviously filled with the spirit of God?" Then Pharaoh said to Joseph, "Since God has revealed the meaning of the dreams to you, clearly no one else is as intelligent or wise as you are. *You will be in charge of my court, and all my people will take orders from you. Only I, sitting on my throne, will have a rank higher than yours.*" Pharaoh said to Joseph, "*I hereby put you in charge of the entire land of Egypt.*" Then Pharaoh removed his signet ring from his hand and placed it on

> Joseph's finger. He dressed him in fine linen clothing and hung a gold chain around his neck. Then he had Joseph ride in the chariot reserved for his second-in-command. And wherever Joseph went, the command was shouted, "Kneel down!" So Pharaoh put Joseph in charge of all Egypt. And Pharaoh said to him, "I am Pharaoh, but no one will lift a hand or foot in the entire land of Egypt without your approval." (Genesis 41:38–44 NLT; emphasis added)

Put in charge over all of Egypt, the famine opened a door of opportunity for Joseph to reunite with his family and save them from starvation. When he finally saw his brothers again, they bowed before him, just like the dreams he shared with them many years earlier. Joseph knew God's hand strategically placed him in this position for such a time as this, and his heart held no anger or resentment.

> Then Joseph said to his brothers, "Come close to me." When they had done so, he said, "I am your brother Joseph, the one you sold into Egypt! And now, do not be distressed and do not be angry with yourselves for selling me here, because it was to save lives that God sent me ahead of you. For two years now there has been famine in the land, and for the next five years there will not be plowing and reaping. But God sent me ahead of you to preserve for you a remnant on earth and to save your lives by a great deliverance. So then, it was not you who sent me here, but God. He made me father to Pharaoh, lord of his entire household and ruler of all Egypt." (Genesis 45:4–8 NIV)

The story of Joseph encourages us to trust God with our lives. Regardless of how dark the circumstance, He truly does have a good plan for each of us. We may encounter suffering along the way to the fulfillment of those plans, but it will be worth it all.

Joseph suffered many things but claimed victory in the end. Through it all, God remained faithful, turning the curses of Joseph's life into blessings. God saw ahead and knew the good plans He had for him, plans the enemy could not destroy.

I am sure through the years Joseph struggled with many questions. He probably wondered what good could come from all the turmoil and injustices he suffered. Would he ever see his family again or his beloved father? Joseph was sure about one thing: he served a miracle-working God. He feared and loved the Lord, and God never forgot him. He faithfully worked all things out, carefully fulfilling the promises He planned for Joseph's life. Plans of restoration, reconciliation, abundance, and a life of favor and blessings. You see, even in suffering, Joseph held out and never gave up. He excelled in every situation and did not use his suffering as an excuse. Whatever he put his hands to, he did it with excellence. What an incredible life lesson this teaches us.

It is important to seek the Lord for direction and with patience wait on Him to answer. We are merely God's instruments and His vessels. If we allow Him to use us for His purposes, even in times of desperation our lives will overflow with blessings. Understanding this principle along with a commitment toward excellence in whatever situation we find ourselves in opens the door for God to do the impossible and the extraordinary in our own lives.

> So you have not received a spirit that makes you fearful slaves. Instead, you received God's Spirit when he adopted you as his own children. Now we call him, "Abba, Father." For his Spirit joins with our spirit to affirm that we are God's children. And since we are his children, we are his heirs. In fact, together with Christ we are heirs of God's glory. But if we are to share his glory, we must also share his suffering. Yet what we suffer now is nothing compared to the glory he will reveal to us later. (Romans 8:15–18 NLT)

Like Joseph, our greatest victories are realized through faithful obedience and perseverance. According to scripture, obedience is learned through suffering. Jesus Christ still stands as our greatest example of this very fact.

After speaking at a church or conference and sharing my life's story, I'm often asked, "How can you be so happy with all you have been through?" The answer to this question is easy. How can I not be happy? What was meant to destroy me God uses to help so many people, and He has truly blessed me with more than I ever dreamed possible. Particularly in the area of family, friends, and purpose. The next most common question: is, "Why do we have to suffer?" My response is quite simple, "Why shouldn't we suffer? Jesus certainly did." Scripture clearly states, "But if we are to share his glory, we must also share his suffering" (Romans 8:17 NLT). This isn't a very popular response; however, it is truth according to God's holy Word.

I desire to bring hope and encouragement to others but will always speak the truth. I'm not a believer in shining someone on just to appease or tickle a person's ears with pretentious, self-serving words. True growth comes when we choose to hear truth, then act on it through healthy changes and choices. When people are hurting and desperate for a miracle, they welcome truth, regardless of how uncomfortable it may be. I'm grateful for those who dared to love me enough to speak the hard, painful truths. Their words brought wisdom into my life, and trust me … I needed it.

Take some time to meditate on the following scriptures. Open your heart to hear God speak wisdom into your life through His words of love and encouragement.

> Although He was a son, He learned obedience from what He suffered and, once made perfect, He became the source of eternal salvation for all who obey Him. (Hebrews 5:8–9 NIV)

> And the God of all grace, who called you to his eternal glory in Christ, after you have suffered a little while, will himself restore you and make you strong, firm and steadfast. (1 Peter 5:10 NIV)

Falling into Faith

For our light and momentary troubles are achieving for us an eternal glory that far outweighs them all. (2 Corinthians 4:17 NIV)

But even if you suffer for doing what is right, God will reward you for it. So don't worry or be afraid of their threats. (1 Peter 3:14 NLT)

Not only so, but we also glory in our sufferings, because we know that suffering produces perseverance; perseverance, character; and character, hope. (Romans 5:3–4 NIV)

For the eyes of the Lord range throughout the earth to strengthen those whose hearts are fully committed to Him. (2 Chronicles 16:9 NIV)

CHAPTER 4

A CHILDHOOD MISSED

When asked what I remember most about childhood, my answer consists of four things: pain, sickness, church, and music. Throughout my young life, I suffered with difficult and painful health complications. By the age of twelve, those complications intensified, but my thoughts and prayers were focused on Mom, not myself. Mother also battled sickness. She suffered with a kidney disease and remained sick until she passed away from cancer in 1994. Many nights, we were awakened by the sound of Dad praying as he bundled Mom up in preparation to go to the emergency room. Mom and I seemed to take turns making trips to the ER, often followed by hospital stays.

Growing up, we watched Mother suffer, but she loved the Lord and possessed an incredible spirit of joy. I am so thankful for a Christian foundation. We made our share of mistakes, but we knew how to pray. This is one of the greatest gifts a parent, guardian, or caretaker can demonstrate and teach a child.

Dad preached on healing, and I believed God could heal Mom. The Bible told story after story of people healed just by asking and believing. I prayed for God to do the same for Mother. Known for being full of questions, I often asked Dad why the Lord allowed her to suffer so much. He always encouraged me to keep praying, and one day she would be healed. Although I did not have the answers, Jesus did. One fact remained. The Bible said, "By His stripes we are healed," and no one could ever convince me Jesus wanted Mom to suffer.

Children have a simple understanding. Without complicating things, they take scripture quite literally. It does not matter how impossible it may seem; their faith is unshakable. A child will pray for something, then resume playing, with no worries or lingering doubts. If it says, "By His stripes we are healed," then we are healed—end of story. This was how my mind worked, and I fully expected my prayers to be answered. Once again, we can understand why God desires for us to become as little children, trusting and unpretentious.

The Bible clearly tells us healing is God's will. As you read and study the scriptures, never again will you doubt God's desire for His children to be healthy and abundantly blessed while on this earth. If someone says, "It is the Lord's will for you to be sick," ask them to show you scripture that supports this opinion. There simply is not one. With that said, there are precious, faith-filled souls who continue to suffer with sickness and disease during their lifetimes. They do not receive complete healing until reaching the loving arms of God. Do I understand this? No. But I trust God and have come to realize there are some mysteries I'll never understand in my finite human mind. Understanding everything is not a priority for me. I believe the need and obsession to understand all things can lead us into a state of doubt, confusion, anxiety, and negative skepticism.

The Bible says, "Study to show thyself approved unto God, a workman that needeth not to be ashamed, rightly dividing the word of truth" (2 Timothy 2:15 KJV). We must diligently study and rightly divide the Word of truth. There is an abundance of Christian books easily available to read and digest. Authors usually have varying opinions and beliefs. Be cautious and make sure what you choose to believe does not contradict God's infallible Word. The Bible is both complex and simple. When studying the Bible, operate in a spirit of faith and ask the Holy Spirit to bring clarity. Faith is the avenue to God and opens the door to the miraculous.

Jesus died a painful death on the cross. His death and resurrection purchased redemption for our sins, and the stripes He bore purchased our healing. If we believe He died for our sins, then we must also believe "by His stripes we are healed." The very definition of the word "salvation" includes divine healing, health, prosperity, abundant blessings, and so much more.

Falling into Faith

We must train ourselves to trust God more than circumstances or the facts as we see them. Believe, even when we do not understand. The key to answered prayer is total unwavering faith and complete trust in God Almighty. Giving into doubt and unbelief hinders God from answering our prayers. The scriptures are clear and precise. As humans, we often complicate them because we want proof and absolutes.

As a child, I understood this truth. A day would come when my heart could no longer hear the simplicity of God's Word. Complicating it with my own reasoning and human limitations, I found myself searching for the "little girl" who once believed God could do anything. In all my reasoning and searching, the Lord never left my side. He patiently waited for that little girl to come out of hiding.

Time went on, and Mom continued to battle sickness, yet our hope remained steadfast in God's power to heal. We witnessed the miracle hand of God time after time, literally bring her back from death's door, and watched as Dad spent many nights fasting, praying, and pacing the floor. Satan took pleasure in attacking our family with sickness, and his attacks on my life soon became painfully strategic.

Because I began singing at three years old, Mother decided to teach me to read, and I fell in love with books. Due to my hyper and curious personality, this occupied my mind and provided exciting places for me to escape. As school age approached, Mom told me about all the books at my disposal in the library and so many new wonderful people to meet. This social butterfly couldn't wait to get started.

Finally, the first day of school arrived. It didn't take long to discover my classmates didn't know how to read, so I decided to help out the teacher by getting everyone up to speed. You can imagine just how well that went over. Apparently, I even gave out daily homework assignments. I do not remember this, but Mother certainly did. She said it took her months to convince me to quit giving out homework and let the teacher do the teaching.

Unfortunately, red flags regarding my health reared their ugly heads in numerous ways. Petite and finicky, mealtimes created stress for our family. Food made me nauseous, and finicky really doesn't begin to describe just how fussy I could be. After eating, nausea quickly took over. Then came vomiting. Hence, a series of doctors' visits began.

It took many years to discover the blood disease I suffered with, resulting in a childhood filled with constant health challenges, such as frequent strep throat, bladder and kidney infections, nausea, vomiting, fever, fainting, headaches, and extreme anemia. I often wondered if I'd be sick for the rest of my life, just like Mother. Many nights I climbed into bed with my parents, tearfully pleading for them to pray for God to heal me. Looking back, this must have broken their hearts.

Feeling like a pincushion, I hated being sick and grew tired of the constant shuffle to different doctors hoping to find answers. Nightly prayer times consisted of me begging God for healing. My prayers went something like this: "Dear Jesus, when I wake up, please let me be well and never have to go to the doctor again. I promise to tell everyone how you healed me. Thank you, Jesus. Amen."

The enemy wanted to rob me of having a normal childhood by filling my days and nights with sickness, pain, and fear. Clearly, he had a stronghold and a generational curse of sickness over our family that desperately needed to be destroyed. Satan is continually at war against the children of God. He uses every opportunity to try to destroy our lives. Sickness and disease seem to be some of his favorite methods of attack. It certainly appeared to be true in our family.

When one looks around at all the hospitals, new clinics, medical buildings, and pharmacies, one might think Satan is winning the battle. Be encouraged; this is only temporary. The warrior is rising up in many Christians around the world. The enemy's reign of terror will soon end as Christians yearn for more of God in anticipation of Christ's return.

I see two diverse groups of Christians today. One group has a fervent desire to seek after God's heart and walk in His favor. They long to further the kingdom of heaven with the salvation message and the truth of His goodness. Then we have a group of Christians that have become complacent. Whatever is easy and doesn't challenge or confront; this is the road they have chosen.

When you hear the word "complacent," what comes to mind? The *American Heritage Dictionary* gives this definition: "Contented to a fault; self-satisfied and unconcerned." Another definition describes it like this: "Smug, unbothered, and untroubled." A Christian should not be any of these things.

The Bible has much to say about complacency, and we should pay close attention to the scriptures. If we heed God's Word, blessings will flow out of our lives, and more importantly, opportunities to share the love of Christ. "For the waywardness of the simple will kill them, and the complacency of fools will destroy them; but whoever listens to Me will live in safety and be at ease, without fear of harm" (Proverbs 1:32–33 NIV).

Allowing complacency in our lives often causes Christians to enter into what I call a convenient *spiritual bubble*. This is where we surround ourselves with everything and everyone "Christian." Although we may feel physically and spiritually safe, it is not a lifestyle that lines up with the example Christ gave us. How can we be a light in the world if we do not reach out to those who do not know our wonderful Savior? Shouldn't we follow the example of Christ? When Jesus walked this earth, He reached out to the broken and hurting everywhere He went. Who are we to do differently?

We must not permit ourselves to be smug, unbothered, or untroubled toward others. Our mission on this earth is to spread the good news of Christ to those who are lost and hurting, as well as encourage and lift up our family in the Lord. If we shut ourselves off from the world, we've made a conscious decision to refuse an important part of our purpose and mission. While there is still time, make a conscious and purposeful decision to be about the Father's business.

Complacency is far-reaching, and the results are never good. The key is to be vigilant and purposeful in our walk with Christ, because the enemy uses many things to cleverly disguise and conceal this disease. When we allow complacency to remain and take up residence, the enemy has a foothold. It gives him places to quietly creep in as he sets his traps of destruction in an attempt to kill, steal, and destroy.

"Be sober, be vigilant, because your adversary the devil, as a roaring lion, walketh about seeking whom he may devour" (1 Peter 5:8 NIV).

So how do we avoid this dangerous pitfall? Be sober and vigilant. We cannot afford to leave any room for complacency. As Christians, we need to agitate ourselves. To agitate means "To put into violent motion; to shake briskly; to excite, consider, discuss."

Revelation 3:2–3 holds important truths on how to avoid this ugly trap and maintain our zeal for the Lord. In summary, it says, "wake up, strengthen what remains, remember what we have received and heard," and lastly, "hold fast, repent, and obey."

Here is some food for thought. We will look at four important words using definitions from *Strong's Greek Dictionary*: sober, vigilant, strengthen, and remember. As you meditate on these words and apply them, complacency will no longer have an opportunity to hinder your love walk between God and humanity.

> **Sober:** To be sober, to be calm and collected in spirit; to be temperate, (calm, cool) dispassionate, circumspect, (watchful on all sides; wary, thoughtful).
>
> **Vigilant:** To watch; give strict attention to, be cautious, active; to take heed lest through remission (relinquishment; give up) and indolence (laziness; idleness) some destructive calamity suddenly overtake one.
>
> **Strengthen:** To make stable, place firmly, set fast, fix; to strengthen, make firm; to render constant, confirm one's mind.
>
> **Remember:** To be mindful of, to remember, to call to mind; to think of and feel for a person or thing; to hold in memory, keep in mind; to make mention of.

I meet Christians in my travels and through my work on a daily basis. Someone once said this to me, "I don't see the point. As long as I've accepted Christ, I feel that is enough." They were curious about my ongoing desire to seek, grow, self-evaluate, and change. I must tell you, this comment truly broke my heart. To become stagnant and complacent is not only sad but can be spiritually dangerous.

I'll use music as an example to express my point. You can pay someone to teach you how to play the piano, even invest in buying a piano, but if you do not continue to practice and use what you've learned, you'll never grow your talent and expand your ability.

People often fear being judged, so they avoid appearing *too Christian*. We have become so politically correct we no longer understand how to debate or disagree in love while standing strong with a solid commitment to our convictions. Many have adopted a belief system that supports a neutral-ground philosophy, stating this is a loving approach. I have dear, wonderful friends from every background and various beliefs. I can honestly say we walk out our friendship in love and respect. They don't expect me to back down from my convictions, but they also know I'm not their judge. I'm their friend who loves them.

To say you love someone but secretly conceal your beliefs and all you hold dear is not love at all. To truly love means you are willing to participate in an honest and true relationship. Warts and all, you love one another. Sometimes, there is no neutral ground; however, respect should always be the foundation of any relationship.

Sin is sin. If I'm condescending and unkind, my actions are not Christian and do not honor God. How can we truly say we love the Lord and live for Him yet approach our differences in anger and hate? The answer is simple: our words say one thing, but our actions speak the truth.

God's love is not in us if we spew hate and hurt others. After all, they are His creation too. Being a Christian does not make us better. We are forgiven because we chose to believe in a merciful God. Experiencing His love and forgiveness fosters humility, accompanied by an overwhelming love for others. God's love should pour out of us like a healing fountain. "Whoever claims to love God yet hates a brother or sister is a liar. For whoever does not love their brother and sister, whom they have seen, cannot love God, whom they have not seen" (1 John 4:20 NIV).

> Jesus said to him, "'You shall love the LORD your God with all your heart, with all your soul, and with all your mind.' This is *the* first and great commandment. And *the* second *is* like it: 'You shall love your neighbor as yourself.' On these two commandments hang all the Law and the Prophets." (Matthew 22:37–40 NKJV)

We were created to be an effective testimony of our loving Creator. Our lives should reflect God's mercy and His ability to heal and restore. It is heartbreaking to see the mediocre lives so many Christians have purposefully chosen to lead. God has blessed them with talents, family, and amazing testimonies, yet it is easier to just exist and become comfortable. I agree, it may be easier at times, but a complacent life is void of true peace and the fulfillment of knowing God in a powerful and life-changing way. This mind-set also spiritually weakens us as battles rage and life delivers pain and despair.

Take a moment to soul search and conduct a self-evaluation. Ask yourself, *Which group am I in?* Are you growing in your relationship with God and humanity, or complacent (smug, unbothered)? Honest, introspective self-evaluation is a necessary tool for growth.

Learning the importance of a growing faith, along with a desire to change self-destructive habits, did not come easy for me. Years of spiritual immaturity, ignorance of God's Word, and a lack of understanding cost me dearly. Through it all, God extended mercy during those times by gently redirecting my steps. Then He lovingly provided acceptance and grace as I dealt with the consequences from my choices. In every experience, God taught me the benefits of waiting patiently on Him and the importance of growing from each life lesson I encountered.

Whatever we go through in this life, it is important to remember we cannot fight Satan using carnal and earthly strategies. Our only hope is in God. The one and only thing that has the power to save, heal, restore, and conquer is the precious blood of the Lamb and God's holy Word. To understand what the Bible says, we must read it for ourselves. Study and learn what the promises and benefits are from walking in obedience. It is not too late to change.

Make a decision to refuse seeds of doubt, unbelief, and the disease of complacency. Don't allow them to cultivate and grow inside your heart and mind. When they come in like an uninvited visitor, they should never become a houseguest and take up residence.

Thoughts are not the problem; it is how we respond to them. If we will confess our unbelief, demolish (utterly destroy) negative thoughts, and replace them with truth, God will extend forgiveness and mercifully bless our obedience.

> For though we live in the world, we do not wage war as the world does. The weapons we fight with are not the weapons of the world. On the contrary, they have divine power to demolish strongholds. We demolish arguments and every pretension that sets itself up against the knowledge of God, and we take captive every thought to make it obedient to Christ. (2 Corinthians 10:3–5 NIV)

Because I repented and humbled myself before God, a bright future awaited me. Everything the enemy stole proved to be a path for God to fulfill His promises. He gave back double blessings (and then some) for all the trials and troubles. The past with its pain and mistakes disappeared from view, forever covered by the blood of Jesus, never to be used against me again. I did not, nor could I ever, do anything to deserve God's mercy, but faithful and true to His Word, the Lord freely offered it without showing favoritism or condemnation.

The Word of God is the same yesterday, today, and forever. He promises a double portion, an everlasting covenant. A life filled with joy, love, health, and abundant blessings awaits those willing to believe and hold out in faith until the fulfillment of God's promises manifest.

> Instead of their shame my people will receive a *double portion*, and instead of disgrace they will rejoice in their inheritance; and so they will inherit a *double portion* in their land and everlasting joy will be theirs. For I, the

> Lord, love justice; I hate robbery and iniquity. In my faithfulness I will reward them and make *an everlasting covenant* with them. Their descendants will be known among the nations and their offspring among the peoples. *All who see them will acknowledge that they are a people the Lord has blessed.* (Isaiah 61:7–9 NIV; emphasis added)
>
> Return to your fortress, O prisoners of hope; even now I announce that I will restore *twice* as much to you. (Zechariah 9:12 NIV; emphasis added)
>
> After Job had prayed for his friends, the Lord made him prosperous again and gave him *twice* as much as he had before. (Job 42:10 NIV; emphasis added)

Serve notice on the enemy today and remind him who your Father is. Do not back down in fear of what terrible attack he may bring. Satan was an angel cast down from heaven due to pride and rebellion. Your Father is his Creator and the Creator of all things. Satan cannot create anything. He can only yield a distorted imitation.

Father God never has and never will be defeated or surprised by anything the enemy cleverly devises to bring destruction upon our lives. Whatever comes our way must go through the Father, for we belong to Him. Therefore, the old saying holds true, "If He brings you to it, He will bring you through it." In the name of Jesus and covered by His blood, we will always have the road map to absolute, overcoming victory. It is up to us to follow it and, with patience, wait. God has not forsaken or forgotten you.

> Have you not known? Have you not heard? The everlasting God, the LORD, The Creator of the ends of the earth, Neither faints nor is weary. His understanding is unsearchable. He gives power to the weak, And to those who have no might He increases strength. Even the youths shall faint and be weary, And the young men

shall utterly fall, But those who wait on the LORD shall renew *their* strength; They shall mount up with wings like eagles, They shall run and not be weary, They shall walk and not faint. (Isaiah 40:28–31 NKJV)

CHAPTER 5

PERSISTENCE PAYS OFF

Healthy and always on the go, I thought Dad was Superman. We fished, played, and prayed together. Building houses as a side job, he put the extra income into the church and paid our ever-growing medical bills. We had a small, struggling congregation oppressed by debt, gossip, and backbiting. Feeling God called him to this church, Dad sprang into action, working tirelessly to rebuild and restore our wounded congregation. It took a while to get the saints prayed up and emotional healing administered to the wounds. Through obedience and perseverance, our little church turned into a loving and growing family.

Arriving home from school one day, tragedy struck. We received a phone call informing us Dad suffered a heart attack and was en route to the hospital. For years, doctors begged him to slow down, but he did not listen. Building houses, taking care of our family, and pastoral duties finally took their toll. The added stress of Mom and I being sick did not help matters either. Trying to do everything without any help, Dad failed to heed the warning signs. In my mind, I could just imagine God saying, "Edward, it's okay to ask for help. Lean on Me, and I'll carry the burden and lighten the load."

> "Come unto Me, all ye that labor and are heavy laden,
> and I will give you rest" (Matthew 11:28 KJV).

Too often, we become so busy making a living we forget to give our cares and worries to God. Learning how to rest in Him is vital to a healthy existence. God gives us the strength to endure and the ability to bring a harmonic balance in every area of our lives. Many times, we just need to stop and ask for help, but we come up with a hundred reasons why we shouldn't, so we don't.

Mom took us to see Daddy; however, hospital rules stated no one under twelve could enter the intensive care unit. Only eleven at the time, I remember thinking, *Surely they won't keep me out*, but I was wrong.

Relatives from Dad's side of the family continued to pile in as we waited to hear news about his condition. Unfortunately, the Grants have never been known to be quiet or patient. Growing more nervous by the minute, I sat conjuring up ways to get into Dad's room.

The time came to make my move, and I slowly walked toward the nurse standing guard by the door. I decided to state my case, hoping compassion would override the rules. Taking a deep breath, I went for it. Without hesitation and very curtly, she stated, "The rules are *not* to be broken." Questions filled my mind: *How can she be so mean? Can't she see my pain? Why is she keeping me from seeing Daddy?*

Feeling angry and more determined than ever, adrenalin kicked in, and something powerful came over me. I hauled off and shoved the nurse aside, burst through the doors, and cried out for Daddy. Hearing the commotion, Mom immediately came out from behind a curtain. She lovingly patted me on the head as I ran to Dad's bedside.

Tubes were everywhere, but he managed to muster up a reassuring smile. I felt helpless as my mind anxiously raced with thoughts of life without him. I remember feeling scared and vulnerable. Daddy was our rock, and we desperately needed him.

Nurse "meanie" soon made her way to Mother, feeling the need to discuss my behavior. I apologized and boldly exclaimed, "I'll pray for Jesus to teach you how to be nice to hurting people."

My intentions were never to hurt anyone or break the rules. Whatever it took, I had to get to Daddy. Apparently, my behavior also disturbed a few of our relatives. Mother told them to leave me alone. Later I found out my parents enjoyed a good chuckle from my little outburst.

Falling into Faith

Jesus must long for us to demonstrate this kind of devotion and determination. If only our love for Him burned so intense, we would boldly push aside every hindrance, just to draw closer to our Savior. Oh, what benefits and blessings await those who strive fearlessly forward and draw near to God.

"Come near to God and He will come near to you" (James 4: 8 NIV).

In Christ alone is fullness of joy. In Him is a place of peace and healing, a place of rest for the weary and brokenhearted. Even when we fail and fall on our face, in repentance we can give our mess to God. He is the Master of turning a mess into a miracle.

Please understand, we should not aimlessly do whatever we please with the hopes God will bless our mess. But if we are truly repentant and turn from walking the path of disobedience, God is forgiving and full of mercy. As you continue reading, you will see my life is living proof of this undeniable truth.

Once we give our situation over to the Father, tests and trials may follow. During this process, a truly repentant heart will experience a profound sense of humility and continue in obedience, in spite of the difficulty.

There are times in our walk with Christ our faith will be tested. Some of these trials are not a result of disobedience; they are simply part of walking "the straight and narrow" and growing in our relationship with Jesus. During these times of testing, we have two choices: *fall* into the pit of despair and unbelief, or *fall* into the hands of God and, with perseverance, stand strong.

A good example of perseverance is the parable of the persistent widow in the book of Luke. This widow needed justice against her adversary; however, the judge in the town neither feared God nor cared about men. Jesus spoke this parable to His disciples and asked a very important question.

> Then Jesus told His disciples a parable to show them that they should always pray and not give up. He said, "In a certain town there was a judge who neither feared God nor cared about men. And there was a widow in that town who kept coming to him with the plea, 'grant me

justice against my adversary.'" For some time he refused, but finally he said to himself, "even though I don't fear God or care about men, yet because this widow keeps bothering me, I will see that she gets justice, so that she won't eventually wear me out with her coming." And the Lord said, "Listen to what the unjust judge says. And will not God bring about justice for His chosen ones, who cry out to Him day and night? Will He keep putting them off? I tell you, He will see that they get justice, and quickly. However, when the Son of Man comes, will He find faith on the earth?" (Luke 18:1–8 NIV)

These are the questions we must ask: Will He find the kind of faith in me that perseveres in prayer, a faith willing to stand on His Word regardless of the obstacles or circumstances? A faith that says, "I may be in pain, but I know my Redeemer lives and purchased my healing and restoration on the cross." A faith boldly proclaiming, "Though undeserving, the blood of Jesus allows me to stand as the righteousness of Christ, and with a grateful heart, I will humbly expect and receive His blessings in my life." God rewards this kind of persistent faith. He is just, good, and merciful. We are His children and joint heirs with Christ. We have the assurance of a loving, faithful Father who longs to bless His children with good gifts.

The Lord mercifully restored Dad back to health. Our church pulled together in love and unity, assisting with household chores, yardwork, and wherever there was a need. The family of God can be an awesome thing.

The thought of losing Dad seemed too painful to comprehend. Until he suffered the heart attack, no one realized how heavy his burden had become. Everyone depended on him for one thing or another. It seemed so natural for us to place our confidence in his ability to fix and handle everything. Dad prayed for us when we were sick, provided for our needs, settled disagreements, and made things right. He truly was our Superman.

Why did this present such a problem? Our focus and dependence needed to be on Jesus Christ. Instead, we were putting too much pressure on Dad to solve all our problems. When dependence is on humankind, the focus is on works and the limited abilities of mere mortals. Humanity is limited. God is not. Once this happens, our priorities get out of line according to God's Word, and we set ourselves up for disappointment. No longer allowing ourselves to grow and mature, we end up placing too much of a burden on someone else to come to our rescue and be our salvation.

There are times when seeking counsel is necessary and full of wisdom; however, as children of God, we carry a responsibility. Instead of running elsewhere for answers about every little thing, we need to walk close enough to the Father and boldly approach the throne of grace for ourselves. As His children, we have this right.

As a chaplain and cognitive behavioral therapist, many people seek my help for guidance during difficult and painful times. There is no shame in asking for help when we are weak, vulnerable, and in pain. If you are a Christian, I always ask about your relationship with God. It is important for me to know how much time you are spending in prayer and studying His Word. These questions are not meant to condemn, but it helps guide my plan to bring hope and healing into a situation.

When we turn away from God because of something a person has done (regardless of their vocation), we have allowed our focus and priority to be on humankind. Our foundation must be firmly built on Jesus Christ. Nothing or no one should be able to shake us off that foundation. How shameful it is for us to allow the mistakes of a human being to interfere or hurt our relationship with a loving and faithful Father.

Challenges and obstacles should be communicated first and foremost in prayer to our Creator, our Deliverer. To successfully grow and mature we must pray, listen, and apply God's Word and principles. Only then can we rise up and exercise our faith. The result of these actions are a life-changing, balanced, and healthy spiritual and emotional life.

I grew up running to Dad for everything, especially spiritual matters.

This is okay if you are a child, but as you spiritually mature, your first instinct should be to seek Christ. My first thought usually went like this: *Dad will have the answer. I don't really need to pray. I'll just ask him.*

This pattern of misplaced priorities repeated itself throughout my life for many years. It took a long time for me to finally realize I needed to seek God first for wisdom and help. He quickly shined a spotlight on this immature area, and the Holy Spirit began a new work of maturity and growth. I am sure Dad breathed a sigh of relief when this growing-up phase started manifesting itself in my actions. Although he never complained, I am certain my problems felt overwhelming to him at times.

Life soon resumed to what we called normal. Mom and I continued battling sickness as uncertain obstacles lay ahead. Even in our weaknesses and human frailties, God remained faithful. He is Jehovah-Shammah, the God who promises to never leave or forsake us.

> The Lord Himself goes before you and will be with you; He will never leave you nor forsake you. Do not be afraid, do not be discouraged. (Deuteronomy 31:8 NIV)

> Then thou shalt call, and the Lord shall answer; thou shalt cry, and He shall say, Here I am. (Isaiah 58:9 KJV)

> But I am poor and needy; yet the Lord thinketh upon me; Thou art my help and my deliverer; make no tarrying, O my God. (Psalm 40:17 KJV).

CHAPTER 6

THE DIFFERENCE BETWEEN HOPE AND FAITH

While studying Luke, chapter 24, I began to understand the difference between hope and faith. After the Crucifixion, two followers of Jesus were traveling the road to Emmaus, discussing everything that happened. As they traveled along, Jesus Himself came up and began walking with them (but they were divinely kept from recognizing Him). He asked what they were discussing. With great sadness, they proceeded to explain the situation.

> He was a prophet, powerful in word and deed before God and all the people. The chief priests and our rulers handed Him over to be sentenced to death, and they crucified Him; *but we had hoped He was the One who was going to redeem Israel.* (Luke 24:19–21 NIV; emphasis added)

The scripture states these men "had hoped He was the One who was going to redeem Israel," which is why they were so disappointed in the recent events of His death. However, prior to the Crucifixion, Jesus said He would be raised to life on the third day (Luke 9:22). Why didn't anyone believe?

When the women went to the tomb to anoint the body of Jesus, they found the stone rolled away, and Jesus was gone. The book of Mark, chapter 16, explains what happened upon their arrival and departure.

> When the Sabbath was over, Mary Magdalene, Mary the mother of James, and Salome bought spices so that they might go to anoint Jesus' body. Very early on the first day of the week, just after sunrise, they were on their way to the tomb and they asked each other, "Who will roll the stone away from the entrance of the tomb?" "But when they looked up, they saw that the stone, which was very large, had been rolled away. As they entered the tomb, they saw a young man dressed in a white robe sitting on the right side, and they were alarmed. "Don't be alarmed," he said. "You are looking for Jesus the Nazarene, who was crucified. He has risen! He is not here. See the place where they laid him. But go, tell his disciples and Peter, 'He is going ahead of you into Galilee. There you will see him, just as he told you.'" Trembling and bewildered, the women went out and fled from the tomb. They said nothing to anyone, because they were afraid. (Mark 16:1–9 NIV)

They left afraid. Where was their faith? After all, it was the third day. When some of the companions went to the tomb and discovered what the women said to be true…where was their faith? Keep in mind, the scripture tells us they had hope, but where was their faith? Why didn't they believe? Jesus addressed their lack of faith in Luke 24:25 (NIV), He called them "foolish and slow to believe."

> When He was at the table with them, He took bread, gave thanks, broke it and began to give it to them. Then their eyes were opened and they recognized Him, and He disappeared from their sight. They asked each other, "Were not our hearts burning within us while He talked with us on the road and opened the Scriptures to us?" (Luke 24:30–32 NIV)

We all need hope, but when hope is mixed with faith, we have a powerful combination. These men hoped in the Savior but lacked faith. After His death, they were even reluctant to call Him the Messiah.

Psalm 62:5 tells us, "Find rest, O my soul, in God alone; my hope comes from Him." Our hope is in God, but it is our faith that makes the decision to believe in Him and boldly "call things that are not as though they were!" (Romans 4:17 NIV).

―⁂―

Every personality test I have ever taken always reveals the same thing; I am an extrovert and optimistic by nature. I have been told these are good traits to have; however, at some point in my spiritual growth, I needed to allow this hopeful optimism to mix with a growing faith. Instead, I stayed in an "I'm hoping for the best, and I hope God will heal me" frame of mind. This mind-set created a perfect atmosphere for defeat and hopelessness. The next stage of my life shined a spotlight on how desperately I needed to understand the difference between hope and faith and how to combine these two very important ingredients in order to mature and grow in God.

The remainder of my childhood and throughout adolescence, I continued experiencing frequent fainting spells, severe bladder and kidney infections, migraine headaches, female problems, and extreme anemia. My white cell count stayed abnormally high due to infections, which resulted in hospitalizations to undergo a series of antibiotic treatments, as well as treatment for the anemia.

Examined and treated by numerous physicians, they could not figure out what was wrong with my blood. Characteristics of the illness appeared much like leukemia and other diseases, but test after test came back negative for everything they suspected.

The doctors did agree on one diagnosis, a small bladder tube (urethra). For the next several years, every thirty to sixty days, I went through a painful dilation procedure to minimize infections and open up the urethra.

The Bible says, "The joy of the Lord is our strength." Being the ultimate optimist, my determination to be known as "the happy one," not "the sick one," stayed strong and steady. Although this attitude of joy did not please the enemy, I remained stubbornly unmovable in my quest. When laughter and joy seemed far away, I took comfort in the scriptures and the support of my parents.

> A merry heart doeth good like a medicine, but a broken spirit drieth the bones. (Psalm 17:22 KJV)

> For I have learned to be content whatever the circumstances. I know what it is to be in need and I know what it is to have plenty. I have learned the secret of being content in any and every situation, whether well fed or hungry, whether living in plenty or in want, I can do all things through Him who gives me strength. (Philippians 4:11–13 NIV)

Shortly after turning fifteen, my urologist requested permission to perform an experimental surgery, with the hope of correcting the urethra. Children were good candidates for the procedure, but due to my age, they barely gave me a 10 percent chance of success. Regardless, infections were spreading to my kidneys and growing more frequent and painful. Grasping for help, we said yes.

During surgery, our family and friends gathered together and prayed. We fully believed God heard our prayers and the surgery would bring healing for my bladder condition. Unfortunately, I was not prepared for what happened next. Within a few days, the doctors realized the procedure failed. I quickly became confused and depressed over the news of no relief for at least one of my many health problems.

Disappointed and apologetic, doctors tried to encourage us by stating the field of medicine changed at a phenomenal pace, and a breakthrough could be just around the corner for patients with my problem. Having grown tired of reassuring words, I turned away and privately thought, *Can't they fix at least one thing that is wrong with me?*

Have you ever prayed and believed God so hard for something, but you did not get the answer you expected? During those times, it is hard to be strong, and unfortunately, the enemy knows this. When we are weak and confused, he takes every opportunity to devise a pity, poor-me

Falling into Faith

trap. At this point, I readily obliged him, and joy no longer prevailed in my world of self-pity and unanswered questions.

I began asking, "Lord, where are You, and why didn't You answer my prayer?" I do not believe God gets upset when we ask questions; however, my heart had become accusatory and bitter. This self-destructive attitude allowed the enemy to steal my peace and joy, replacing it with fear and discouragement.

You may be at a place of desperation in your own life, a place where nothing makes sense. You have done all you know to do, and it still is not enough. You may even be questioning God as you seek answers to tough questions. Have you ever felt like screaming, "God, where are You? Do You hear me? Do You care? Do You really love me? What is the point?"

Due to the fall of humankind, Satan is the ruler of this world, and we are his prey. Scripture tells us, "And whoever shuns evil becomes prey" (Isaiah 59:15 NIV). We must not forget God is always at work on our behalf warring against the enemy's attacks, but there are times we may never fully understand a situation or have an answer. It is in those moments of frustration we need a maturing, growing faith. In moments of despair and uncertainty, it is vital we learn to "lean not on our own understanding" (Proverbs 3:5 NIV) and trust the Lord Almighty to "make the crooked paths straight" (Isaiah 45:2 NIV).

Be encouraged and remember an important truth—God is more powerful than Satan, and He gave us a promise, "A righteous man may have many troubles, but the Lord delivers him from them all" (Psalm 34:19 NIV). God's Word does not say we will understand all our troubles, but it does say He will "deliver us from them all." Although we are not promised a life of ease, a life free from worry and problems, we are promised deliverance. This truth brings a great deal of peace to my soul.

Have you ever watched a cat stalk its prey? Slowly and methodically it moves, with its eyes fixed on the target. Nothing can distract it. Satan preys on the children of God using this same method. The only way of escape is to know, trust in, and apply God's Word. We must fix our eyes and ears on our Creator; no other report should be trusted. Even when things do not make sense, our complete hope and faith must be in the resurrection power of Jesus Christ. The slightest distraction due to unbelief, anxiety, or pain gives Satan the opportunity to "kill, steal, and destroy."

> "Be sober, be vigilant, because your adversary the devil, as a roaring lion, walketh about seeking whom he may devour" (1 Peter 5:8 NIV).

As you continue reading my life's story, you will understand why I emphasize knowing the Word, trusting God, and the importance of application. Too many times, I crashed and burned due to believing Satan's lies. My eyes failed to stay fixed on Jesus and His report. A need for everything to make sense, constantly analyzing, and questioning why I didn't or couldn't understand, became a source of great downfall.

Humans look at things through the eyes of flesh. If we could see our circumstances through spiritual eyes, doubt and fear would not overwhelm us. You see, God is not going to allow anything to come our way that He is not willing and able to bring us through.

There is a remarkable story in the Bible regarding seeing with spiritual eyes. The king of Aram was at war with Israel. The prophet Elisha warned the king of Israel where the Arameans would be. The Israelites were repeatedly one step ahead of them. This enraged the king of Aram, so he summoned his officers together to find out who the traitor was among them.

> "None of us, my lord the king," said one of his officers, "but Elisha, the prophet who is in Israel, tells the king of Israel the very words you speak in your bedroom." "Go, find out where he is, the king ordered, so I can send men and capture him." The report came back: "He is in Dothan." Then he sent horses and chariots and a strong force there. They went by night and surrounded the city. When the servant of the man of God got up and went out early the next morning, an army with horses and chariots had surrounded the city. "Oh my lord, what shall we do?" the servant asked. "Don't be afraid" the prophet answered, *"Those who are with are more than those who are with them."* And Elisha prayed, *"O Lord open his eyes so he may see."* Then the Lord opened the servant's eyes, and

> *he looked and saw the hills full of horses and chariots of fire all around Elisha.* (2 Kings 6:12–17 NIV; emphasis added)

In response to Elisha's prayer, the Lord opened his servant's eyes, and he saw the protecting, mighty, and heavenly host surrounding them. What an amazing boost of faith.

The devil wants our spiritual eyes blinded with lies and deceptions. Keeping our focus on flesh and circumstances always gives him the upper hand. If we will build up our spiritual self by feeding on the Word of God and speaking truth over our situation, we too will see and feel the very presence of God's mighty army of protection.

Walk in daily communion with the Holy Spirit; purpose to take in more of God and His Word than the world and its lies. Begin to watch and weigh every word before speaking. This is a constant work in progress for me. However, I've seen firsthand how miracles manifest when we do these things. Remember, we are prey to Satan; therefore, we must put on the armor of God to fight against his attacks.

Do not be afraid to reveal everything to the Father in prayer. You see, He already knows. Nothing you can say will ever stop Him from loving you. He longs for us to commune with Him. Don't just talk to God when you're hurting or in need. Talk to Him when you are happy and full of joy. He loves an honest and grateful heart full of praise.

How would our earthly parents feel if we only talked to them when we needed or wanted something? This kind of selfish and self-centered attitude will cause any relationship to suffer. Too often, this is how we treat God.

We have a direct line to this magnificent Creator of life through prayer, communion, praise, and obedience. Reading God's Word and talking to Him daily should come as naturally as eating and breathing. Having the truth of the living God inside us and acting on it turns Satan's attacks into awesome opportunities for the Lord to reveal Himself as our Healer, Deliverer, the great I Am.

I grew up talking to the Lord but rarely listening. I failed to realize a healthy, mature relationship consists of two people communicating. We limit His ability to bless and manifest miracles in our lives when we are doing all the talking. You see, He is the one with the answers. I am so thankful He remained patiently at work in my heart.

You may ask, "How does God talk to someone?" He speaks in many ways. I have found most of the time He speaks to me through His Word and the Holy Spirit, "that still small voice." What is that still small voice? Scriptures explain that once we receive Christ as our Savior, the Holy Spirit dwells within us. It is a living spirit of God constantly directing and instructing us to walk according to His Word.

Several times in my life, God has spoken to me so powerfully it felt as if someone was sitting beside me talking. This is a truly humbling experience. He can speak through many avenues: dreams, visions, friends, strangers, and ministers. Do not box God in; He can speak any way He chooses. The Bible tells us in the book of Numbers, chapter 22, He even spoke through a donkey.

Allow me to spotlight a critical issue and render a caution: we must not carelessly and loosely state, "God spoke to me and said …" unless He truly did. It is a violation of the commandment, "Thou shall not take the name of the Lord thy God in vain." The Amplified Version brings a sobering clarity to this commandment. It is not just talking about profanity.

> You shall not take the name of the LORD your God in vain [that is, irreverently, in false affirmations or in ways that impugn the character of God]; for the LORD will not hold guiltless *nor* leave unpunished the one who takes His name in vain [disregarding its reverence and its power]. (Exodus 20:7 AMP)

Yes, God speaks to His children, but too often He gets credit for things He had nothing to do with. There are hurting people who are in desperate situations and just because someone advised them, "God spoke to me and said (so and so), and you should do (such and such)," they have ended up with additional pain and devastation. This one statement has caused so much damage within the body of Christ.

If someone constantly says, "God spoke to me and said …" a big red flag goes up, and I begin observing the fruit and life of that individual. This is not judging; it is doing what scripture tells us to do, "test everything." We will discuss this scripture further and in depth in a later chapter.

Growing up in church, we often heard people say, "God said so and so." When it did not work out, they claimed He changed His mind or God meant something else. We noticed the same thing happening when we were missionaries. In 1 Samuel 15:29 (NIV), it clearly says, "He who is the Glory of Israel does not lie or change His mind; for He is not a human being, that He should change His mind." Another scripture confirming God's steadfastness is in Malachi: "I the LORD do not change" (Malachi 3:6 NIV).

It is important to understand the character of God our Father. According to scripture, He does not call someone to do a certain thing, only to recant and say, "Oops, sorry, I changed My mind." Study this for yourself, and it will help you discern the truth.

Many will use scripture to argue this point, stating God changed His mind several times in the Old Testament; however, as you study the Bible, you will discover He did not contradict Himself. God clearly gave an option to people living a life of sin and idolatry. If they repented and turned from their wicked ways, He would not bring wrath and judgment upon them. A choice was given: repentance or wrath.

Because of God's mercy and grace toward His creation, intercession for the lost and those who stray from the Lord is of critical importance. God will always reserve the right to bring redemption instead of wrath when repentance has been chosen over continued sin.

> And if I say to a wicked person, "You will surely die," but they then turn away from their sin and do what is just and right-if they give back what they took in pledge for a loan, return what they have stolen, follow the decrees that give life, and do no evil-that person will surely live; they will not die. None of the sins that person has committed will be remembered against them. They have done what is just and right; they will surely live. (Ezekiel 33:14–16 NIV)

When I feel God has spoken to me about something concerning

another individual, first I make sure what I heard lines up with scripture. Next, I ask the Lord to show me if this is something I am to intercede and pray about or share with that person. If it is something I am to share, I begin the conversation by saying, "Take this to God in prayer and ask Him to confirm the truth."

I do not want to assume at any time I am not capable of making a mistake. I am an emotional woman who is sensitive, opinionated, and hormonal. If I am in error (and yes, it has happened), I am the first to say, "Forgive me." When it is God, the Holy Spirit will reveal the truth and confirm what has been said. The fact is we are fallible. Humans make mistakes, but God does not. One more thing to remember, the fruit will follow. Inspect the fruit, and the truth will be clear.

Throughout my life, different individuals have given me words from God. When this happens, my spirit immediately bears witness or I feel strangely uneasy. Regardless, I carefully weigh the words against the Bible. If it checks out, I give it to the Lord and ask for confirmation (unless He has already confirmed it).

> Jesus replied, "I have already told you, and you don't believe me. The proof is the work I do in my Father's name. But you don't believe me because you are not my sheep. My sheep listen to my voice; I know them, and they follow me. I give them eternal life, and they will never perish. No one can snatch them away from me, for my Father has given them to me, and he is more powerful than anyone else. No one can snatch them from the Father's hand. The Father and I are one." (John 10:25–30 NLT)

What a glorious promise. We can hear the voice of God because we belong to Him, and no one can snatch us out of His mighty hands. We are His sheep; He is our Shepherd. Talk to your Shepherd; ask Him to open your spiritual eyes and ears. You will find He is anxiously waiting to reveal Himself to you in wonderful and exciting ways.

Falling into Faith

I eventually stopped pouting about the failed surgery and asking, "Why, why, why?" It amazes me how patient God is toward His children. He never once screamed, "Shut up, Donna! You are driving me crazy!" Thankfully He is not impatient like so many of us (myself included). I am truly grateful He lovingly and mercifully stuck around, constantly working on my heart and mind. Another year passed, filled with many challenges. Faithful and true to His word, the Lord stayed by my side, always wooing me to draw closer to Him.

One Sunday morning a few weeks before my sixteenth birthday, a young man walked into our church. Sitting at the piano preparing the music, I looked up and watched as he made his way to a seat. Stepping down from the platform, I went over to welcome him to the service. He introduced himself as Bob Wilcox, stating he was in the military and stationed at Eglin Air Force Base. Bob appeared quiet and shy. Although I could not put my finger on it, there was something about this guy I really liked. We were immediately drawn to one another, and a close friendship soon developed.

Bob possessed a presence of someone who trusted God with his life. You did not have to ask; you just knew he loved the Lord. We enjoyed spending time together, and he always made me feel accepted and happy. Being the typical teenager, I did not know how to appreciate this gift of friendship, nor did I recognize God's hand at work.

In time, our friendship blossomed into courtship. Mom and Dad really liked Bob, although he was older and in his early twenties. Bob's maturity and thoughtfulness made him easy to love. Unfortunately, my health continued to be a huge obstacle. The closer we grew, the more obsessed I became about not becoming a burden to Bob due to sickness. I often shut down, withdrew, and became distant. In my heart, I felt he deserved better than I could ever give him. Bob continuously reassured me, but my head could not grasp someone loving me that much. In my mind, I was damaged goods. Bob put up with a lot during our on-again off-again relationship.

Instead of seeking God for guidance, I reasoned things out for myself. Regardless of how mature I may have been about some things, the fact is a teenager does not possess much wisdom. During those young and impressionable years, I became a slave to feelings. Many years ago, I heard a very wise statement, "Feelings make great servants but terrible masters."

Despite spiritual immaturity, when I fell on my face in failure, I earnestly sought God for help and answers. He lovingly showered me with love, peace, and forgiveness. The desire to serve Him remained strong. Even when I chose the wrong path, God used those very mistakes to teach and mold me into something useful for His glory.

Sunday nights after church, our youth group often went out for pizza or burgers. We shared hours of laughter and mischievous fun. The Bible tells us a cheerful heart is medicine to the body, and it certainly lifted my spirits. Very few people understood the importance these little outings held for me. For a short while, I forgot about pain and sickness, as it brought a sense of normalcy and much-needed laughter. Friends and fellowship are necessary and vitally important to our overall mental and emotional well-being. Accountability partners and healthy relationships are also key to a harmonic balance and growth.

Physically, things took a turn for the worse. Serious female complications surfaced with unpredictable and heavy menstrual periods, followed by ovarian cysts. As doctors continued running tests, I battled constant anemia, fainting spells, and numerous infections, sending me in and out of the emergency room and hospital for treatment. Doctors remained baffled, unable to find the reason why my white cell count stayed so high and infections plagued me continuously.

There were other problems as well. Always the perfectionist, I desired to please everyone. Unrealistic expectations and overly critical of myself, anxieties often turned to constant worry. This behavior eventually caused a bleeding ulcer, resulting in more hospitalizations and additional daily medications.

One semester in high school, I received a B in home economics. This sent my world crashing down around me because a B ruined my A average. Feeling as though I let everyone down, I boarded the school bus in tears. When I arrived home, Mom tried to console me. Nothing worked. Finally, she called the teacher and requested a conference. Sympathetic to my situation, the teacher advised Mom I could do a make-up assignment.

In those days, home economics consisted of sewing and cooking. I cooked without a problem, but sewing frustrated me something awful. Fortunately, Mom sewed beautifully. She provided the instructions and one-on-one attention needed to bring my grade up to an A. I still remember her reassuring words, "Okay, little Miss Worry Wart, it's not the end of the world. Just follow my instructions, and you'll do just fine."

In and out of the hospital so frequently, I could no longer attend high school. The principle and teachers were kind and helpful. They gave my assignments to Mother, making the necessary arrangements for me to complete my studies at home and graduate early. None of my classmates contacted me, and I lost touch with everyone. When you are chronically ill, people often pull away because they don't know what to do or say. It is isolating and emotionally painful.

The year I turned eighteen, my parents surprised me with a very special gift. They arranged for me to record a gospel album. Singing and testifying about Jesus is all I ever wanted to do, and this was a dream come true. If I left this world, at least I would leave a testimony of God's love through music.

As the day approached, I nervously prayed, *Dear Lord, please don't allow health complications to land me in the hospital and hinder the album.* God heard my prayer and granted me the strength to complete the project. Whatever the cost, I purposed to work for the Lord until my time on earth ceased. The enemy did not like this stubborn determination, and he did not plan to sit idly by.

> Humble yourselves, therefore, under God's mighty hand, that He may lift you up in due time. Cast all your anxiety on Him because He cares for you. Be self-controlled and alert. Your enemy the devil prowls around like a roaring lion looking for someone to devour. (1 Peter 5:6–8 NIV)

Word about the album spread as churches began asking me to come for concerts and services. Health complications made it apparent I could not travel alone. My cousin Rhonda and I were very close, and she lived only a short distance away in Pensacola, Florida. She had been earnestly seeking God's will for a new direction in her life. Although Rhonda shared my desire to reach the lost, the thought of public speaking made her panic and break out in a sweat. Despite being extremely shy and quiet, the Lord put it on her heart to become my traveling companion. It is amazing how God knows just who and what to bring into our lives to fulfill His will and purposes.

Rhonda lovingly and meticulously handled details like driving and equipment setup. Her only stipulation, I could not call on her to speak in front of people. However, she was amazing during times of prayer. Rhonda possessed the precious gift of an intercessor and prayer warrior. Our opposite natures worked well together as her mature, mild manner brought a balance to my hyperactive personality.

Being in ministry with me held many challenges. I fainted easily and with no warning whatsoever. One minute we were driving down the road or walking through a grocery store talking and laughing, and then—bam. I passed out cold. We always seemed to find humor in the situation. At the time, it sure beat crying.

As the days and months passed, I continued suffering with intense migraines, severe pain in my back and sides, infections, anemia, and high temperatures. Rhonda became a pro at pulling off the road for me to throw up as we traveled to and from services. It was not a pretty sight. Through it all, Rhonda's prayers carried us from destination to destination with the patience and compassion of a saint. Amazingly, it is the laughter and times of prayer I remember most, not the pain or frustration.

Together we witnessed God move on our behalf in mighty and miraculous ways. Pulling up to a church or concert venue, we prayed for God's healing touch and anointing. The Lord never let us down. As soon as I stepped on the platform or stage to sing and minister, all nausea and pain immediately disappeared. Singing my heart out, I testified of God's goodness and prayed for people. In those moments, I felt a faith strong enough to move any mountain. When service ended and we headed home, sickness usually returned with a vengeance. Some may say, if God is so good why did He allow the pain to return? Keep reading my story and you will soon understand just how the Lord truly does work all things out for the good.

One night in a small country church, a lady came forward for prayer. She desired healing from a kidney infection. Standing there with a fever

Falling into Faith

and kidney infection myself, I thought, *How in the world can I pray for this lady and expect results?* Suddenly, an overwhelming compassion for this sweet lady and a warrior-type spirit arose within me. Rhonda and I began speaking God's Word of healing over her body. As we stood together united in prayer and faith, the Lord miraculously healed her. The fever and pain immediately disappeared. I spent years in a confused state of mind, wondering why God did not heal me too. The truth is I could believe for her but not for myself. I needed to let go of this self-imposed defeatist attitude and believe God's promises also applied to me.

I diligently studied the Bible and knew the scriptures; however, I lacked understanding. I could not see myself through God's eyes. Instead, I saw an "always going to be sick, this is my cross to bear" image staring back at me. On the outside, I appeared to have complete confidence and poise, but on the inside, I felt broken, damaged, and completely unworthy of asking anything from God.

Feelings of inadequacy, along with accepting and tolerating things the Lord desired for me to overcome limited His ability to perform a greater miracle in my life. The devil deceived me into thinking I somehow deserved this; therefore, it must be God's will. In the South, we call this stinkin' thinkin', and it will always hinder God's best in our lives. Whether we realize it or not, when we choose to entertain these kinds of thoughts, we are living in condemnation (believing a lie) and are no longer in agreement with God. Christ died and shed His precious blood so that *all* His children can be overcomers, not just a chosen few.

Without openly admitting it, I also suffered with a works mentality. I thought if I worked hard enough for God, eventually He'd consider me worthy of healing. It is not about works, talents, abilities, or how many scriptures we can quote. The Bible clearly states, "Our righteousness is as filthy rags." Working for God nonstop will not make us good enough. He longs to be merciful to us, and the key to His great mercy is faith.

If you are a student of the Bible, you may be thinking about the scriptures in James concerning faith and works. For the sake of clarity, let's look at them.

> What does it profit, my brethren, if someone says he has faith but does not have works? Can faith save him? If a

brother or sister is naked and destitute of daily food, and one of you says to them, "Depart in peace, be warmed and filled," but you do not give them the things which are needed for the body, what *does it* profit? Thus also faith by itself, if it does not have works, is dead. (James 2:14–17 NKJV)

Faith without works is dead because true faith produces a harvest of blessings brought forth from our commitment toward obedience. Obedience requires work; however, we absolutely must remember what God says about the importance of faith itself. "And the Scripture was fulfilled which says, 'Abraham believed God, and it was accounted to him for righteousness.' And he was called the friend of God" (James 2:23, NKJV). Abraham's faith in God and his willingness to believe was the beginning of an amazing miracle and stirred God's heart to the point He called Abraham *friend*.

My life continued to be interrupted with doctors and hospitals. Forced to face the inevitable, I could no longer travel. Rhonda and I said goodbye to our days on the road but never stopped believing for a miracle. Despite the setbacks, the Lord found ways to use us for His glory.

God is not looking for perfect vessels to get the job done. None of us earthlings are perfect. All He truly wants is a heart and life striving after Him in willing obedience.

CHAPTER 7

HONEYSUCKLE AND VANILLA

During one of my bouts with sickness, a cyst developed on my left ovary with a serious infection. Before long, my bladder and both kidneys were also infected, sending my white cell count soaring dangerously high. Running out of options, doctors scheduled a partial hysterectomy and exploratory surgery. I panicked when they said *hysterectomy*, but they assured me I could still have children one day. With any luck, they hoped the exploratory surgery might reveal some answers. We did not believe in luck. but we believed in prayer, and that is what we did. *Pray*.

They did not find the answers we hoped for, but I received some pain relief for a brief period; however, this only proved to be a small lull before a very troubling storm.

With traveling behind me and after a time of recuperating, I resumed working as the music and youth minister in Dad's church. This was not a paid position due to the size of our congregation, so I went in search of a job. When you live in a small town, everyone knows you (or of you), and because of my numerous health problems, I wasn't sure anyone would be willing to hire me. God's favor shined through, and He mercifully opened a door of opportunity at a local bank with great health benefits. Because of my physical condition and the need for health insurance, this proved to be a huge blessing.

The next few months, life played out like a nightmare. Extremely thin and unable to keep food down, everyday living presented a heaping dish of discouragement and physical pain. Regardless of how hard I tried, I could not seem to catch a break. Heavily medicated, I suffered with memory loss, a poor appetite, and confusion. My employer never knew what physical disaster might strike from one day to the next. Through it all, God's mercy and favor prevailed.

One night after coming home from work, I passed out several times trying to get to bed. Experiencing severe pain in my sides, excessive menstrual bleeding, and a high temperature, my parents frantically called the doctor and rushed me to the emergency room. In my heart, I knew something bad was happening. With the hospital forty-five minutes away, I lay in the back seat of the car crying. Mom and Dad tried to hide their desperation and panic, but I could see it in their eyes. We all prayed together as fear gripped our hearts.

What a scary time this must have been for my parents. As the years passed, we rarely spoke about that long ride to the hospital. Parents want to fix things for their kids, but they could not fix this or simply kiss and make it go away.

The enemy comes in like a flood when we are weak from praying, vulnerable from sleepless nights, and tired from pain and worry. He attacks without mercy when we are physically and emotionally weary from praying for a miracle we are not seeing. It is in those moments the Word of God must be rooted deep in our hearts. Beyond a shadow of doubt, beyond all circumstances and no matter how hard or painful the situation, we must know God is willing and able to keep His Word. If we do not stay focused on God's truth, Satan's attacks will beat us down.

I do not mind telling you, we were worn out from the struggle, and things were headed downhill fast. Everyone prayed for a miracle while a team of doctors hovered about discussing their next plan of attack. Feeling they must have overlooked something from the previous surgery, they decided to operate again. In no shape to argue or question, they assured us everything possible would be done to avoid a complete hysterectomy. I was terrified.

Weary from pain and uncertainty, I prayed for God to heal me or take me home. Before heading off to surgery I reminded my parents, "If things look really bad, God will give us a miracle. Don't worry and have faith. I don't want a hysterectomy."

Family members began arriving as everyone joined together in prayer. Amanda, my three-year-old niece, is who I remember most from that night. She was a sweet bundle of joy, and best of all, she loved her aunt Donna. Judy, Amanda's mom, hid her in a laundry basket to sneak her into the room. She crawled up in bed next to me, patting my face, telling me Jesus was going to make it all better. She appeared so full of faith while the rest of us felt overwhelmed by the circumstances and bad reports.

Amanda's childlike faith is what God longs for us to demonstrate toward His promises, even in the worst of times. When life throws us a curve and does not seem fair, childlike faith is often hard to find. That's when we must dig deep and choose truth.

Small and frail, doctors worked to stabilize and prepare me for surgery. Little did I know, in a few short hours my faith would experience a tremendous blow. Life as I knew it soon changed forever.

During surgery, I began losing a lot of blood, and my pressure dropped dangerously low. My female organs were in terrible shape, and I continued to hemorrhage. The situation turned critical quickly, and it appeared the doctors' efforts were failing. In a desperate attempt to turn the situation around, one of the physicians went to the surgical waiting room and asked for permission to proceed with a hysterectomy. With pressure mounting, my parents said, "Yes." I received numerous pints of blood that day, which put me at risk for other complications. In 1979, blood was not tested for the AIDS virus. Years later, God's mercy and protection from this disease revealed itself in a miraculous way.

Waking up in recovery, I asked for Mom and Dad. Hardly able to talk, I whispered, "Everything's okay, isn't it? They didn't have to do the hysterectomy, did they?"

Tears rolled down Daddy's face, and he said, "Baby, you are going to be okay, they got everything." Asking him what he meant, Dad said the doctors did not have a choice; the hysterectomy was necessary.

Seeing my pain and despair, Mama said, "Donna, don't worry about not being able to have children. You've had enough pain in your life, and God has great things in store for you."

Something happened in that moment. I can't explain it except to say a part of me died that day. Living lost its appeal. Feeling hopeless, I found myself constantly whispering this simple prayer, "Please, God, take me home. I don't want to live here anymore."

The crushing disappointment of only being nineteen years old and robbed of ever having children, along with continued and constant pain, hindered my ability to remember, "When bad things happen, God is still on the throne." I went through a season of anger and bitterness toward God for allowing the hysterectomy. I even felt He added insult to injury by choosing to let me live, especially with what happened next.

I never felt anger toward my parents because of the hysterectomy. I realized they were desperately trying to save my life the only way they knew how. Ultimately, God had the final say. Even in this season of rebellion, His love and protection stayed faithful. He is an amazing Father, and His love is unconditional.

Nothing takes God by surprise. He knew what that fateful day held for me. Did this stop His good plans for my life? Oh no. His plans were going to be wonderfully accomplished, despite the enemy's attempts to kill and destroy. The road ahead stretched long and hard, but one day blessings would come from the curse.

To this day, I truly believe if the hysterectomy had not happened, God would have miraculously sustained my life, for He is the giver and taker of life. I wasn't leaving this world until He fulfilled and accomplished everything He planned. His Word promises, "The Lord will fulfill His purpose for me" (Psalm 138:8 NIV). "Being confident in this, that He who began a good work in you will carry it on to completion until the day of Christ Jesus" (Philippians 1:6 NIV).

You may ask, "Well, Donna, what if you died on the operating table?" The answer is simple. I am still alive today, so obviously God's work in my life wasn't finished. He alone will decide the moment I take my last breath on earth, because it is His breath in my lungs. Although hard times lay ahead, the Lord stayed faithfully by my side.

When life is hard and seems unfair, remember we are God's children, and we belong to Him alone. He is all-powerful and all-knowing with great plans for each of us.

> Blessed is he who has regard for the weak; the Lord delivers him in times of trouble. The Lord will protect him and preserve his life; He will bless him in the land and not surrender him to the desire of his foes. The Lord

> will sustain him on his sickbed and restore him from his bed of illness. (Psalm 41:1–3 NIV)

The greatest weapon we can use in moments of pain and confusion is praise. Years passed before I understood the power of this praise principle. The Bible says, "Be joyful always; pray continually; give thanks in all circumstances, for this is God's will for you in Christ Jesus" (1 Thessalonians 5:16–18 NIV). Notice it says give thanks in *all* circumstances. It doesn't say *for* them but to give thanks *in* them.

Trusting God is a 100 percent commitment, even when nothing makes sense and the Lord seems a million miles away. We must trust Him when the outcome is totally different from what we think it should be, when there have been no revelations and no still, small voice. We must remain steady and willing to stand firm with unwavering faith, even though we cannot see or understand a reason for or reason why we are facing certain situations and challenges. God rewards this kind of faith, and it is essential in fighting spiritual warfare and receiving a miracle.

Shadrach, Meshach, and Abednego were three young men who understood this principle and knew what it meant to trust God. King Nebuchadnezzar was furious because they refused to bow down to his image of gold. With conviction, they stood firm, even if it meant death.

> Shadrach, Meshach and Abednego replied to him, "King Nebuchadnezzar, we do not need to defend ourselves before you in this matter. If we are thrown into the blazing furnace, *the God we serve is able to deliver us from it, and he will deliver us from Your Majesty's hand. But even if he does not*, we want you to know, Your Majesty, that we will not serve your gods or worship the image of gold you have set up." (Daniel 3:16–18 NIV; emphasis added)

I love how boldly they held on to their convictions. Their decision to trust God regardless of the outcome is an amazing testimony of passion and courage. Even if He did not deliver them, these young men purposed to stay true and faithful. Did God let them down? Absolutely not. He rewarded their faith and delivered them in a miraculous way.

When I meditate on this story, it leaves me with a question: will He find this kind of faith in me? As my journey continued, it became evident the testing of my faith had only just begun.

When doctors came in with their facts, our faith took a beating, but God's mercy continued to carry us through. You see, God is not interested in facts. He already knows the information mere mortal humans are able to obtain. Gathering and receiving information about any situation is using wisdom, but it does not determine the outcome when we entrust our lives to Father God, our Creator. Facts and information enable us to be specific and focused in prayer; however, the only true and unmovable report is God's truth. We must ask, "What does He say about our lives? Does His Word say we are to be sick or well, poor or blessed?"

In the book of Numbers, chapter 14, Moses sent spies to explore the land of Canaan. They returned reporting the facts as they saw them with their natural eyes. In summary, they said, "Are you crazy? We cannot attack those people; they are too big and strong. We seemed like grasshoppers next to them. We would have been better off if we died in Egypt or in the desert."

Their report angered God. He called it an evil or bad report. Why? Did they lie? No. So, what was the problem? Let's look at the scriptures and explore the issue.

> They gave Moses this account: "We went into the land to which you sent us, and it does flow with milk and honey. Here is its fruit. But the people who live there are powerful and the cities are fortified and very large. We even saw descendants of Anak there." (Numbers 13:27–28 NIV)

> Then Caleb silenced the people before Moses and said; "We should go up and take possession of the land, *for we can certainly do it.*" But the men who had gone up with him said we can't attack those people; they are stronger

than we are. *And they spread among the Israelites a bad report.* They said, "The Land we explored devours those living in it. All the people we saw there are of great size. We saw the Nephilim there (the descendants of Anak come from the Nephilim). We seemed like grasshoppers in our own eyes, and we looked the same to them." (Numbers 13:30–33 NIV; emphasis added)

Rather than trust the God who brought them through so many unimaginable challenges, the Israelites chose to believe the unbelieving fact finders and continued to grumble. Well, guess what? Those fact-finding reporters were struck down with a plague and died, while the ones they influenced due to unbelief lived out their lives in the desert, forbidden to enter the promised land.

Only Joshua and Caleb came back with a report based on faith in their powerful God, instead of what their eyes saw and the facts about the situation. In summary, they said, "The same God who parted the Red Sea, performed miraculous signs and wonders in Egypt and the desert, supplied food, water, and even prevented our clothes from wearing out will victoriously go before us and make a way." Joshua and Caleb found favor with God due their unshakable trust in Him. They were rewarded for their faith and allowed to enter the promised land, partaking in its rich bounty.

Why is faith in God so important? The Word says without it we cannot please our Father. One interpretation of "please" in Greek is, "to come into full agreement." When we choose to believe and speak things that are contrary to the truth (God's Word), we are choosing to come out of agreement with God. In doing this, we are actually saying to our Creator and the Creator of the universe, "I really don't trust You." Let's take it one step further; it is also exalting ourselves above God Almighty and His infinite power and wisdom by placing our trust in our own limited ability to understand and comprehend.

Too often, we allow our trust in God to be hindered because we perceive He did not meet our needs. God answers prayer according to faith. If God answered according to need, there would be no purpose or reason for faith. We all fall short in this area at one time or another. To see a radical move of God's power in our lives, we must learn the truth and choose to grow.

When we quit hearing the Word of God, we don't receive. Faith comes by hearing the Word. Once we hear, then we can choose to do something important—obey. What does obedience look like? Someone willing to hear, believe, receive, and expect.

After the hysterectomy, I felt God let me down because He did not meet my needs. Like the spies sent to explore the land of Canaan and came back with a faithless report, focusing only on the facts opened doors of doubt and unbelief to take root and grow in my heart.

> Therefore, we do not lose heart, though outwardly we are wasting away, yet inwardly, we are being renewed day by day. For our light and momentary troubles are achieving for us eternal glory that far outweighs them all. So *we fix our eyes not on what is seen, but on what is unseen, for what is seen is temporary, but what is unseen is eternal.* (2 Corinthians 4:16–18 NIV; emphasis added)

These scriptures shine a light on something so important in our faith walk. It is where we "fix our eyes" in the hardships and battles that makes the difference between defeat and victory. If our faith is truly in God, we won't lose heart. We may experience occasional moments of despair along with questions regarding our situation, but once discouragement attempts to take up residence, we'll quickly kick it to the curb. When true faith in God is present, a mature Christian will choose to rise up and not stay down and out.

Overwrought with despair, all I could think about was another wasted year filled with hospitals, surgeries, blood transfusions, and pain. Barely eighty pounds and looking like a walking skeleton, thoughts of never being able to have children consumed me. In fact, it invaded my mind and spirit like a parasite. A parasite is dependent on its host for survival. It must be in the host to live, grow, and multiply; it cannot live independently. The bitterness I allowed inside my heart was the host, and it grew and penetrated every area of my life.

I left the hospital with some minor stomach pains, but the doctors assured us they were temporary. By the time we arrived home, the pain intensified with each passing hour. Throughout the night, I awoke drenched in sweat. Mom repeatedly changed my gown and sheets.

The following day, my temperature spiked as the pain continued with a vengeance. I remember literally screaming out in despair. This terrified my parents because I could tolerate pain better than the average person. Mom called the doctor, and he told them to bring me back to the hospital ASAP.

X-rays revealed adhesions throughout the abdomen wrapping around and blocking the intestines. This caused a serious bowel obstruction. I was rushed into surgery, and the doctors removed over six feet of adhesions, which included a small portion of my intestines. This seemed hard to believe considering my weight and size. The small intestine is about twenty feet long, and the large intestine is about five feet long. The human body and all its intricate details is quite an amazing machine. How anyone in the field of medicine can doubt there is a God is beyond my comprehension.

After a time of healing and noted improvement, I returned home. Surely nothing else could go wrong. If only this had been true. While lying on the couch and visiting with a friend from church, I smelled a terrible odor and noticed my gown appeared wet around the incision area. I told my friend something was wrong and please go get my parents. He quickly said goodbye as Mom and Dad rushed in to check on me. Mom lifted my gown to see if the stitches were intact, and to our horror, there was a hole in my stomach. The stitches had burst open. Dad called the doctor in a panic. Once again, Dad was told to get me back to the hospital ASAP because it must be gangrenous. All the way there, I cried and screamed, "God, please let me die! I can't take this anymore!"

When we arrived, everyone was in tears. My parents could not console me, and they were just as distraught. Only Jesus could deliver me out of this painful abyss, but the only deliverance I wanted was death. Heaven held a much greater appeal than living one more minute on this earth.

As the surgeon entered the room I quickly informed him, "I'm prepared to die and do not want another surgery." Taking my family out to the hallway, he advised them due to my state of mind and physical condition, putting me to sleep presented too many dangers. The doctor felt my only chance of making it through this ordeal meant doing the procedure with me fully awake. Although I faced a risk of going into shock, they felt certain I would never wake up from anesthesia. My poor parents reluctantly agreed, and the doctor proceeded without anesthetic.

I don't remember a lot about the procedure except feeling intense pain and anger. The entire time, I pleaded with God to take me home and said some *not so nice* things to the doctors. Tubes were everywhere, up the nose and down the throat, with needles in my arms, neck, and chest. The tubes were pumping poison and infection out of my body and into large tanks that looked like scuba diving equipment. They stitched a large needle into my chest, which administered medication to my heart. Helpless and hopeless is how I felt. If only I remembered what David said, "When I am afraid, I will trust in You. In God, whose Word I praise, in God I trust; I will not be afraid, what can mortal man do to me?" (Psalm 56:3–4 NIV).

During this period of time, I was in a coma-like state of unconsciousness. Doctors met with my parents and prepared everyone for the worst. They told Mom and Dad they did not expect me to live past twenty-four hours. Mom told me later Dad could hardly talk for several days after that, and the doctors suspected he was in shock.

After a number of days passed and I continued to live, I began experiencing periods of consciousness. I remember waking up and seeing sad faces everywhere. Daddy looked so pale and lost, as though he was a million miles away. If I tried to talk, the tubing crimped in my stomach, setting off a loud alarm. To fix the tube, the nurses had to bring it up and reinsert it back down my throat and stomach. The pain was excruciating.

During these tubing procedures, the needle in my chest had to stay in place and not move. Mom often assisted the nurses by gently holding my shoulders down and keeping me still. I remember Mama locking eyes with me as if to say, "I love you, baby. Hang in there. It's going to be okay." Trapped in this painful nightmare and unable to run away or verbalize my thoughts, I screamed out in my mind and begged for God to take me home. With great compassion, everyone worked tirelessly to keep me alive ... whether I wanted them to or not.

An amazing thing happened after one of these agonizing tube episodes and another lapse into unconsciousness. A beautiful figure appeared by the bed with a bright light shining all around. The colors surrounding me were stunning, with amazing brilliance and clarity. Immediately sensing this was an angel, I thought God answered my prayer and I finally made it to heaven, but then I realized I was still in the hospital bed. I recall thinking how cruel of God to leave me in the bed. Not even a second later, an indescribable peace flooded my weary heart. The angel picked me up in its arms as we waded through what looked like a sea of infection and pollution. With a firm yet compassionate tone, the angel rebuked me for praying to die. It stated: "Do not pray to die. God hears the prayers of His children. Many children will pass through your arms and be blessed. There is still a work for you to do. You will not leave this earth until your work is complete." My spirit stirred with humble appreciation and a shot of much-needed faith. Despite my angry and bitter heart, God still loved me enough to send a guardian angel to bring comfort and hope.

During times of unconsciousness, I heard people talking. Nurses speculated about how long I would live or if I'd even make it through their shift. As the days and weeks passed, the angel stayed with me. In moments of discouragement when I wanted Mother, it spoke in a reassuring, motherly voice. In times of fear and panic when I wanted Dad, it spoke in a strong, firm, fatherly voice. Whatever I needed, the angel became, whether it was a mother's gentle touch or a father's firm assurance.

The angel brought something else very special to the room. The entire time it stayed with me, I smelled the most beautiful fragrance. The best way I know to describe it is a combination of honeysuckle and vanilla. The smell of infection, gangrene, and medication disappeared. Every moment of every day, it carried me in its arms, speaking scriptures of hope, blessings, and life.

> Never will I leave you; never will I forsake you. (Hebrews 13:5 NIV)
>
> I can do all things through Christ which strengtheneth me. (Philippians 4:13 KJV)
>
> Being confident of this, that He who began a good work in you, will carry it on to completion until the day of Jesus Christ. (Philippians 1:6 NIV)
>
> But he said to me, "My grace is sufficient for you, for my power is made perfect in weakness." Therefore I will boast all the more gladly about my weaknesses, so that Christ's power may rest on me. (2 Corinthians 12:9 NIV)

The number of scriptures the angel spoke are too numerous to write. It still amazes me how loved I felt as the Word of God miraculously sustained me. Difficult obstacles lay ahead, but thanks to this heavenly visitation, I knew God still loved me.

Psalm 91 is evidence God sends His angels to watch over and protect His children. In fact, my angel did *exactly* what is written in verse 11.

> For He will command His angels concerning you to guard you in all your ways; *They will lift you up in their hands,* so that you will not strike your foot against a stone. You will tread upon the lion and the cobra; you will trample the great lion and serpent. Because he loves Me, say the Lord, I will rescue him; I will protect him, for he acknowledges My name. He will call upon Me, and I will answer him; I will be with him in trouble, I will deliver him and honor him. With long life will I satisfy him and show him My salvation. (Psalm 91:11–16 NIV; emphasis added)

CHAPTER 8

DAUGHTER, WHERE IS YOUR FAITH?

We began questioning why so many things went wrong. Much to our dismay, the information we received came a little late. Doctors recommended a radiation treatment after the hysterectomy due to several things. First, they stated it proved effective in preventing excessive keloid scarring. Second, they hoped the radiation might stop or slow down whatever was happening with my blood and causing so many infections. We agreed to the procedure, not being informed of any serious side effects.

Unfortunately, an adverse reaction to the treatment created adhesions and scar tissue to rapidly and aggressively form, wrapping around my intestines. The result was an extensive bowel obstruction, which caused the tissue to become infected and unable to heal. Within a very short time, my stomach literally burst open due to an aggressive infection and gangrene.

Not being advised of the side effects, we were understandably upset and began asking why we had not been informed. The doctors assumed the radiation dosage was too low for any complications, so they chose not to say anything. Too late to undo the damage; their assumptions proved wrong.

To keep the wound free of infection, the bandage had to be changed three to four times a day. Simply stitching my stomach back up wasn't an option because it would burst open again, causing more infection. The wound had to heal gradually from the inside out. It is important to note how wonderfully medicine has changed and improved since 1979.

There are so many new medical products that would have been helpful in the wound-healing process; however, those things were not available at that time.

The road to recovery grew even longer and more painful; however, I remained thankful for the caring people God placed in my life. The nursing staff became very dear to our entire family. The day I left the hospital, they presented me with a special pillow to use while recovering to prevent sores from developing on my inner legs and knees. I was so small and skeletal one of the nurses actually made the pillow to fit my frail frame. Everyone signed the pillow with words of love and encouragement. They all commented about the special purpose God must have in store for me. They knew only a miracle brought me through this whole ordeal alive.

Leaving the hospital became quite comical. When my parents initially rushed me back, I did not bring any other clothes except the gown I came in. While waiting for the discharge paperwork, Dad secretly slipped out and went across the street from the hospital to the mall. My sweet daddy went shopping for me...all by himself. He wanted to purchase something special for me to wear home. Something comfortable that didn't require high heels. What he brought back caused quite a stir—a size-zero white jumpsuit, with "pit crew" and gas station names written across pockets and sleeves. To complete the outfit, he also purchased a pair of tennis shoes. No one could believe it. Robbie was the tomboy. I'm the prissy one. It didn't matter. He beamed with excitement while everyone else quietly chuckled. Not having the heart to say, "Daddy, what were you thinking?" I proudly put it on, thankful to have such a loving father.

Dad wasn't done surprising us. Apparently, in his state of shock, he went to the Dodge dealership and traded cars but couldn't remember what he bought. When the nurse wheeled me down, Dad went to get the car. He came back in the hospital with a puzzled look on his face. Mama looked at him and said, "Edward, what's wrong? We want to go home."

Daddy looked at her and said, "Mary, I can't find the car, and don't get mad, but I think I did something. I seem to recall being at the Dodge dealership the other day, and I think I traded cars."

Well, let me tell you, my 4'10" mama had a good ole-fashioned hissy fit. She started fussing right there in the lobby in front of God and everyone. It was a Catholic hospital with very sweet nuns sitting at the front desk. Mama proceeded to bark orders for the nuns to get her a phonebook. They immediately complied. She looked up the number for the dealership and called asking for a manager. She told them who she was and asked if Dad traded cars. They confirmed he did. Then she scolded them real good. As we say in the South, Mama was *fit to be tied*. She asked how in the world they let Daddy trade a car when he was clearly in no shape to even go buy bread or milk. After giving them a good tongue lashing, she asked what kind of car he bought. They told her it was a black four-door LeBaron with red interior. The final thing she said before hanging up was, "You better not sell our car because Edward will be bringing that thing he bought back." Then bam. She hung up.

Although pain gripped my entire body, I remember holding my stomach and laughing until I cried. When Daddy drove up to the door with that car, Mama went off again like a woman possessed. She fussed all the way home … the entire forty-five minutes. I lay in the back seat laughing, crying, and thankful to have such crazy parents. All Daddy could do was say, "Yes, Mary. I'm sorry, Mary. I'll get our car back, I promise." Once Daddy fixed the car situation and got rid of what Mama called "the most hideous thing I've ever seen," we were all able to laugh about Daddy going temporarily insane.

It took some time, but I eventually found myself thanking God for not answering my cries to end the misery and take me home. I am so glad I did not leave this world before experiencing the joy of walking in His abundant blessings while on this earth. The enemy mistakenly counted me out and completely defeated. Praise God for His sustaining Word: "I can do all things through Him, who gives me strength" (Philippians 4:13 NIV).

Just to prove God cares about every little thing, before entering the hospital for my second surgery, I felt a direct leading of the Holy Spirit to be financially responsible. God miraculously provided health insurance through work, but I did not want my parents burdened with my bills. As a bank teller in 1979, I took home about $400 a month. Thankfully, my only debt was a car payment of $154.10, which included insurance (yes, I still remember the exact amount to this very day). After praying about my finances, I decided to pay my bills three months in advance. Between savings and checking, I had enough to make the payments. Three months later, I returned to work, making the next car payment on the fourth month, not even one day late. God truly cares about every little thing.

Mom and Dad were concerned about me going back to work with a hole in my stomach. Medication helped with pain management, but changing the dressing at work had to be a priority. Determined to get back on my feet, I felt I could handle it. The doctor wrote a note stating I could return, as long as I took care of changing the dressing during the day. Demonstrating a great deal of patience and support, my boss welcomed me back with open arms. Self-conscious and terrified people might find out about the gaping hole, I asked her to keep my condition private, and she kindly agreed.

Each day consisted of continuous pain and fatigue, but I refused to quit. Doctors made sure I was fully medicated at all times. This later became another obstacle to overcome. The enemy will use every means possible to destroy us.

I refer to the next decade of my life as "the foggy years." The Lord must have been asking, "Daughter, where is your faith?" During this time, doctors were so perplexed about my condition they stopped running tests and simply wrote prescriptions for every symptom, pain, and infection. Not being able to find the source of my problems frustrated them terribly. Their answers or quick fixes usually came in the form of a pill or shot. Due to remaining heavily medicated throughout these years, it is amazing I functioned normally at all.

By the age of twenty, I was a full-blown emotional mess and felt like damaged goods in every sense of the word. As a woman, I truly looked at myself as worthless. Any form of positive self-esteem was nonexistent. Bob tried to hang in there and stay on the roller-coaster ride, but he finally had enough. He could not penetrate the wall I put up and the constant pushing away. To be honest, I felt relief. I was convinced he deserved so much better than me.

During our relationship, we talked about many things. I knew Bob longed for a little girl of his own one day, and I could never give that to him. His assurances of lasting love and God's ability to work things out did not matter. I remained stubborn and utterly certain that being stuck with me would absolutely ruin his life forever. After our last breakup, we maintained a tense friendship filled with sad regrets.

Desperately needing a change of scenery, I accepted a job offer in New Orleans and signed up for some college classes. At the time, I thought makeup, a big smile, and stylish clothes hid everything; however, the truth has a way of rising to the surface. Longing to experience some kind of normalcy, my parents hesitantly agreed to let me go. Extremely naïve, in poor health, and in a mental la-la land (due to staying heavily medicated trying to manage the pain), I embarked on this new journey. My earthly possessions consisted of makeup, plenty of medication, lots of pretty clothes, and shoes.

Dad took me all over New Orleans trying to find a suitable place to live. I could not afford very much, but he was determined to find a safe place, regardless of the cost. We soon found an adult-only apartment complex, with twenty-four-hour security, only a block from my job. Finding it hard to leave her baby, Mom decided to stay a few extra weeks to help me unpack and make sure I was okay.

When Mom left to go back home, I quietly decided to take a "spiritual break." Thinking no one would ever know, I privately thought, *Everyone needs a break from church and God at some point in their life, don't they?* The enemy loves it when we entertain these kinds of ideas and act on them, because they usually lead to painful and poor choices.

Although God miraculously sent an angel to comfort and rescue me from death's door, seeds of bitterness and anger stayed harbored in my heart concerning the hysterectomy, no more Bob, years of pain, and overall loss. Through it all, the Lord never stopped loving and protecting His little lost and hurting sheep. His love stayed unconditional and true.

"For I am with you and will rescue you" (Jeremiah 1:19 NIV).

After a few weeks of not attending church, I felt a strong nudging from the Holy Spirit. That still, small voice seemed to boom in my ear, "Donna, you should be in church. You need fellowship, and more importantly, you need Me." Deciding to heed the nudge, I got dressed and went to a church located approximately twenty minutes from the apartment. As I arrived, a beautiful young lady named Denise came over and welcomed me. Sensing my despair and being sensitive to the Holy Spirit, she became a loving and devoted friend. If I missed a service, Denise showed up at my door expressing concern and offering gentle encouragement.

One Sunday while the choir was singing, I felt overwhelmed with conviction. I could not run to the altar fast enough. Ashamed of how I blamed God for everything, He flooded me with His love and forgiveness as the anger melted away. Denise stayed right by my side, praising God for answered prayer. Through obedience, she allowed herself to be instrumental in bringing me back to the Father. Today, she continues to be a precious friend. Both Denise and her husband are ministers in Louisiana.

A few months passed, and another serious kidney infection set in. Just to keep going, I increased the amount of pain medicine I took. Every day, I ran a high temperature while standing a straight eight to ten hours in high heels and swollen feet. The next thing I knew, the bottom of my feet burst open. Unable to work and in desperate need of help left only one option—going back home. Feeling like a failure, I resigned from my job and waited for Mom and Dad to come rescue their pitiful little girl.

As soon as we returned home, they took me straight to the ER, and I was admitted to the hospital. After receiving a few units of blood and antibiotics for infection, I recuperated and started searching for a new job. God's hand of favor always shone through when I looked for employment. I did not withhold information regarding health issues, and yet I never experienced a problem finding work. Amazingly, prior employers gave good references in spite of my unpredictable attendance record. The only explanation for this is God's mercy and divine favor.

Receiving a job offer with Civil Service, I agreed to move to West Palm Beach for a ninety-day training period. After the ninety days, they offered to transfer me back home to one of the nearby military bases. Weighing about eighty-nine pounds and just getting over another major obstacle, I somehow convinced my parents I could handle it. Although they voiced many reservations, they understood my intense desire to do something productive with my life, so they reluctantly loaded up the car, and we headed further south.

Within a month, another serious infection hit, and the doctors in West Palm immediately suspected leukemia. When the test results came back, just like all the doctors before them, they realized their assumptions were incorrect. They attempted to diagnose the problem but could not find the answer either. The physician in charge was very kind and contacted Civil Service concerning the situation. The government notified me, stating they would honor my time in West Palm and allow an early transfer to a base closer to home after my release from the hospital. The favor of God once again came to my rescue.

Upon my return, I received some unwanted news. Bob became engaged to someone I knew from a nearby church. I went to him in tears pleading for another chance, but he could not risk the disappointment. Heartbroken, I tried to accept the fact he found happiness with someone else. The day of his wedding arrived, feeling more like a funeral as I realized how foolish I had been and how empty life felt.

Several more years passed filled with numerous hospitalizations, depression, and so much more. In fact, the majority of the next few years became a blur. I honestly have very little recollection regarding many of the events that transpired. My most profound and clear memory happened in 1983, which I will detail in the next chapter.

I considered writing about some of the difficulty I encountered throughout those foggy years, but most of the information is secondhand. I cannot objectively write about things relayed to me that I only remember in parts and pieces. Some things are so painful I consider even slight memory loss a blessing.

In relationships, I made poor choices and suffered many things; including painful abuse, betrayal, and rejection. My state of mind was a spaced-out, drug-induced existence. By the grace of God, I miraculously stayed employed, although I have very little memory of events, people, and places.

Throughout these foggy years, I discovered how cruel people with ulterior motives can be who prey on and take advantage of those who are weak and vulnerable. The saddest part is most of them were in the church. Through this experience, God stayed faithful and used the worst times of my life to teach me a lesson on loving others without judgment or condemnation; this continues to be a daily work in progress. When you have been wounded and hurt, it tends to make you more empathetic and caring to those in distress who have not led perfect lives. Like it or not, this applies to all of us.

In an effort to help others who have gone through or may be going through something similar, I want to use my situation as an example and take this opportunity to speak specifically to the church. Heaven knows I was messed up in every sense of the word, but all too often "Christians" turn to gossip and condemnation. In my particular situation, I am sure they felt fully justified. However, before reacting or responding, we should ask an important question, "What is the loving thing to do?"

Those who do not know Jesus are closely watching our lives. Many of the people gossiping and pointing a finger had no idea the amount of pain I struggled with and the medication I took just to function and deal with the constant pain. Some knew, but it didn't matter. They also did not consider the years of disappointment and torment involved from doctors running test after test trying to find answers and coming up with none. To make matters worse, having a hysterectomy so young created a severe hormone imbalance. Although I took monthly hormone shots, my levels were never regulated, and I was anything but sane. In fact, the shots caused additional challenges, which included severe migraines and extreme nausea. Many years ago, they put women like me in asylums, and sadly, I understand why.

We live in a world full of hurting, lost, and messed-up souls who desperately need God. Many of these precious people will not darken the door of a church because of how we treat one another while proudly calling ourselves Christians. The word "Christian" means Christlike. It is not about making perfect choices, doing all the right things, an impressive church attendance record, and being able to quote more scriptures than the person next to us. It is about loving people, reconciliation, and bringing the lost to the knowledge of Christ.

When a brother or sister begins slipping and straying away from a godly path, loving them does not mean ignoring the problem; however, if we love God and want to obey His Word, we must do as the Bible says.

> Brothers, if someone is caught in a sin, you who are spiritual should restore him gently. *But watch yourself, or*

> *you also may be tempted. Carry each other's burdens, and in this way you will fulfill the law of Christ. If anyone thinks he is something when he is nothing, he deceives himself. Each one should test his own actions.* (Galatians 6:1–4 NIV; emphasis added)

If we are not careful, we can also fall into temptation as well as hinder God's best in our own homes and lives. You have probably heard the statement, "God doesn't like ugly." Responding and reacting in unloving and judgmental ways is a kind of ugly God does not turn a blind eye to. He will bring justice to the situation in His own time.

Everyone on the planet needs love and acceptance, regardless of their dark circumstances. The believer going through a hard time and the lost who don't know Christ need reassurance and examples of our Father's ability to save, heal, and beautifully restore what has been broken and shattered. Regardless of who is to blame or how it happened, we must share the good news in word and deed of a loving God who has an amazing plan for every single one of us. He is not waiting to beat us over the head when we fail. With love, He longs to bring us into a close relationship with Him. He alone has the power to use our situation to make us stronger and wiser.

Let's look at a commandment Jesus gave to all of us. If we choose to put this into practice, lives will be changed, and miracles will happen. By choosing to do as Christ commands, bondages are broken, hearts are mended, and the wounded receive healing. People will actually desire to be a part of the body of Christ, not run away screaming or duck behind something when they see us coming.

> Jesus replied: "Love the Lord your God with all your heart and with all your soul and with all your mind. This is the first and greatest commandment. And the second is like it: Love your neighbor as yourself." (Matthew 22:37–39 NIV)

When God called me into ministry, He knew the direction my life would take. He did not call me with plans to take it back because of mistakes and failures. We must remember, nothing ever takes Him by surprise. One of my favorite scriptures is, "For God's gifts and His call are irrevocable" (Romans 11:29 NIV). This truth offers comfort to those of us who have gifts and calls but have not walked a perfect path. Once again, this applies to all of us.

Years of pain, uncertainty, and confusion took their toll. Holding down a full-time job proved difficult. To the bewilderment of many onlookers (myself included), employers were usually very good to me, and I'm forever grateful. I learned how creative, sovereign, slow to anger, and rich in mercy the Lord truly is. If a willing vessel is nowhere to be found, He is more than able to reach across the heavens to bring compassion and love to one of His hurting kids. As the song says, *He will make a way where there seems to be no way.*

Just to express how good God is, I stayed the course and finally received my specialized ministry diploma with studies in youth, counseling, and music ministries. While working with Civil Service (and the state of Florida a few years later), I also received additional training and certification in substance abuse counseling and mental health. After a few more years, I continued my studies and pursued a bachelor of science degree in counseling psychology, graduating magna cum laude with a 3.89 GPA.

Oh, but wait … God wasn't done. He continued restoring my life, using all the pain and disappointments as a pathway to help others. Some years later, I returned to school and received a master's degree in theology, chaplaincy certification and ordination, a PhD in counseling, and certification in cognitive behavioral therapy and rational living therapy, level III. To my utter amazement, I graduated with honors; summa cum laude, with a 4.0 GPA.

Yes, I worked hard to accomplish these things, but God deserves the praise and glory. His unrelenting tenacity to show Himself powerful in my life remained steadfast and uncompromising. He never gives up on us even when we give up on ourselves.

> Now all glory to God, who is able, through his mighty power at work within us, to accomplish infinitely more than we might ask or think. (Ephesians 3:20 NLT)

CHAPTER 9

HIS MERCIES FAIL NOT

During the foggy years I spoke about earlier, there is a vivid and profound event that changed the course of my life. One October night in 1983, I came home from work very sick and headed straight for bed. Within hours, I began babbling and hallucinating due to infection and a high temperature. Around two in the morning, my parents wrapped me in a blanket and rushed me to the hospital.

In the emergency room, visiting from Emory Hospital in Atlanta, Georgia, was a doctor who just happened to be a liver and spleen specialist. He came to town for a medical conference and decided to use the emergency room computers to check on research data before heading home to Atlanta. As they wheeled me to a room, the staff began discussing my case. Because my symptoms sounded all too familiar to him, this doctor joined in and started asking questions. Within moments, he walked over to Mom and Dad, introduced himself, and asked for permission to do an examination and order additional tests and x-rays. In tears, they said, "Yes, please help our daughter."

When the results came back, the doctor rushed into our room exhibiting a great sense of urgency. He could not believe what he was seeing because my spleen was massively enlarged and my liver was also grossly enlarged. The reports showed severe abnormalities. Bombarding my parents with questions, he asked, "How long has she had this problem and who is treating her spleen and liver?"

Mom and Dad stood speechless. Finally, mom spoke up and informed the specialist, "We did not know anything about a problem with Donna's spleen or liver, and we have taken her to more doctors than you can imagine."

The doctor went into high gear barking out orders to the staff. My temperature stayed dangerously high, and as the medical team worked feverishly to bring it down, no one could comprehend the profound future impact of the events taking place. My parents later told me what the doctor said to them: "Her spleen has to be removed, and although the x-rays show her liver is enlarged with abnormalities, this doesn't mean it is diseased; however, it's a sign of an underlying problem, which in this case I feel certain has to do with the spleen. We must proceed quickly and make sure the liver is not damaged as well. If it is, we are looking at a critical situation possibly involving a transplant, but we will cross that bridge when and if we come to it. Pray for a miracle."

Amidst all the commotion, Mom said I looked at them with tears streaming down my face and said, "Could it be possible someone has finally found what's been wrong with me all these years? I can't take another disappointment." My parents agreed; however, they expressed a sense of renewed hope, which according to them enveloped us in that emergency room as if God Himself was present and guiding every move the medical team made. I can tell you this: He most definitely was present and in complete control.

It did not take long for all the test results to come back. They also requisitioned x-rays and charts from a number of the doctors I had seen. After carefully reviewing reports from the previous eight years, every test revealed an abnormally enlarged spleen with gross abnormalities. Fifteen at the time of the first x-rays and cat scans, my spleen was over three times the normal size with a slightly enlarged liver and gross abnormalities. Eight years later, my spleen and liver more than doubled from the first scans with severe abnormalities.

When you have infection, it is not unusual for your spleen to slightly enlarge; however, year after year, tests showed the size of both my spleen and liver increased with gross abnormalities. In big letters, all reports indicated, "Enlarged spleen and liver, gross abnormalities present."

Repeatedly, doctors pressed on my swollen side as I cried out in pain, yet they continued to misdiagnose the problem. I struggled with constant anemia, infections, the need for numerous blood transfusions,

Falling into Faith

and constant antibiotics. To make things worse, a few doctors (not all) arrogantly expressed, "This is most definitely psychological and psychosomatic. Your daughter just needs a good psychiatrist." They were cold, hard, and showed no compassion. So many times, I really did think I was just going crazy.

We soon found out the extent of their oversight: unnecessary surgeries, physical internal damage, medications with harmful side effects, and tremendous emotional distress caused from the hysterectomy and years of suffering. The revelation proved incomprehensible and tragic.

The specialist discussed a transport to Emory Hospital in Atlanta where doctors specialized in these kinds of diseases. My spleen needed to be removed and evaluated ASAP. After meeting with my parents, he realized the hardship it would place on them by sending me six hours away. A pastor cannot always pick up and leave town due to their many responsibilities. Dad was willing, but the doctor understood the stress this could potentially cause for everyone. Mom's health was very poor, so this created additional problems. With these things in mind and the critical nature of the situation, the doctor called a surgeon from Pensacola and arranged for the operation to be performed there. I actually felt excited with an overwhelming sense of peace. Finally, there was a reason for all the years of pain. If my liver turned out okay, the prognosis looked very good.

Our youth pastor started a prayer chain with churches near and far. Being in a military community, many people came and went, but our family's friendships remained strong. Throughout the US and around the globe, friends and family joined in prayer. Our prayers are not hindered by distance, and I am so thankful for praying believers.

Surgery went exceptionally well, although my spleen ruptured as they were removing it. The doctors did an amazing job. Best of all, my liver test came back negative for any disease or damage. It just needed some time to heal. God truly heard our prayers. The surgeons were amazed at not only the size but the condition of my spleen. Tests showed a severe form of splenomegaly, and my spleen had most likely been diseased from childhood. Without getting too technical, it was a rare medical anomaly.

Now that the medical professionals knew the root cause of my problems were physical and not psychological, the doctors involved in my case decided to run even more tests. They also discovered my hormone levels were horrendously out of balance. This did not come as a surprise to us. For years, Mom begged doctors to check my hormone levels, but they assured her everything was fine. One of the new doctors working on my case, stated, "I'm amazed you're not swinging from the rafters." Little did he know just how irrational and downright crazy I had been at times since the hysterectomy. There are absolute memory gaps in my life where I have no (or very little) recollection, dating back to 1978. The doctor stated due to the disease, medications, and hormone levels, I suffered with intermittent confusion and periods of temporary memory loss.

So many questions began to have answers once properly diagnosed and treated. The reason I threw up after every meal became clear. My stomach expanded for food, causing it to press against the enlarged and diseased spleen, setting off a cycle of problems resulting in pain, nausea, and vomiting. Constant anemia and the need for blood transfusions with this disease answered another mystery that had plagued me for years. In fact, the mystery to all my physical misery was finally solved.

The spleen produces antibodies, and it removes old and abnormal red blood cells, platelets, and other damaged cells from circulation, reusing whatever parts it can. It also filters out bacteria and parasites from the blood and lymph that have been killed by white blood cells. A diseased spleen cannot filter these impurities properly; hence, a person's blood is seriously affected. Due to my condition, the white cell count soared from constant infections, and the ability to fight off infection was gone. Basically, my immune system was nonexistent. Antibiotics only worked temporarily as infections constantly attacked my body. Another mystery solved.

Upon reading and learning the signs of a diseased spleen, I became angry. For years, my symptoms read word for word right out of the medical journals. Examined and treated by so many physicians, it seemed incomprehensible no one correctly diagnosed the problem. I started asking some pretty tough questions: "Why did I have to suffer for so many years, and more importantly, could the hysterectomy have been avoided? And what about my hormones? Wasn't it obvious to everyone I was more than a little batty? You would think a doctor with a nineteen-year-old patient who underwent a complete hysterectomy would keep an eye on her hormone levels, wouldn't you? Oh, and what about the swelling and constant pain in my side where the spleen is located? Why, please tell me why you didn't check on my spleen! My questions were never answered, but they sure made people nervous.

A well-known lawyer from Miami heard about my case and flew to Fort Walton for a consultation with us. We never found out how this lawyer knew about my situation, although we suspected a nurse who cared for me on the day shift contacted him. She was visibly shaken by the oversight. The lawyer stated I would never have to work another day in my life if we allowed him to sue the doctors and hospitals. It sure sounded good, but something felt terribly wrong. How could I sue doctors who tirelessly worked to keep me alive for so many years? Several of them truly agonized over my situation and desperately sought answers. The ones who stated I should find a good psychiatrist certainly needed a jolt; however, it felt wrong.

The cold, hard truth stared me in the face; nothing and no amount of money could take away the suffering or pain of never having children. Complicating life's pain and injustices with bitterness and revenge is never a good option. Choosing to trust God, I gave it all to Him. His Word tells us He will bring justice to our cause and make the crooked paths straight.

We met again with the attorney, and I advised him I did not want to sue. Without hesitation, Mom and Dad supported and honored my decision. Memories of yesterday held too much pain. Only God could restore and bring healing. At least now I had answers and hope.

After I made the decision not to sue, the Lord brought to light what actually transpired as Satan spent years trying to destroy me. This revelation came through a dream I had one night after our final meeting with the attorney. Just as God uses people and things (whatever He desires) to carry out His plans, the enemy also uses anyone and anything to fulfill his schemes of destruction. The Lord opened my eyes to see how the doctors were blinded by Satan and unable to see the problem.

Yes, God is more powerful and could have removed the blinders; however, the *why* is not for me to ponder. Dwelling on *what if and why* is never constructive. I had already lost too much valuable time consumed with sickness, hospitals, and unanswered questions. The fact is, God is God, and I am not. His ways are higher, and some things will remain a mystery until the day we are called home. My mind and emotions needed to heal, so I put it in God's hands. The weight of the burden had been too heavy.

Word spread like wild fire: "Donna's not crazy; she's really had something wrong with her." People began calling and apologizing for unkind things they said or thought through the years. Not understanding how to deal with my constant battle of sickness, they found it easier to criticize and, like many of the doctors, speculated it must be psychological. In many ways, I felt vindicated but sad and lonely. You see, by this time, friends were few and far between. I appreciated everyone's honesty and desire to make things right, but life seemed easier when I did not know for sure what they thought. Making recovery more difficult were those painful foggy years, of which I had little recollection. What I could recall brought feelings of hurt, confusion, betrayal, and tremendous shame.

To forgive others proved so much easier than forgiving myself. Have you ever wondered why that is? The answer is a carefully crafted plan of Satan to keep us beat down and unfruitful. When we forgive ourselves, we are not consumed with self-pity and play-by-play regrets. It is very liberating. I knew what I had to do, and Paul said it best. "Forgetting what is behind and straining toward what is ahead, I press on toward the goal to win the prize for which God has called me heavenward in Christ Jesus" (Philippians 3:13–14 NIV).

Science has proven the effects of bitterness and unforgiveness are as devastating as any cancer or disease. For believers, these things will destroy the spirit of the living God that is alive within us. In fact, it grieves the Holy Spirit.

Learning to forgive myself took time. With determination and a restored hope, I chose to fight for my future and embrace a brand-new beginning. It felt amazing to plan for a new and healthier tomorrow.

Many challenges lay ahead. People suffering from chronic illness for prolong periods of time normally take all kinds of medication on a regular basis, resulting in addiction. I, too, had fallen into this trap. Since doctors continued to write the prescriptions, I felt justified. That is called denial and avoidance.

There were other complications too. I had scarring on my left kidney, and the doctors stated I would always experience problems with my nervous system because of all the surgeries, nerve damage, and internal trauma caused by the diseased spleen. The results of these complications were occasional kidney infections, interstitial cystitis, chronic back pain, and my blood pressure soared high and dropped low, creating severe headaches and constant hand tremors.

One day, I ran out of a grocery store in tears, leaving everything on the checkout counter because I could not stop shaking long enough to sign a check. If only credit and debit cards were as popular and easily available back then. Equally embarrassing was trying to hold a microphone when I sang. At least when I played the piano, my hands were constantly moving. Everyday living consisted of daily medications for pain, nerves, and blood pressure. Through the years, I simply learned to medicate and tolerate.

For some time, I remained a broken and hurting young woman, desperately in need of complete healing and deliverance. It is hard to help others with any degree of success when you are a mess yourself. You cannot hide behind makeup, an outgoing personality, and fancy clothes forever. The truth will eventually come out. With any addiction (or habitual negative behaviors), honesty and transparency must be embraced for a successful healing process to begin. Only then can you become the overcoming child of God you were meant to blossom into.

As the Holy Spirit brought healing and maturity to my mind, soul, and body, I began realizing the devastating effects of certain destructive behaviors. I continuously repeated a cycle of making the same mistakes over and over. My insecurities were numerous and out of control, causing me to look for love and fulfillment in people or things. I repeatedly chose relationships that were unhealthy because I felt so undeserving of anything good.

Wanting to be loved is natural, but if a relationship brings pain and abuse, something is wrong. Stop and seek God for help. We must be aware of an important fact; friends, mates, jobs, money, power, success—all these things and more—can become little idols we set up to make us feel better about ourselves or fill a void. This is not God's way, nor does it lead to His best. "Seek first the Kingdom of God, and all these things shall be added unto you." We often allow our emotional pain to create an impatience. The result of this behavior usually leads us to make seeking things the first priority, then we try to fit seeking the things of God into the equation. It simply does not work, because God must be our first priority. Thankfully, our heavenly Father is patient, "slow to anger and rich in mercy."

> But you, O Lord, are a God of compassion and mercy, slow to get angry and filled with unfailing love and faithfulness. (Psalm 86:15 NLT)
>
> It is of the Lord's mercies that we are not consumed, because His compassions fail not. They are new every morning; great is Thy faithfulness. (Lamentations 3:22–23 KJV)
>
> Like a father pitieth his children, so the Lord pitieth them that fear Him. (Psalm 103:13 KJV)
>
> But the mercy of the Lord is from everlasting to everlasting upon them that fear Him, and His righteousness unto children's children. (Psalm 103:17 NIV)

CHAPTER 10

CHALLENGES, CHANGES, AND GOD'S AMAZING GRACE

The next few years presented many challenges, changes, and a brand-new Donna. In the midst of it all, the Holy Spirit remained faithfully at work mending and restoring all the past hurts. Addictions were broken, and I could see the light of hope at the end of the tunnel.

One memory I could not shake had to do with Bob. I often wondered if anyone would ever make me feel as loved and accepted as I felt with him. By this time, we were no longer communicating, and I missed my friend. I often slipped into the self-destructive world of *what if*. Shaking those moments off, I forged forward but never stopped hoping the best for him and praying he was truly happy.

Tremors continued to be a constant source of embarrassment and frustration. I finally found a doctor who took the time to see if anything new in the world of medicine could help. My medical history intrigued her, and she showed a genuine interest in helping me overcome the constant tremors, blood pressure issues, and headaches.

Scheduling an MRI and CAT scan, she hoped to pinpoint the specific areas of nerve damage. Consulting with a few of her colleagues, they decided to gradually wean me off pain and nerve pills and try a certain type of blood pressure medication used for controlling tremors, headaches, and fluctuating blood pressure. Eventually the headaches and tremors were under control, and for the first time in years, I experienced steady and calm hands. I could even hold a microphone when I sang without shaking. Hallelujah, restoration had begun.

During this time of restoration and hope, I received a disturbing letter from the hospital in Pensacola informing me of a high probability of health problems associated with the units of blood I received from 1975 to 1983. They requested I make an appointment as soon as possible. A large percentage of patients who received blood from the blood bank the hospital used during that time period developed various types of hepatitis or the HIV/AIDS virus.

No one knew very much about the AIDS virus at this time, and scared does not begin to describe my state of mind. I made an appointment and received the necessary tests. Although the results came back negative, the doctor advised me to be tested every six months for the next five to ten years. Having survived so much already, I stood in faith and gave the situation to God. I continued being tested, and God faithfully proved Himself powerful and mighty on my behalf.

Putting thoughts of hepatitis and HIV/AIDS behind me, I felt strong enough to return to some form of counseling and finish what I started years prior. Although the Lord continued to bless my life, I did not feel *complete* as a woman, and I longed for happiness in my personal life.

Instead of seeking God first for the best career path for my life, I decided to begin applying for jobs at counseling offices and mental health hospitals. Longing for a sense of value and worth, I set out to help others who were less fortunate and in distress.

An adolescent rehabilitation center offered me a position, and I happily accepted. Day after day, I witnessed the painful effects of abuse as I tried to help precious, hurting children. Unable to simply close the door and leave it behind, I went home every day stressed out to the max. Still feeling empty and incomplete, confusion lingered followed by unanswered questions: *Why isn't God blessing all my hard work? Why am I not happy?* This works mentality continued to show up and rise to the surface. Despite these misguided efforts, God knew my heart and graciously showered me with His mercy and love. You see, at that time, I failed to understand something important: the Lord rewards obedience, not good intentions, honorable professions, or anything else we cleverly come up with to justify why we do what we do.

In a secular counseling setting, there are guidelines that must be adhered to when it comes to discussing anything relating to faith and God. Although I carefully obeyed the rules and regulations, God's amazing grace opened many doors of opportunity. As a believer, I knew only Jesus could truly heal the hurt and remove the painful scars.

Several years passed along with burnout and frustration before realizing, *Hey, Donna, don't you think this career choice is a big mistake for now? You haven't even worked through your own issues.* I'm stubborn, so I dug my heels in and tried to push through.

Emotionally, there were so many unresolved issues in my life. Being around negativity and constant problems without complete healing in these areas hindered my ability to truly help others. It also added extreme stress and anxiety, which I found myself incapable of handling in a healthy manner.

To be a successful therapist and counselor, it is important to walk in wisdom when it comes to your own life, because it can take a toll on you personally, spiritually, and physically. I longed to find fulfillment and someone who would love me, and I desired to minister to hurting people. Unfortunately, in my pursuit of those things I failed to walk in wisdom. This sent me down many directions, just not the right ones.

I've spent many years in ministry and counseling and have observed some important things regarding relationships. Much of the wisdom I've gained is a direct result of my own failures; others are by examples and causation of environmental factors. One critical issue seems to be the desire for another person to make us feel important, needed, and whole. A close and continual relationship with Jesus Christ is the only thing capable of bringing anyone a sense of acceptance and wholeness. Our mates, family, children, or careers only define a portion of who we are; however, they cannot complete us, fill every void, or right every wrong. To demand this in a relationship places unrealistic expectations on those we love. It also causes strife and unnecessary emotional pain. Marriages, friendships, and families are torn apart and destroyed every single day due to the following key issues: selfishness, insecurities, not letting go of the past, wrong motives of the heart, and unrealistic expectations.

Pride is usually the source of these issues. When we refuse to humble ourselves to God, our mates, or anything we perceive is a roadblock in the quest to having it our way, we are in jeopardy of destruction. Scripture clearly tells us, "Pride comes before downfall." When we find ourselves demanding our rights and being unwilling to bend, pride is definitely rearing its ugly head, and we are no longer acting in love.

Too often, we fail to recognize what love should sound or look like because it interferes with getting our own way or our own agenda. I am not proud of this, but I regularly responded in ways love *is not*, and a downfall was inevitable. The next phase of my life will show the desperate measures I pursued trying to find love and happiness. It also reveals my level of immaturity when it came to truly knowing how to love and be loved.

So, where do we find the guidelines for love? The following scriptures clearly define love and its behavior. As you read the description of what love is and how it behaves, make the decision today to be a hearer and doer of the Word. If you choose well, your relationships will flourish.

> Love is patient, love is kind. It does not envy, it does not boast, it is not proud. It is not rude, it is not self-seeking, it is not easily angered, it keeps no record of wrongs. Love does not delight in evil, but rejoices with the truth. It always protects, always trusts, always hopes, always perseveres. Love never fails. (1 Corinthians 13:4–8 NIV).

CHAPTER 11

FRIENDS AND FAREWELLS

Speaking from a grateful heart for what God brought me through and a desire to walk in forgiveness, I won't go into specifics about the few things I remember from the foggy years. With that being said, some explanation is necessary. During those uncertain and challenging times, I longed for someone to love. Someone who wouldn't see me as incomplete or a woman of no value because of the inability to give birth to a child. Having experienced abuse during those painful years, I longed for a healthy, loving relationship. You see, healing from damaging, emotional scars takes time. It's a process. When we choose to rush through the healing steps or seek others to fill the void, we will face difficulty with added sorrow and no peace.

As I continued to heal from years of disease and the toll it took on my body, I eventually met a nice Christian young man who was in the military. He asked me out, and on our very first date, he casually stated, "There is something you should know. I like kids, but I have no desire to ever have children of my own. I need to know how you feel about this if you want to date me." Completely blown away, I proceeded to tell him about the hysterectomy and all the years of pain and suffering. I recall going home that night with this thought: *Okay, Lord, this must be the person you are bringing into my life. It won't bother him that I can't have kids. He'll accept me just the way I am.*

Convinced this was the hand of God, within nine weeks of our first date, we became husband and wife. Whew! I suppose it is an understatement when I say this area of my life lacked maturity and godly wisdom. We married so quickly we did not take time for premarital counseling. I do not recommend this for anyone. Naturally, the situation concerned Mom and Dad because my husband and I barely knew one another. I, on the other hand, assumed the Christian aspect solved everything. Big mistake.

Although terribly naïve, once we said, "I do," we entered into a covenant with one another. More than anything, I wanted to be loved. Determined to be the best wife possible, I forged ahead believing all my insecurities would somehow cease to exist and marriage fixed everything.

As time passed, our marriage began to disintegrate. I found daily comfort from reading the Bible, along with volunteering in the music and youth department at Dad's church. I also worked as a counselor for an adult recovery facility. Unfortunately, my career choice added more stress to our marriage.

After a few years, my husband received orders to Germany for two years. The military doctors recommended I remain in the States because of all my previous health issues. To save money, I moved in with Mom and Dad until his two-year tour ended.

A number of things transpired before my husband's departure, sending feelings of inadequacy and insecurities spiraling out of control. Sadly, I actually sighed with relief when he left. I am sure he felt the same way. Longing for the blessings of God, we sought forgiveness from one another, but dividing walls remained. We corresponded by writing letters and one monthly phone call, but our conversations were brief. In the eighties, communication options were limited, and calling from one country to another was very expensive.

We soon learned a painful lesson; when Christ is no longer Lord of your home, Satan has a stronghold that can destroy everything and anything good remaining. We were a world apart in more ways than simply geography.

With my husband in Germany and feeling alone, the Lord opened an unexpected and wonderful door of opportunity … in the form of a friend. One Sunday morning, a beautiful young woman visited our church. She was tall and thin with long, dark, flowing hair. As the service ended, she made her way to the altar and rededicated her life back to God. Wanting her to feel supported, I went and knelt beside her as she prayed. At one time, she had served the Lord but, like so many of us, allowed circumstances and painful experiences to hinder her commitment to follow God.

As she rose to her feet the scripture "old things are passed away; behold, all things are become new" became alive and real to me in a powerful way. This young lady became transformed right before my eyes. She looked like a completely different person. My new friend truly was a brand-new creation. A peace and happiness beautifully replaced the bondage she knelt down with.

We went to lunch after church, and she shared with me how her husband moved out of their home, stating he no longer wanted to be married. She struggled with the pain of divorce and losing someone she deeply loved. The process of divorce is never easy, regardless of the circumstances or who is to blame.

As our friendship and strong bond of trust continued developing, we studied the Bible together and shared beautiful times of laughter and tears. A safety net surrounded us like a shield, allowing the most intimate feelings and thoughts to be exposed and expressed. During this time of discipleship, the Lord began to manifest the gift of discernment in my life. It was an intimidating but humbling experience.

Many of us carry around scars and memories of past hurts. They seem too great to bear and too devastating to share with anyone. My friend kept one of these painful secrets closely guarded and tucked away. She would not even allow herself to tell me. God gently and patiently waited, longing to heal the hurt in her heart and abundantly restore all the things Satan stole from her life.

One night we attended a Christian concert. The singer began sharing a testimony when the Lord spoke something directly to me concerning my friend. It felt as if God Himself sat down beside me and whispered in my ear. An overwhelming love and compassion consumed every cell of my being. Beyond a shadow of a doubt, I knew my dear, sweet friend urgently needed assurance of the Father's unconditional and unrelenting love for her.

I leaned over and said, "God not only loves you, but He desires to heal and restore your broken heart and life. His love is without boundaries or conditions, and He is about to reach past your mistakes and failures and give you a miracle. He is not angry; you are His daughter, and He truly loves you." Grabbing her by the hand and putting my arms around her, we walked outside to the parking lot. With the anointing of the Holy Spirit, I shared an intimate and painful issue God showed me about her past. It was something I had no way of knowing or even suspecting. We stood for a moment shaking and broken before the Lord as we clung to one another in praise and gratitude for God's forgiveness, healing, and restoration.

Heading back to her house, our praise and fellowship continued past midnight into the early morning hours. After that night, her hope and faith received an incredible boost as she forged ahead into complete emotional and spiritual healing. Standing in awe of God's mercy and power, I too felt a sense of renewal and expectation.

> No, in all these things we are more than conquerors through Him who loved us. For I am convinced that neither death nor life, neither angels nor demons, neither the present nor the future, nor any powers, neither height nor depth, nor anything else in all creation, will be able to separate us from the love of God that is in Christ Jesus our Lord. (Romans 8:37–39 NIV)

If reading this story brings up unresolved issues in your own life that have been carefully tucked away in a secret corner of your heart, let me encourage you to turn those things over to Jesus *today*, for He alone has the power to heal and miraculously restore. Christ urges us to come to Him, and He will give us rest. There is a miracle of healing waiting for you right now. The only way to receive it is to give everything over to the heavenly Father. His arms are open wide waiting for you to run in and find rest.

> Come to Me, all you who are weary and burdened, and I will give you rest. Take My yoke upon you and learn from Me, for I am gentle and humble in heart, and you will find rest for your souls. For My yoke is easy and My burden is light. (Matthew 11:29–30 NIV)

Falling into Faith

My husband completed his two-year assignment in Germany and came home. He never said much about his time away; however, he casually stated he didn't attend any Bible study group or church regularly. We talked about things he could participate in on the base once he got settled, but he chose not to attend any of them. This revelation scared me because of our already troubled marriage.

I am not talking about legalism. We are not saved by the law or how often we attend church, but Satan is cunning and deceptive. When we stop meeting together in fellowship with likeminded people, our lives are open to temptation and so much more. Without accountability, we are left to our own devices. Meaning, we have to figure things out for ourselves by using our own limited reasoning. This is a dangerous place to put ourselves, particularly when we are struggling in certain areas. It is important to be faithful in the things that keep us strong and accountable. Even when we fail miserably, *if with a repentant heart we rise up and call out to Him, He will forgive and come to our rescue.*

Over the years, my failures were too many to count. One thing I learned early in life is the importance of staying in fellowship with believers. Without these personal connections, the road back is filled with difficulty and additional challenges to overcome.

As Christians, we are free to serve from a heart of love and obedience. God does not reward those who attend church regularly out of obligation, His Word says He rewards the *faithful*. One definition of faithful is, "true to one's word, promises, or vows." Being faithful and good stewards of all God has blessed us with is of utmost importance to the Father. Knowing this, we should examine our priorities and honestly discover why we choose to not heed and obey the scriptures. Remember, "The little foxes spoil the vine."

After a few long discussions, my husband and I made a promise to get back on track, put the past behind us, and make God a priority in our marriage. The next step … honoring our commitment and being obedient.

Within a brief period of time, we received orders to Plattsburgh, New York. Feeling a fresh start might be just what our marriage needed, we began making plans to leave. Although excited about a new beginning, I dreaded leaving my wonderful new friend and loving parents.

After many tears and sad farewells, we left Florida and moved to Plattsburgh. Upstate New York is beautiful, although the winters tend to be humid and cold. The colors and changes of the seasons left me speechless. Bundling up like a kid, the first time it snowed I played outside until my hands, feet, and face were numb. I loved it. Florida beaches are gorgeous, but this topped anything I had ever seen.

We soon settled into our new home and community. As time ticked by, I found myself daily reorganizing, cooking, and cleaning like a woman possessed. Bored from not enough to do, I needed a job and a reason to get up. With only one vehicle, I had to find something to do from home or on the military base.

While grocery shopping one afternoon, I saw a sign in the commissary window advertising for home daycare providers. This enabled me to work with children in a positive way, without all the heartbreaks. My husband agreed and seemed delighted with the decision. I filled out the paperwork, took the classes, and received my certification.

Before long, I enrolled two babies and three three-year-olds. My life went from bored to busy very quickly, but I loved it. These children became my very own extended family. Sensing my loneliness and need for companionship, their parents included me in outings and activities. They were wonderful people, willing to share their lives and children. As marital woes grew more intense, the love I received from these families helped lessen the moments of depression and despair. A marriage in decay is a painful and exhausting existence. We both bore the responsibility of what happened. Tired of struggling, we simply learned to tolerate, ignore, and exist. This is a recipe for failure in any marriage.

Two years passed, and my little ones were growing more every day. While busy planning a birthday party for one of them, I received a phone call from home. Dad and Mom were both on the line, but Dad said something I did not want to hear, "Baby, Mama's been diagnosed with non-Hodgkin's lymphoma, and they found a number of tumors all over her body. Can you come home?"

Mom tried to sound strong and tough, but I could hear pain and fear in her voice. Between shock and tears, I said, "I love you both, and I'll be on the first flight out. Mama, you are going to beat this."

Like many mothers and daughters, we often clashed during my

teenage years. Our struggles with constant illness created a bond and division throughout childhood and adolescence. The main reason for the tension had to do with the fact we were undeniably so much alike in our opinionated and stubborn personalities. After the hysterectomy, something changed between us. I needed Mom's strength just to keep sane, and this created a strong and unshakable friendship. I could tell her anything, and it seemed she saw right into my heart. At the same time, Mom trusted and confided in me. Being a pastor's wife is often challenging, and she could not open up to just anyone. It was an honor to be her daughter and to experience an adult relationship with her.

Our parents always gave us their unconditional love and support. Now it was our turn to be there for them. Numb and unable to process a rational thought, I hung up the phone and bluntly stated, "Mama has cancer, and it isn't good." Then I turned to go upstairs and began packing. To this day, I cannot remember what happened to the birthday party I was planning. The next day, I said a tearful goodbye to my husband, the children, and their families.

What happened next is best described as God's amazing grace in action. I took a ferry to Vermont and boarded a small plane en route to a larger airport. Thoughts of how hopeless cancer sounded and the possibility of losing Mother weighed heavily on my mind. I sat in my seat praying, when a man touched my hand and said, "Hi, I don't want to bother you, but is there anything I can do?" The compassion and love of Jesus shone in his eyes as he offered to pray with me. I quietly thought, *God, is this another angel?* A floodgate of emotions broke, and I proceeded to sob and tell him the whole story. At that very moment, I knew God sent him to soothe my hurting heart.

The miracle of this meeting soon became clear to both of us. He had recently flown to a small remote town in Vermont to visit with his elderly mother and was on his way home to Florida ... Fort Walton Beach to be exact. God is so awesome. Never leaving my side, we shared the same flight schedule and connections, allowing us the opportunity to pray and talk. I shared stories from my childhood, and we enjoyed some much-needed laughter in between bouts of tears and heartache.

During a layover, I called home to check in, and Mom answered the phone. She tried to sound upbeat, but I could tell she was scared.

I hung up sobbing uncontrollably. This precious man rushed toward me with arms opened wide. God knew just how to get His arms of love around me.

Home at last, we entered the airport where my family awaited. Introducing my new friend, we shared the sequence of events that brought us together as everyone hugged and cried. We said goodbye and promised to stay in touch.

Several months later, this gentleman and his wife surprised me by attending one of our church services. My new friend's wife possessed the same spirit of compassion and love as her husband. The family of God is a glorious thing.

Within a month of my arrival, the military granted my husband a humanitarian assignment back home. Over the next four months, our marriage completely dissolved, and I felt numb. Needing peace and help, we began counseling with a Christian therapist. Facing the giants in our lives is never easy.

Unable to fix our marriage, struggling with depression, and emotionally drained, my focus stayed centered on Mom. I became the main caregiver for her and Dad. He felt so lost and became despondent. The love of his life was withering away in front of his eyes. Heartache engulfed me to the point it often hurt to breathe.

CHAPTER 12

MAMA SAYS HELLO TO JESUS

Chemotherapy is a word I learned to strongly dislike. Doctors gave us facts and information; however, they could not predict how Mom's body would tolerate the treatments. We were given two scenarios, one good and one bad. They felt hopeful and optimistic, if no serious complications occurred. Her overall health seemed to be the greatest concern. Mom always said if ever faced with cancer, she'd refuse chemotherapy, but to our surprise, she decided to accept the treatment. Seeming at peace with her decision, we pressed forward into the unknown. We knew God could heal her with or without chemo, so we did the best and only thing we knew to do … pray for a miracle.

Mom talked about heaven a lot during this time. One day she looked at me and said, "I want you to know I am looking forward to meeting Jesus face-to-face, and just think, baby, I'll never have another day of pain, pills, and suffering."

The next four months, the family took every opportunity to spend time with Mom. We laughed, cried, and shared stories of days gone by. She did not sleep well at night due to nausea and pain, so Dad slept on the other side of the room where he studied and prepared his sermons, and I slept on the floor next to her bed. We talked privately for hours during the night about her concerns and the dreams she had for each one of us.

Dad and I were the primary caregivers; however, Dad's health was also in jeopardy due to stress and heart problems. Robbie lived a few hours away, and her son, Chad, was in junior high school, but they came home often. Larry, Judy, and Amanda lived in town and helped as much as they could. Judy worked full-time yet never failed to be available with a helping hand. Amanda and Chad lavished their granny with lots of love, and she enjoyed the attention and quality time they spent together.

My parents loved each other deeply. Mother was only fifteen when they married, and Dad became her everything. In sickness and in health, through good times and bad, they were truly there for one another.

Although Mother battled sickness most of her life, she always found a way of bringing humor into our home. She was a firecracker in every sense of the word, and people loved being around Mom. Her infectious laugh created joy and waves of laughter. When Mama laughed, everyone joined in.

Dad's desperation over Mom's illness grew with each passing day. Suffering with high blood pressure and heart problems, mounting stress caused him to succumb to a stroke. Thankfully, it was mild and did not result in paralysis. We had always seen Dad as the rock of the family but soon realized Mama was the emotional glue holding things together.

God mercifully intervened, and Dad made a full recovery. On the funny side, during the stroke episode, Dad made several wacky and strange comments. Mama spent the next month taking every opportunity to let people know Dad finally jumped off the deep end. She laughingly stated, "It finally happened. Edward lost his ever-lovin' mind."

My failing marriage concerned Mom. Constant reassurance from me did not sway her from worrying. We were living in her home, and she saw firsthand the lack of affection and indifference. We basically lived separate lives. Mom also understood the painful void I felt from not having children. When I lived in New York, we spent hours talking on the phone and laughing about all the things the babies I cared for got into. My husband and I discussed adoption, but he could never make the commitment. Our desires for a family were very different. I eventually reconciled myself to the fact adoption was not an option; case closed. Knowing all of this, Mama never stopped praying for us. The last month of her life, she shared many personal and prophetic things with me. In time, every one of them proved true.

Christmastime soon arrived. Decorations, lots of presents, and the smell of ham and sweet potato casserole filled the house. Everyone sensed

Falling into Faith

this might be our last Christmas with Mom. More tumors were found the previous month, and the doctor intensified the treatments. After running more tests, we were told there were no signs of improvement. Chemotherapy was discontinued and replaced with comfort measures only.

Mom was so frail and weak, but she mustered up the strength to play the piano. We all gathered in the living room to sing and praise God. After a time of worship, we ate and exchanged presents. Having Mother with us was the most precious gift for all of us that year, and we are forever thankful.

Later that night, Mother made an unexpected request; she wanted my sister and I to sing at her funeral. Pleading with her to reconsider, she refused to hear any excuses. Mom stated she did not want anyone ruining her favorite songs at her very own funeral. Robbie and I knew exactly what she meant. She did not like it when singers failed to pronounce their words properly or sounded too twangy or nasally. Mama always said, "When you sing for the Lord, you should do your very best, and for heaven's sakes, don't sound like you're whining." We wanted to grant her request, but how? Mom was so weak and barely eighty pounds due to cancer and chemo, but make no mistake about it, she always had the final say and it was in your best interest to listen.

Simple everyday tasks proved difficult for Mom when we were growing up because of pain and infection from the kidney disease she suffered with. But she refused to allow anything to keep us from getting to our music lessons. The ultimate perfectionist, she worked long hours every week teaching us the importance of giving God our best when we sang or played the piano. She made us practice repeatedly, saying, "Girls, you can't bless someone with the words of a song if they can't hear or understand what you are saying. If you're gonna do it ... do it right!"

Mom imparted her love and gift of music to us, and although we failed to appreciate it at times, we love her dearly for it. Knowing the sacrifice she made and how she felt, we would have to find the strength to sing at her funeral should Jesus choose to take her home to heaven.

On New Year's Day, things took a turn for the worse as Mom began struggling to breathe. Fearing the onset of pneumonia, we rushed her to the hospital. The drive felt like an eternity as every breath grew harder for her to take. When we arrived at the emergency room, she literally began gasping for air. Mom always said she never wanted to be on life support, but turning critical so fast, Dad only had seconds to make the decision. Before we realized it, doctors and nurses were hooking her up to tubes and machines. Feeling this would be temporary, we all prayed she understood.

Things continued happening way too fast. We were not ready to let Mom go. How do you prepare to lose someone you love? We all felt like robots just going through the motions of walking and breathing.

Afraid to leave the hospital, we slept in the waiting room. We only left one time to get clothes and other things we needed from home. Seven days later, the family stood around Mom's bed hand in hand, singing in harmony her favorite songs. While we sang "Beulah Land," Mama slipped into the arms of Jesus. She was only sixty-three years old. In the natural, we wanted to fall apart, but the mercy and comfort of the Holy Spirit held us together.

Dad walked around in a daze. His wife and best friend of forty-nine years was gone. Only the good Lord could sustain him through this. Going through the motions, we proceeded to do all the things you are supposed to do when a love one dies. By the grace of God, we sang at the funeral and miraculously made it through without breaking down.

Mom received the ultimate healing—never again to suffer pain, sorrow, or sickness. What a glorious thought. It would be selfish to want her back. One day, we will see her again, and what a reunion that will be. Thoughts of heaven are more wonderful because she is there. Mama truly left a mark and legacy of love.

Her death brought about many changes. After almost sixty years of faithful ministerial service to the Lord, and thirty-two of those years spent at Wright Assembly in Fort Walton Beach, Dad announced his retirement. With Dad retiring and Mom gone, I felt utterly lost. My communion with the Lord grew cold. Longing for a change, I could no longer tolerate things that were wrong in my life by simply ignoring them. My husband and I continued counseling, hoping for the best. Many painful things came out during these sessions, giving us an understanding as to why we faced so many difficulties. It appeared most

Falling into Faith

of our problems were a direct result of unresolved issues from our past and childhood trauma.

The counselor released me from further sessions but continued counseling with my husband. After a few more months passed, and no longer willing to stay in the struggle, we filed for divorce. Everything was finalized a few months prior to our tenth anniversary.

The day of our divorce, we went to lunch together and asked one another for forgiveness. We knew according to scripture we must be willing to forgive if we expected God to forgive our sins. We hugged, cried, and said goodbye. As I walked away that day, I felt both sadness and an unexpected peace.

God's will is not divorce; however, if we repent and humble ourselves before the Lord, He will forgive and bring restoration. Contrary to what many religious Organizations believe, divorce is not an unpardonable sin.

> For if you forgive men when they sin against you, your heavenly Father will also forgive you. But if you do not forgive men their sins, your Father will not forgive your sins. (Matthew 6:14–15 NIV)

Desperately wanting God's forgiveness, I once again allowed shame and condemnation to drag me into a pit of despair. I continued to wonder, *How many more mess-ups will God allow before He slaps me into a fiery eternity?* Obviously, I viewed God as a hard taskmaster, instead of the loving, merciful Father He is.

In time and with the help of the Holy Spirit, my life made a dramatic and lasting change. God planned to restore and resurrect things I assumed were forever history—His abundant blessings, along with "His gifts and call." The restoration process included teaching me a valuable lesson on forgiving one's self and the joy and peace it brings. An amazing journey to freedom awaited me as I chose to fall into the hands of a loving God.

CHAPTER 13

IT'S TIME TO GET REAL

Using God's holy Word as our guide, the focus of this chapter is about church (the body of believers), hypocrites, and forgiveness. Jesus is very direct when it comes to these matters. The scriptures point toward the truth of God's Word and offer clear instructions on how to live together in love and harmony with a spirit of peace and reconciliation.

Let me clarify something. This is not about a building. It is about the body (or family) of believers, which includes churches, missions, cell groups, house churches, and so on—wherever we come together in unity and fellowship, professing Christianity.

The entire body of Christ desperately needs godly wisdom in dealing with sin issues of every kind. When we choose disobedience, there will be consequences. We may find ourselves facing various levels of brokenness, along with emotional, spiritual, and physical scars. Although we are free to make whatever choices we want in this life, we are not free from the consequences of those choices. With that said, when people are hurting, they need truth accompanied by love and encouragement, not condemnation and additional wounds. Even when they are at fault or have been reckless and foolish. No one is without sin, and none of us are perfect.

Statistics show Christians have as much difficulty forgiving one another as unbelievers. Therefore, we cannot ignore those within the family who continue to condemn people to hades, humiliate, and shoot our wounded. There are entirely too many souls lost and dying without Christ because of witnessing the unloving ways we treat one another, all in the name of the Lord. This must break the Father's heart. It is no wonder we are not seeing miracles and souls saved in our churches on a grander scale. The world does not want what we have, and who can blame them?

Every year, the number of people leaving the church increases at an unbelievable rate because they cannot find the support and acceptance they are desperately seeking. This is wrong, and we must change. Jesus Christ is the *only* lasting answer to the hurts of this world. Although the Bible tells us to hate the sin, we must love the sinner. This is not a cliché; it is truth.

Every man, woman, and child has value and worth in God's kingdom. It is not our job to decide who is worthy of His mercy and forgiveness. We must repent, turn from our wicked ways, and serve in love, staying focused on our mission of reconciliation. "All this is from God, who reconciled us to Himself through Christ and gave us the ministry of reconciliation" (2 Corinthians 5:18 NIV). The ministry of reconciliation means to reach the lost so that they can be reconciled to Jesus Christ, and restore the wounded back to the Savior.

On a positive note, we have seen and heard of churches throughout America offering divorce, abuse, and other kinds of care and counsel necessary for a healthy overall well-being. After some research, I discovered these programs are on the rise, and I pray they continue to increase in number and wisdom.

Jesus illustrates compassion for His children and their worth in the kingdom with the parable of the lost sheep. Our Creator, the Savior of the world, set the example for us. Who are we to show any less compassion for the lost and hurting than He did?

> But if anyone causes one of these little ones who believe in Me to sin, it would be better for him to have a large millstone hung around his neck and to be drowned in the depths of the sea. (Matthew 18:6 NIV)

> See that you do not look down on one of these little ones. For I tell you that the angels in heaven always see the face of My Father in heaven. What do you think? If

a man owns a hundred sheep, and one of them wanders away, will he not leave the ninety-nine on the hills and go look for the one that wandered off? And if he finds it, I tell you the truth, he is happier about the one sheep than about the ninety-nine that did not wander off. In the same way your Father in heaven is not willing that any of these little ones should be lost. (Matthew 18:10–14 NIV)

Notice He says, "But if anyone causes one of these little ones *who believe in Me to sin.*" He is referring to "His sheep" or "children of faith." This parable is about those of us who believe but are hurting, misguided, or lost. Whatever the label, it is about the believer who unfortunately gets off track.

Ask yourself, "Do I receive or despise others? Do I judge or encourage? Does my attitude cause others to stumble, or does it edify and offer hope?" Meditate on these questions and ask the Holy Spirit to reveal areas in your life that are not Christlike. Be prepared to repent and turn from walking a self-righteous, judgmental, and destructive path.

Now let's talk about one of the most popular reasons individuals leave the church—hypocrisy. Yes, it is a legitimate problem, but there are just as many hypocrites outside the church as there are inside. So, how do we differentiate between the two? First of all, believers should know better! Scripture tells us "But you are a chosen people, a royal priesthood, a holy nation, a people to be his very own and to proclaim the wonderful deeds of the one who called you out of darkness into his marvelous light" (1 Peter 2:9 ISV). As representatives of Christ, we are instructed to be "doers" not "hearers" only of God's Word: "Do not merely listen to the word, and so deceive yourselves. Do what it says" (James 1:22 NIV). Obeying these scriptures and consistently putting love into action will prevent deception and hypocrisy. So why don't we? I believe the answer to this question is self-righteousness and pride.

From Genesis to Revelation, pride appears to be a main root of sin. Some may argue the "fear of man" is the problem; however, when we fear doing the right thing because of another person's response or opinion, we are actually exalting them above God. *Webster's Dictionary* describes pride as "a high opinion of one's self, person, or object." So we should ask ourselves this question, "Whose opinion should matter, God our Creator, or humanity, His creation?" The only way to avoid being deceived and resolve this issue is to put into practice what the Bible says: "Demolish arguments and every pretension that sets itself up against the knowledge of God, and we take captive every thought to make it obedient to Christ" (2 Corinthians 10:5 NIV).

Because of pride, we are afraid to be "real," causing us to put on a false face. We tend to judge and criticize others, trying to hide our own shortcomings. Choosing this behavior creates a lifestyle of hypocrisy in action and opens the door to deception. Somehow, we fool ourselves into believing no one sees us as we truly are. We might fool a few people for a short time, but eventually the truth will rise to the surface.

Self-righteousness is a feeling or display of moral superiority. It is derived from the belief that one's actions or opinions are of greater virtue and superior to the opinions and thoughts of others. As you can see, pride must be a vital source of fuel in a person's life in order to attain the characteristics and actions of a self-righteous individual.

In a therapeutic setting, it is proven those who exhibit these behaviors are often narcissistic by nature. Narcissism is the pursuit of gratification from vanity or egotistic admiration of one's own attributes. For instance, narcissists believe they are right and everyone else is wrong. Ultimately, their opinions are the only ones that matter. They do not consider your feelings or opinions because they are insignificant and of no consequence to them. It is a sad and lonely existence because most of the time they alienate those around them, particularly friends and family.

Writing my story caused me to seriously take on the task of self-evaluation, challenging me in the area of hypocrisy. Being real meant telling many painful, pitiful, and shameful things about my life. Reading about the mistakes I repeated over (and over) again probably made you think, Man, *this woman really needs to get a clue,* and I agree. Recalling and sharing all the sordid details made me feel the same way; however, my heart's desire was to get my love walk right between God and humanity.

Those who are serious about their love walk will tell the truth at the risk of ridicule, gossip, and shame. They will humbly reveal all for the sake of forgiveness and saving someone else from pain and suffering. This is where a hypocrite parts ways with a genuine believer. A hypocrite cannot risk this kind of exposure. It is more important for them to continue in deceit and denial than truth and love. On the other hand, a genuine Christian will hold tightly to the fact they are washed in the blood of the Lamb and 100 percent forgiven. Receiving and not letting go of God's truth enables us to be vulnerable, sincere, fruitful, bold, and real. The truth shall set you free.

Those within the church who suffer from a works mentality often gravitate toward the life of a hypocrite out of pure exhaustion. They ignore their own issues and focus on pointing out other people's faults and shortcomings, mistakenly thinking they are camouflaging their own. Usually they volunteer for anything and everything, eventually wearing themselves out. Too tired from doing but not hearing, they become cranky, judgmental, and unfulfilled. Although they put on a fake smile and give you a hearty handshake, you will often see the negative results within the dynamics of their personal life.

Unfortunately, I know a lot about this. For many years, I was one of these misguided worker-bee souls. To this day, it continues to be something I must pay careful attention to. When you are raised in a minister's home, there is often an expectation from those within the church. We are to dutifully volunteer, overextend, and give of ourselves to the point of exhaustion. At least that was my experience growing up. Even today, my downfall is feeling the need to say yes to everything asked of me. This is unhealthy, personally destructive, and unwise. When I fall into this pit, I become so weary that the only smile I can muster up is a fake one; however, my loved ones catch the brunt of my exhaustion.

To conclude the hypocrite subject, let's look at how this affects the body of Christ—the church. As long as fallible human beings try to navigate relationships and interact with one another, there will be problems. Godly wisdom and learning to love ourselves and others paves the way toward healing. It also promotes spiritual growth in our own lives. Without it, hypocrisy can manifests in many different ways.

To recap, you know you're in a danger zone when these things occur: gossip, critical spirits, neglecting your own family but saying yes to everything and everyone else, taking your frustrations out on your family, and harboring bitterness and unforgiveness while smiling and pretending all is well. Philippians 4:8 teaches us what is good and right.

> Finally, brothers and sisters, whatever is true, whatever is noble, whatever is right, whatever is pure, whatever is lovely, whatever is admirable—if anything is excellent or praiseworthy—think about such things. (Philippians 4:8 NIV)

Now, let's shift our focus to forgiveness. What do we do when Mr. or Ms. Loose Lips mistreats, judges, or even falsely accuses? Moreover, what do we do when someone hurts us in painful ways when we are not at fault? These can be difficult situations, especially if you are a target of unjust actions and motives. Trust me, I've been there.

Regardless of the sin or situation, the scripture is clear. If we do not forgive, we will not be forgiven. Is this fair? Not always; however, it's not about what is fair. It is about doing the right thing according to God's Word. So why don't we? It boils down to relinquishing our pride, humbling ourselves, obedience, and our willingness to make a good and right choice. We have all been given *free will* to make our own choices. Choose well, and God's blessings will follow.

> For if you forgive men when they sin against you, your heavenly Father will also forgive you. *But if you do not forgive men their sins, your Father will not forgive your sins.* (Matthew 6:14–15 NIV; emphasis added)

It is important to understand what forgiveness means. Forgiving is not forgetting or even trusting. There are painful experiences many of us have endured that we will never forget; however, the power of forgiving causes anger and bitterness to flee and opens the door to healing. Memory can serve as a testimony of God's restoration power, as well as an amazing opportunity to help others who are hurting. When past hurts replay in your mind, offer praise to God for what He has brought you through. Pray earnestly and study the scriptures on forgiveness. Seek God for guidance and help. With purpose and determination, resist feelings of bitterness, condemnation, and anger.

Depending on the situation, trusting the individual (or individuals) we have forgiven is not always an option or even wise. With the help of the Holy Spirit and God's amazing grace, we can overcome the pain and walk in love. Obedience to God's Word and seeking His wisdom will also help you know what to walk away from.

If you are struggling in this area, ask the Holy Spirit for help as you apply forgiveness and stay in the Word. It will sustain your very life and lead you down a path of healing—a path that promotes a growing, liberating, and healthy love walk between God and humanity. Peace will saturate your mind and heart like a cleansing rain pouring over you. There is freedom and joy when we choose to walk in forgiveness.

Allow me to drive this point home before moving on. There is an old saying that states, "Unforgiveness is like drinking poison and expecting the other person to die." Think about this for a moment. Rationally speaking, holding on to unforgiveness does not make sense.

Another sobering fact to consider is this: if we do not forgive, we will spend eternity with the very hypocrites we despise so badly. This is not my opinion; it is God's Word. Remember, "But if you do not forgive others their sins, your Father will not forgive your sins" (Matthew 6:15 NIV).

When we pray, harboring bitterness and unforgiveness toward anyone hinders God's ability to forgive us of our sins. You see, God does not change, He does not lie, and He abides by His Word. Willful, purposeful sin will not be permitted in heaven. The Lord will not force us to choose obedience, it is up to us. If our desire is to spend eternity with Christ our Savior, we must forgive, and then we too will be forgiven.

When I reflect back on the forgiveness God has extended toward me, it becomes abundantly clear my response must always be to forgive. Make a decision today to serve the Lord in love, striving to do the right thing regardless of anything or anyone. Ask the Holy Spirit to reveal areas of pride or bitterness in your heart. Then, simply repent and choose truth. Doing this creates a beautiful love walk, and your life becomes powerfully fruitful. The hurt you have overcome becomes a testimony and source of strength for others as they face the giants in their lives and the battlefield of unforgiveness.

The subject of forgiveness is a serious issue within our Christian communities. Pray for the body of Christ as a whole. If you are not currently attending a church due to a past issue or hurt, ask God for healing. Find a church you and your family can call home, with a shepherd who has a heart for discipleship and ministers in spirit and truth. Choose to become a vessel of hope, love, and compassion to those inside and outside the church. This saying holds true: become part of the solution, not the problem.

> If My people, who are called by My name, will humble themselves and pray and seek My face and turn from their wicked ways; then will I hear from heaven and will forgive their sin and heal their land. (2 Chronicles 7:14 NIV)

No one knew better than Jesus and me how off the mark I drifted at times in my life. Mercifully, God heard my cries of genuine repentance. I did not deserve His forgiveness, but He freely gave it. For too many years, I failed to receive this precious gift, hindering God's blessings in my life and limiting His ability to use me to the fullest for His glory.

Although I will never get back those wasted years, I believe by sharing my story, someone's life will be enlightened. My prayer for anyone reading this is to take a leap of faith. Don't allow another minute to be wasted and consumed by unforgiveness. Choose today to forgive those who have hurt you, and forgive yourself for every mistake and poor decision, past or present. You have nothing to lose but so much to gain. Learn to walk in freedom, no longer bound by shame and condemnation.

The Bible tells us, "Therefore there is *now* no condemnation for those who are in Christ Jesus" (Romans 8:1 NIV; emphasis added). The time is now. Jesus Christ has set us free from the bondage of sin. If I had spent my entire life making all the right decisions and never straying, I would not be considered a more worthy or acceptable candidate to receive God's forgiveness.

Once we genuinely repent, a turning will follow. Instead of disobedience, we choose the path of obedience. Then we can rest in the fact that when God sees us, He sees red, the blood of atonement. By His grace and His strength, we can walk in the spirit of truth here and now, without the baggage of condemnation.

> Because through Christ Jesus the law of the Spirit of life set me free from the law of sin and death. For what the law was powerless to do in that it was weakened by the sinful nature, God did by sending His Son in the likeness of sinful man, in order that the righteous requirements of the law might be fully met in us, who do not live according to the sinful nature but according to the Spirit. (Romans 8:2–4 NIV)

It is of utmost importance to become knowledgeable in what the Word says about love and forgiveness. The next step is to walk it out. This will help us understand how to "lovingly restore" our brothers and sisters who are making unhealthy and ungodly choices, causing them to waver in their faith and creating havoc in not only their lives but also the lives of others.

We are instructed to "restore gently" a believer who is caught in sin. We must resist flesh and our own opinions. In other words, resist self-righteous and prideful behavior. Regardless of the sin, refuse to be an instrument of doubt and unbelief about our Redeemer's ability and willingness to forgive a truly repentant heart. We too can fall into the same temptations. Godly wisdom is essential. According to His Word, sin is sin. Humans categorize and measure the severity of sin, deciding which one is worse than another, but not God. He is just and good. Do I understand this? *No.* Do I trust Him? *Yes.*

Regardless of how intelligent you are or how many degrees you may hold, mere humans do not possess the wisdom or love necessary to handle many of the sensitive and painful situations we encounter in this world, but we have a heavenly Father who does. He will generously pour out His wisdom on all who ask. "If any of you lacks wisdom, he should ask God who gives generously to all without finding fault, and it will be given to him" (James 1:5 NIV).

> Brothers, if someone is caught in a sin, you who are spiritual should *restore him gently. But watch yourself, or you also may be tempted.* Carry each other's burdens, and in this way you will fulfill the law of Christ. *If anyone*

> *thinks he is something when he is nothing, he deceives himself. Each one should test his own actions.* Then he can take pride in himself, without comparing himself to somebody else, for each one should carry his own load. (Galatians 6:1–5 NIV; emphasis added)

Jesus Christ makes the process easy to understand. We are to restore gently, watch ourselves so that we do not fall into temptation, carry each other's burdens, test our own actions, and be careful not to think more highly of ourselves than we ought. Simply put, walk in the fear of the Lord.

As we continue reading in Galatians, scriptures 7–10 provide a wealth of information when it comes to "walking out" a life of love with a godly character.

> Do not be deceived. God cannot be mocked. A man reaps what he sows. The one who sows to please his sinful nature, from that nature will reap destruction; the one who sows to please the Spirit, from the Spirit will reap eternal life. Let us not become weary in doing good, for at the proper time we will reap a harvest if we do not give up. *Therefore, as we have opportunity, let us do good to all people especially to those who belong to the family of Believers.* (Galatians 6:7–10 NIV; emphasis added)

Daily renewing our minds in Christ will keep our love walk in check as it brings restoration and reconciliation within every aspect of our lives. Walking in love and obedience creates an atmosphere of expectancy for miracles and healings to manifest. This is my prayer, and I believe it is an obtainable goal within the entire body of Christ.

Because of the destruction and pain caused from bitterness, unforgiveness, hypocrisy, and pride, I want to close this chapter with a few more important points. God longs for His children to be emotionally healthy, but choosing these dangerous behaviors hinders stability, reconciliation, love, and growth.

When Jesus walked this earth, He left many beautiful examples of humility and the power of forgiveness. By grasping this concept and receiving truth, we will see miracles in a greater, more powerful way in our homes, communities, and churches.

Let's begin with a story about a woman with a sinful past. We will read the story in its entirety, due to the importance of the message.

> Now one of the Pharisees invited Jesus to have dinner with him, so He went to the Pharisee's house and reclined at the table. When a woman who had lived a sinful life in that town learned that Jesus was eating at the Pharisee's house, she brought an alabaster jar of perfume, and as she stood behind Him at His feet weeping, she began to wet His feet with her tears. Then she wiped them with her hair, kissed them and poured perfume on them. When the Pharisee who had invited Him saw this, he said to himself, "If this man were a prophet, He would know who is touching Him and what kind of woman she is, that she is a sinner." Jesus answered him, "Simon, I have something to tell you." "Tell me teacher," he said. "Two men owed money to a certain moneylender. One owed him five hundred denarii's, and the other fifty. Neither of them had the money to pay him back, so he canceled the debts of both. Now which of them will love him more?" Simon replied, "I suppose the one who had the bigger debt canceled." "You have judged correctly," Jesus said. Then He turned toward the woman and said to Simon, "Do you see this woman? I came into your house, you did not give Me any water for My feet, but she wet My feet with her tears and wiped them with her hair. You did not give Me a kiss, but this woman, from the time I entered, has not stopped kissing My feet. You did not put oil on My head, but she has poured perfume on My feet. Therefore, I tell you, her many sins have been forgiven, for she loved much. But he who has been forgiven little loves little." Then Jesus said to her, "Your sins are forgiven." The other guests

> began to say among themselves, "who is this who even forgives sins?" Jesus said to the woman, "Your faith has saved you; go in peace." (Luke 7:36–50 NIV)

It was customary in those days, and a gesture of hospitality, to wash someone's feet when they entered your home. While Jesus reclined, with His feet extended away from the table, the woman began weeping, wetting His feet with her tears. Then she wiped the Lord's feet with her hair. She did for Him what the Pharisee did not.

This woman loved Jesus deeply. Her love for Him was not the basis for her forgiveness. She took a leap of faith. Without faith, this would not have happened. Jesus stated these powerful words, "Your faith has saved you; go in peace." Her sins were gloriously forgiven. By faith, she dared to believe and receive God's forgiveness.

I love this story, for I too have been forgiven much. It never ceases to amaze me how merciful and gracious God is to all His children. Next, we will read what happens after true repentance and forgiveness is received and embraced in our lives.

> After this, Jesus traveled about from one town and village to another, proclaiming the good news of the Kingdom of God. The twelve were with Him, and also some women who had been cured of evil spirits and diseases: Mary (called Magdalene) from whom seven demons had come out; Joanna the wife of Cuza, the manager of Herod's household; Susanna and many others. *These women were helping support them out of their own means.* (Luke 8:1–3 NIV; emphasis added)

These women were never the same once Jesus came into their lives. They embraced His forgiveness and walked in peace and humility. Their faithful service supported Jesus and His disciples in spreading the good news to a lost and dying world. No longer living in condemnation or the shame of their past, they were gloriously and mercifully forgiven. How liberating and beautiful are the mercies of God.

CHAPTER 14

BY THEIR FRUIT YOU WILL KNOW THEM

As Christians, we have a responsibility to know and understand God's Word. We are instructed to "study to show thyself approved unto God, a workman that needeth not to be ashamed, rightly dividing the word of Truth" (2 Timothy 2:15 KJV).

One topic of confusion among so many believers is the subject of judging. Almost everyone knows the scripture "Judge not, that ye be not judged" (Matthew 7:1 KJV), but do we understand what it means? As Christians, we should not judge self-righteously or hypocritically; however, Christ repeatedly commands us to evaluate people's characters, particularly those who confess to be followers of Christ. What does the fruit from their lives produce? Are they genuine? Do their actions line up with their words? "You can identify them by their fruit, that is, by the way they act. Can you pick grapes from thornbushes, or figs from thistles?" (Matthew 7:16 NLT).

If you want to know God's formula for discerning a person's intent or authenticity, here is some biblical insight. "Yes, just as you can identify a tree by its fruit, so you can identify people by their actions" (Matthew 7:20 NLT).

There is a story in the Bible about a woman caught in adultery, and it is a perfect example of the wrong kind of judging. It deals with sin, finger-pointing, deceit, and ultimately forgiveness.

More than one person is responsible and participates when committing adultery; however, only the woman stood accused. Provision had been made for the man to escape, using this incident as a stage to trap Jesus. They obviously underestimated who they were dealing with.

> But Jesus went to the Mount of Olives. At dawn He appeared again in the temple courts; where all the people gathered around Him, and He sat down to teach them. The teachers of the law and the Pharisees brought in a woman caught in adultery. They made her stand before the group and said to Jesus, "Teacher this woman was caught in the act of adultery. In the law Moses commanded us to stone such women. Now what do you say?" (John 8:1–5 NIV)

The Bible tells us they used this question as a trap because the Romans did not allow the Jews to carry out death sentences. If Jesus had said to stone her, He could have been in conflict with the Romans. If Jesus said not to stone her, He could have been accused of being unsupportive of the law. Stoning was not a prescribed manner of execution unless the woman was a betrothed virgin. The law also required the stoning of both parties involved; therefore, the trap was set.

What Jesus did next was brilliant. He spoke of throwing a stone; therefore, He could not be accused of failure to uphold the law, yet the conditions He gave for throwing the stone prevented anyone from doing so. His wisdom is astounding and powerful.

> But Jesus bent down and started to write on the ground with His finger. When they kept questioning Him, He straightened up and said to them, "If any one of you is without sin, let him be the first to throw a stone at her." Again, He stooped down and wrote on the ground. At this, those who heard began to go away one at a time, the older ones first, until only Jesus was left, with the woman still standing there. Jesus straightened up and asked her, "Woman, where are they? Has no one condemned you?" "No one, sir she said." "Then neither do I condemn you," Jesus declared, "Go now and leave your life of sin." (John 8:6–11 NIV)

Can you imagine what this woman must have been thinking? I have heard varying opinions about what Jesus wrote on the ground, but I am particularly partial to the one suggesting He wrote down all the sins of the accusers. That would certainly shut me up.

Hopefully, this story causes us to think twice before eagerly pointing a self-righteous and hypocritical finger of accusation and judgment. There is only one person who walked the earth without sin, and His name is Jesus Christ.

Although we are not to hypocritically judge or condemn others, scriptures tell us to test and evaluate a person's fruit and character. It is appropriate to ask questions such as: Do their words and actions line up? Do their lives portray the fruits of the Spirit? Do they bless and edify, or bring confusion and tear down? When they fall short, do they make excuses or accept responsibility and repent?

If you are not sure what to look for, Galatians clearly tells us what kind of fruit must be evident in the life of an individual who claims Christianity. It does not mean a Christian will get it right every time and never make mistakes; however, when he or she falls short, a Christian will be honest and repentant, and a change will take place.

> But the fruit of the Spirit is love, joy, peace, kindness, goodness, faithfulness, gentleness and self-control. Against such things there is no law. Those who belong to Christ Jesus have crucified the sinful nature with its passions and desires. Since we live by the Spirit, let us keep in step with the Spirit. Let us not become conceited, provoking and envying each other. (Galatians 5:22–26 NIV)

Now that we understand the kind of fruit a Christian produces, the next step is to prayerfully heed the warning signs and seek truth. We live in a world where truth is often hard to come by. There are those who walk around in clever disguises, but their lives resemble a destructive hurricane. They usually leave a path of hurting and wounded people due to their actions and choices. Most of the time, it is because they too have been wounded in some way. Regardless of the why, ask the Holy Spirit for discernment and wisdom when dealing with the ferocious wolves hovering about. They desperately need our prayers but not necessarily our company.

> Watch out for false prophets. They come to you in sheep's clothing, but inwardly they are ferocious wolves. *By their fruit you will recognize them.* Do people pick grapes from thorn bushes, or figs from thistle? Likewise every good tree bears good fruit, but a bad tree bears bad fruit, and a good tree cannot bear bad fruit, and a bad tree cannot bear good fruit. Every tree that does not bear good fruit is cut down and thrown into the fire. *Thus, by their fruit you will recognize them.* (Matthew 7:13–20 NIV; emphasis added)

We talked in the previous chapter about how to gently restore someone who is caught in sin, but what do we do when a believer continues to choose an ungodly path? According to scripture, we have a responsibility to the Lord, the body of Christ, and ourselves. Sin behavior does not only hurt the person involved but also destroys and wounds others. This is why the Bible clearly states light has nothing to do with darkness. If we continue to be part of a person's life who chooses to walk in sin yet claims to be a Christian, we too can fall into the same temptation. I know this to be a fact from my own personal experience and also from seeing many of the children God has given us fall into these destructive traps.

We must not grieve the Holy Spirit. We cannot make people choose what is right according to scripture, but we can love and encourage them to turn away from sin so blessings can be restored to their lives. 1 Corinthians chapter 9 offers great insight on what is expected from us when dealing with these issues. It is a hard word, but it must be adhered to if we expect God's blessings.

If we faithfully put these instructions into practice, a hypocrite could not last long in our churches without truly repenting or fleeing. Just imagine a congregation full of people who are transparent, honest, and accountable to God and others in word and deed. Think about the impact this would have on our families, communities, and the world.

> I wrote to you in my letter not to associate with sexually immoral people—not at all meaning the people of this world who are immoral, or the greedy and swindlers, or idolaters. In that case you would have to leave this world. But now I am writing to you that you must not associate with anyone who claims to be a brother or sister but is sexually immoral or greedy, an idolater or slanderer, a drunkard or swindler. Do not even eat with such people. What business is it of mine to judge those outside the church? Are you not to judge those inside? God will judge those outside. Expel the wicked person from among you. (1 Corinthians 5:9–13 NIV)

Paul was not instructing the church to disassociate themselves from unbelievers. In fact, he says if we did, we'd have to "leave this world." On the contrary, he is instructing the believers not to associate with those who say they are Christians yet live like the world. To be blunt, their fruit stinks, they are living a hypocritical existence, and association could cause a Christian to compromise and sin. The scriptures we just read tell us, "Do not even eat with such people."

Total perfection will not be achieved on this earth. We all fall short; however, we should be striving for holiness, not trying to find ways to sin. Keep in mind the true difference between a hypocrite and a genuine Christian: those with truly repentant hearts will humble themselves, make a change, and cease from walking down a sinful and destructive path.

There is another responsibility we have as God's children: keep our tongues from evil. This is not the time to call up a friend and share the bad news about someone who has blown it. Gossip is hurtful and can hinder or delay an individual from getting right with God. We must pray and intercede, not gossip and tear down.

> If anyone has caused grief, he has not so much grieved me as he has grieved all of you, to some extent, not to put it too severely. The punishment inflicted on him by the majority is sufficient for him. Now instead, you

> ought to forgive and comfort him, so that he will not be overwhelmed by excessive sorrow. I urge you, therefore, to reaffirm your love for him. (2 Corinthians 2:5–8 NIV)

In these scriptures, Paul is speaking about a particular person who was caught in a serious offense in Corinth. Church discipline had been imposed, and this individual displayed true repentance. In summary, Paul urges the Corinthians to "forgive and comfort him, so that he will not be overwhelmed by excessive sorrow … reaffirm your love for him."

Even though discipline is painful and difficult, God's love remains constant. His Word says He loves those He chastises. If we choose to humble ourselves during times of discipline, the result will be a strong and growing relationship with the Father. Every relationship in our lives will benefit from the wisdom we obtain during these times.

> Endure hardship as discipline; God is treating you as sons. For what son is not disciplined by his father? If you are not disciplined (and everyone undergoes discipline), then you are illegitimate children and not true sons. Moreover, we have all had human fathers who disciplined us and we respected them for it. How much more should we submit to the Father of our spirits and live. Our fathers disciplined us for a little while as they thought best; but God disciplines us for our good, that we may share in His holiness. No discipline seems pleasant at the time, but painful. Later on, however, it produces a harvest of righteousness and peace for those who have been trained by it. *Therefore, strengthen your feeble arms and weak knees Make level paths for your feet, so that the lame may not be disabled, but rather healed.* (Hebrews 12:5–13 NIV; emphasis added)

God does not contradict Himself, change His mind, add to or take away from His Word. His promises are *Yes* and *Amen*. To live a life pleasing to the Father, we must put into practice what the scriptures teaches us, "strengthen our feeble arms and weak knees, and make level paths for our feet." Why? So the lame will walk, the blind will see, and the lost will find Jesus. To accomplish this awesome task, we must endure discipline. The outcome will produce a "harvest of righteousness and peace."

Never lose sight of the fact God is constantly at work in our lives to fulfill His plans and divine purposes. I can assure you it is for our good, and blessings will follow. Just as a child receives discipline in their growth and maturity, our spiritual lives grow and mature through discipline as well. There is no getting around it; discipline is a necessary part of our Christian growth.

How can the body of Christ achieve a healthy balance and produce lasting kingdom fruit? We must be prepared by studying God's Word and not keep it to ourselves. We are called to preach, teach, mentor, and love. Even if you are shy and quiet, there is no free pass.

Remember, part of our love walks includes correction, rebuke, and encouragement. Most of the time, we are preaching and teaching through our actions. Our lives reveal who we belong to and our level of commitment to the things of God.

> In the presence of God and of Christ Jesus, who will judge the living and the dead, and in view of His appearing and His kingdom, I give you this charge: Preach the Word; be prepared in season and out of season; correct, rebuke, and encourage, With great patience and careful instruction. (2 Timothy 4:1–2 NIV).

> All scripture is God breathed and is useful for teaching, rebuking, correcting and training in righteousness, *so that the man of God may be thoroughly equipped for every good work.* (2 Timothy 3:16–17 NIV; emphasis added)

> Finally, brothers, whatever is true, whatever is noble, whatever is right, whatever is pure, whatever is lovely; whatever is admirable—if anything is excellent or praiseworthy-think about such things. Whatever you have learned or received or heard from me, or seen in me

put it into practice, and the God of peace will be with you. (Philippians 4:8–9 NIV)

Losing Mom, the pain of divorce and other broken relationships, along with so many regrets and confusion from the foggy years plagued my mind. Depression carefully weaved its way in, leaving me with feelings of great sadness and hopelessness. Before my life made a truly dramatic and positive change, I made a decision to stop the insanity by humbling myself and enduring some much-needed discipline.

Through it all, I came to understand the blessings that come from true obedience and the peace God extends when he sees a heart genuinely humbled and seeking after Him.

Below are some steps I followed as my journey of spiritual growth and maturity continued. Like most things, it was a process, but Donna finally started growing up.

1. I asked God for an understanding of scripture.
2. I opened my heart to apply what I learned.
3. I sought wisdom to discern fruit.
4. I chose to bear the burdens of others with love and compassion.
5. I worked with others in unity and love.

CHAPTER 15

OVERCOMING DEPRESSION ...
IT'S TIME FOR SOME THERAPY

Many of us have walked through the valley of depression, struggled with low self-esteem issues, and other debilitating mental health challenges. The majority of young people God brought into our lives faced these painful battles. My own struggles have been a wonderful testimony in helping others and are the very reason I became a counselor and chaplain. Father God turned my ashes into something beautiful, and it did not happen by accident. His plans for my life were strategic and powerful.

A positive change began when I wholeheartedly aligned with Christ and chose His truths instead of keeping my focus on the ever-present circumstances. You see, to experience genuine results, a person must be willing to face the giants in his or her life with sincere honesty and pure determination, regardless of the dysfunction surrounding them, including the turmoil and internal pain. Then comes the challenging part: a purposeful decision to change your thinking and actually choose to do something about it.

Accomplishing this task means we must prepare for spiritual warfare. It is not a journey for the faint of heart. Breaking free from longstanding generational curses and understanding the significance of renewing our minds in Christ on a daily (and sometimes minute-by-minute) basis is filled with obstacles and uncertainty. Once you take this step of faith, your outlook will never be the same. As you begin seeing positive results, defeat and negativity will no longer dominate and control your existence.

In preparing for this chapter, I spent long, sleepless hours in prayer and research. First, I reflected upon the many years I've worked in the mental health field and observed firsthand the miraculous results patients received when they cried out to God and placed their faith and trust in Him. God has given men and women wisdom to help those who are emotionally and physically sick, but we are mere humans. The greatest results are achieved when a partnership is formed between God and humans.

Second, I strategically investigated the positions and teachings of institutes and doctors who are not affiliated with Christianity, and several things caught my attention as I studied their findings. They share numerous common perceptions and key points Christian counselors embrace concerning depression and other mental health issues.

As a mental health professional, I've seen painful and debilitating effects caused from depression and other mental health disorders; however, our heavenly Father is the Maker and Creator of our minds and bodies. He alone intricately created this amazing thing we call our brain and the remarkable machine we call our body. Father God completed this task with more intelligence and attention to detail than any mere human being will ever comprehend. Incredibly, all believers have direct access to the very one who holds the answers to all of those perplexing issues we face at some point in life, including deliverance from depression.

A counselor who uses God's Word as his or her foundation when creating a care plan for the client's total health and well-being will experience success and breakthrough. Of course, the client must be willing to dig deep, stop tolerating things that do not belong in his or her life, resolve to change, and place total faith in God.

I'm living, breathing, and joy-filled proof that change and mental stability are possible. To all my friends and family, stop laughing … I'm as stable as a blonde can be who was born with Grant blood flowing through their veins—Ha!

One of my certifications is in rational living therapy (RLT). It is a form of cognitive behavioral therapy (CBT), and I have found it is highly effective when helping a client with depression and other mental health challenges. RLT is a motivational therapy that utilizes rational motivational interviewing techniques to help the client effect positive change. It utilizes empirical research in the areas of linguistics, cognitive development, learning theory, general semantics, neuro functioning, social psychology and perceptions, and linguistics. I strongly recommend seeking a Christian therapist who uses this approach as part of their care plan.

In an effort to gain understanding and wisdom, let's pay close attention and analyze each one of the three common viewpoints on the subject of depression shared by experts in the mental health field. As we go through each one, it will astound you to discover how their findings line up with the Word of God. After we have gained a general understanding about depression and its causes, then we will look to the Bible for answers on how to break free from this curse and find healing.

Before we begin, make a decision to receive and apply this information to your life. Remember, there is power in application. You are not alone. Jesus Christ will guide you through to victory. In and through Him, you can overcome.

COMMON VIEWPOINTS CONCERNING DEPRESSION SHARED BY MENTAL HEALTH EXPERTS

I. The causes of depression are not fully known; however, it is most likely a combination of genetic and biological factors, medical causes, as well as lifestyles and environmental factors. Using the information I have gathered, let's break these down in an effort to gain an understanding about what each one means:

    A. **Genetic and Biological:** Some types of depression tend to run in families, suggesting a genetic link; however, depression can occur in people without family histories of depression. Researchers have been able to determine that to some degree, depressive illnesses can be inherited. What appears to be inherited is a susceptibility (or vulnerability) toward depression. What does this mean? If we have a close family member who has been diagnosed as clinically depressed, we may inherit a tendency to develop the illness. It does not mean that we are destined to become depressed.

B. **Medical Causes:** Diseases that affect the brain, such as Parkinson's, multiple sclerosis, and Alzheimer's can cause depression due to the disease process. Health problems causing chronic pain or disability can also trigger depression. The risk of depression is highest when the physical problems cause major changes to someone's lifestyle. Depression is often common in diseases affecting the immune system, such as lupus, or the body's hormone levels. Hypothyroidism (a condition caused by low levels of thyroid hormone) commonly contributes to depressed moods and fatigue. It is important to note, hormonal imbalances of any kind can bring about depression.

C. **Lifestyle Factors:** The three major lifestyle factors usually common in those diagnosed with depression are lack of exercise, poor diet, and substance abuse.

1. **Lack of exercise:** Exercise has been proven to be a critical key in fighting depression. Studies have determined exercise is not only a huge mood booster but is as effective, if not more so, than antidepressant treatment. Researchers have found exercising as little as three times a week can lift the symptoms of depression, and daily walks of thirty minutes (or more) are even more effective.

2. **Poor diet:** Poor eating habits can wreak havoc on your mood, not to mention your body. Junk food and sugary snacks can cause rapid changes in blood sugar, resulting in a temporary high followed by a crash and burn. The same is true of caffeinated beverages. And if you aren't eating enough complex carbohydrates, lean protein, and produce, you probably aren't getting enough of the nutrients your mind and body need. I know this isn't fun to hear, but if we

desire a healthy mind and body, then we must change our ways and educate ourselves.

    3. **Substance abuse:** Some people abuse alcohol and drugs in an effort to self-medicate and ease their symptoms of depression; however, studies show substance abuse itself causes depression. Alcohol is particularly dangerous because it acts as a depressant that slows down brain activity. Another problem is the use of marijuana. Studies show excessive use can also lead to depression. What about uppers, such as amphetamines and cocaine? They initially stimulate the nervous system, but when the effect wears off, depression often follows. None of these options are healthy choices.

  D. **Environmental Factors:** Life stressors such as relationship issues, financial difficulties, death of a loved one, or medical illness can cause depression to manifest. Environmental factors encompass actual physical surroundings as well as cultural or social background situations.

II. *Thinking* is always involved and is a common pathway to depression. The good news is you can control your thinking. You can actually choose what you allow your mind to dwell and focus on. Learning to control your thought life, or what some experts call *pathway of thinking*, is a powerful aid in controlling the onset of depression.

III. There is no one answer for what causes depression, yet there appear to be at least four pathways to depression: physiology, stress, learning, and thinking.

  A. **Physiology:** This is simply the study of the function of living things, including processes such as nutrition, movement, and reproduction. *Webster's Dictionary* tells us it is: "a specific response by the body to a stimulus, as fear or pain that disturbs or interferes with the normal physiological equilibrium of an organism." An example of this can be a lack of energy due to being overweight, which can ultimately lead to depression. Obesity can cause diabetes, hypertension, inflammatory effect, and organ dysfunction involving cardiac, liver, intestinal, pulmonary, endocrine, and reproductive functions. Simply put, if we change our eating habits and gain an understanding about why we overeat, we can lose weight, become healthy and energetic, and feel better about ourselves.

B. Stress: At some point in our lives, we all come to know what stress is, even children. They may not understand their problem is stress related; however, when stress happens, they will react to it in various ways. In adults, emotions go haywire, tempers flare, or some people shut down and keep things bottled up inside. (I am not one of those people, although I am sure my family wish I'd give it a try.) A simple definition for stress is this: "The action on a body of any system of balanced forces whereby strain or deformation results." Basically, stress distorts and causes unnatural strain to the point of harm.

C. Learning: Learning is where we gain knowledge or acquire experience, an ability, or skill to become aware or informed. Throughout our lifetimes, we are continuously learning, and we are never too old to learn something new or a better way of dealing with life and emotions. Choices … It is all about choices.

D. Thinking: As stated previously, studies have proven we can control what we choose to dwell and focus on. Changing our thought life is vital to conquering depression. Thinking is where we reason, analyze, invent, or conceive something. It is a belief or opinion, such as, "I think so." In thinking, we have a conscious mind to form beliefs, opinions, and so on which means we can control our thoughts.

Now that we have read what mental health experts agree on in regard to depression, let's look at God's Word for help on how to break free. As we go through these points, get ready to not only receive truth

Falling into Faith

but to take the next step and apply what you learn. Application is the key. A miracle of deliverance is waiting for you. Choose well and choose life.

Depression is living under the curse, and Jesus redeemed us from the curse through His death and resurrection. Settle it in your mind today; depression is not something God conjured up to humble or teach us a lesson. This isn't part of our Lord's character. Your body is the temple of the Lord, and you belong to Him; therefore, depression has absolutely no right to dwell in you. Every part of your being belongs to God, including your mind. Now is the time for you to take back your mind and body.

To understand more about blessings and curses, read Deuteronomy, chapter 28. You will discover the blessings that come from obedience and the curses reaped from disobedience. Keep in mind we are redeemed from the curse through the precious blood of Christ. In the name of Jesus, we have the right to be set free, healed, and restored in every way.

> Christ purchased our freedom [redeeming us] from the curse (doom) of the Law [and its condemnation] by [Himself] becoming a curse for us, for it is written [in the Scriptures], cursed is everyone who hangs on a tree (is crucified); To the end that through [their receiving] Christ Jesus, the blessing [promised] to Abraham might come upon the Gentiles, so that we through faith might [all] receive [the realization of] the promise of the [Holy] Spirit. (Galatians 3:13–14 AMP)

The Word tells us through faith the blessings promised to Abraham are for us as well. So what about Abraham? He was a man blessed by God, not because of works but because of his faith. Faith is crucial in our walk with God. "And everything that does not come from faith is sin" (Romans 14:23 NIV).

If Abraham's good deeds made him acceptable to God, he could have bragged about it. But that is not God's way. His way is to walk by faith, because works cannot save us. The scriptures tell us, "Abraham believed God, and God counted him as righteous because of his faith" (Romans 4:3 NLT).

> "But people are counted as righteous, not because of their work, *but because of their faith in God who forgives sinners*" (Romans 4:2–5 NLT; emphasis added).

To sum it up, anyone who puts their faith in Jesus Christ through the gift of salvation has the right to seek after and receive the blessings of God; however, our faith will produce works as we walk out our lives in obedience. There is hope, there is healing, and there truly is bondage-breaking deliverance.

Depression is a spiritual battle. The Bible says, "Be not grieved and depressed, for the joy of the Lord is your strength and stronghold" (Nehemiah 8:10 AMP). If the enemy can't snuff out our lives, he will use whatever means possible in an attempt to kill, steal, or destroy our joy. You see, if he takes our joy, he can successfully rob us of fruitful and happy lives. He desperately wants to keep us from living a victorious existence by consuming our minds with thoughts of pain or despair. His tools are a combination of any and all things negative and destructive.

The enemy is on a mission to steal our destiny. He longs to destroy our Christian testimony and the hope of living a powerful, overcoming life. There is no greater joy than to serve God. But to be effective, our lives must reflect the blessings of God, or our words mean nothing.

When someone is suffering with depression, he or she may be living and breathing, but that individual does not feel truly alive. One of my patients described it this way: "I felt invisible, as though I barely existed; however, I watched other people living their lives."

Make no mistake about it, this is war. Can we win this battle? Absolutely. We must remember what the Bible tells us, "You are from God, little children, and have overcome them; because greater is He who is in you than he who is in the world" (1 John 4:4 ISV).

We have a promise from Jesus Christ, "I can do all things through Christ which strengtheneth me" (Philippians 4:13 KJV). There is no battle too hard for God. He can do anything but fail, and He longs to bring healing to every area of our lives.

Don't Give Up

Choose to believe God not only has the power to heal, but He wants to heal you. In the hard times, praise Him and speak His truth. Even when you don't feel like it, do it anyway. Learn the importance of aligning yourself with God's truth every day. Realize you have a choice in the matter.

Stop agreeing with the enemy and start believing in the all-powerful God of heaven and earth. He is our Creator and the Maker of all things. Dive into His holy Word and find out what He says about our past, present, and future.

His forgiveness is immeasurable, His mercy is incomprehensible, His love is all-consuming.

You are God's child, and the enemy does not have any right to your life unless you allow him access. We give him permission with our words, which is why the Bible tells us the tongue has the power to speak life or death. In other words, watch your mouth.

I cannot stress this enough: discover truth by reading what the Bible has to say, then speak His truth, not the enemy's lies. When you consistently and with purpose begin doing this, God will bring forth a miracle in your life.

> "The tongue has the power of life and death, and those who love it will eat its fruit" (Proverbs 18:21 NIV).

CHAPTER 16

BEAUTY FOR ASHES, JOY FOR MOURNING

Have you ever been driving along and—*bang*—you hear a crash and feel pain? Suddenly your brain says, "Hey, I've just been in a car accident." It's a funny thing how the sound of medal bending and airbags going off in your face can make a lasting impression. Physically, I seemed to be in one piece, but my little Daytona was totaled. Then I remembered, *Man, I just paid this car off and got a brand-new paint job*. The saying is true, "Some days are better spent in bed." With that said, I'm thankful for the accident because God used this unwanted interruption to reveal something important.

The other driver involved did not suffer any injuries and received a lot less damage to his vehicle. I felt pain down my back and neck, with visible burns and bruises caused by the airbag and seat belt, but looking at my car made me thankful for the safety equipment in cars today.

Paramedics hovered about, insisting I go to the emergency room, reassuring me it was in my best interest. Unable to stand up straight due to pain, with great hesitation and a bit of pouting, I finally agreed to go.

On the way to the hospital, I felt a soft lump, about the size of a small pea protruding from the left side of my neck. The paramedics saw it too but thought it may have been there before the accident. I advised them it was never there before. The doctor in the emergency room took x-rays, and everything checked out fine except for a few bruises, burns, and pulled muscles. According to the doctor, the lump had nothing to do with the accident and insisted I make an appointment for further tests. I said okay, anxious to get home and cry on Daddy's shoulder.

Just in case you are interested, the accident was my fault. Cars stopped for me to cross through an intersection, but they failed to notice someone approaching in the far left-hand lane. Actually, a man in a van saw the oncoming car but continued to motion for me, thinking I could make it, so I happily forged ahead. You should never do this. Take my word for it.

Approximately two months later, the lump appeared a bit larger and bothered me when I wore a turtleneck or any kind of collar. I decided to make an appointment and get it checked. The doctor stated it looked like a very small soft tissue growth, not commonly associated with a malignant type tumor and absolutely nothing to worry about. He scheduled outpatient surgery to remove it. No big deal … right?

Several days later, the doctor left an urgent message on my voice mail, insisting I call him ASAP to discuss the tumor. My mind raced with panic and questions. *Did he say tumor? When did this pea-size lump (of which I had absolutely nothing to worry about) turn into a tumor?*

The timing stunk, to say the least. Barely a year had passed since we lost Mom to cancer, so I made a decision to keep this to myself. My poor father still walked around in a daze. One more very important thing … *what about Bob?* You see, something amazing happened. Literally days prior to hearing the word "tumor," Bob came back into my life.

Bob attended Mom's funeral, and it was the first time in years I had seen him. We didn't even speak to one another. He tried talking to me, but I looked away. Just seeing him caused my heart to hurt because it added to my overwhelming feelings of loss.

After my divorce and mom's passing, I continued living at home with Dad. One afternoon while washing my car in the driveway, Bob drove by. He wanted to talk. Bob just couldn't understand why I had been so cold and distant at Mom's funeral. We engaged in small talk, but I remained distant. Finally, I blurted out, "The past is the past, and we both just need to get on with our very own separate lives." After my little hissy fit, Bob shared with me how his marriage of fifteen years was over. Although the marriage did not last, God blessed them with a beautiful daughter. Her name is Traci, and interestingly enough, we share the same birthday, February 6.

Falling into Faith

As we discussed problems we both experienced in our marriages, my heart raced, and I excitably thought to myself, *Good heavens, it's been seventeen years. Does Bob realize I never stopped loving him?* At that moment, I decided to tell him how I felt and let the chips fall where they may. I wasn't about to waste any more time. I looked him right in the eyes and said, "Bob, I need you to know something, I still love you and probably always will." We both just looked at each other as tears ran down our faces.

Our conversation soon turned to the past. We discussed the self-destructive mess my life became after the hysterectomy and how everything changed when they properly diagnosed the disease I suffered with for so many years. The more we talked, I realized how much I missed my friend and how good it felt to be with him once again.

Facing Dad and Bob about this new health crisis would not be easy, so I made a decision not say anything until I knew the facts. Thankfully, the doctors worked me in that day as I nervously prayed and tried to keep my emotions in check.

With great trepidation, I walked into the doctor's office ready to discuss the "tumor," but his countenance said it all. He started off with, "I'm sorry but …" You know the report is bad when a doctor begins with those words. Then he said something my brain refused to accept. "The results came back as a malignant soft tissue sarcoma in the third stages of cancer. The cancer is very rare, and it's imperative to see a specialist immediately. Your car accident was a blessing in disguise. It appears the impact caused the tumor to become visible. I'm sorry to have to give you this news, but please let me know how things turn out. I wish you well."

When he finished talking I began laughing. Standing up, I said, "Okay, thanks, Doc." My response concerned him. I reassuringly said, "I've cried enough over the years about my health. I might as well try something new." As I headed to the door, he stood up and stated I needed support. He asked to call someone for me. I quickly said, "No thanks," and without hesitation hurried to my car.

After driving a short distance, I pulled over on the side of the road. Reality hit me like a ton of bricks. I tried to collect my thoughts and make sense of what I heard. *Rare cancer … stage three … I wish you well.* Then I became angry. *What? How can this be? I spent my whole* life suffering with a blood disease, surviving insurmountable odds, including escaping death. This cannot be happening. I'm finally enjoying life without the constant dread of pain and hospitals. On top of everything else, I have to go home and tell Daddy and Bob.

Arriving home, I sat in the driveway and prayed. There are some moments in life I believe we keep with us as long as there is breath in our body. This was one of those moments. I bowed my head and prayed, "God give me the strength to tell Daddy. He depends on me so much since Mama went to be with You. He needs me, and oh yeah, please, Father, don't let me die. I'm just starting to enjoy life. Remember the angel You sent to my bedside when I lay dying in the hospital? It said, 'Many children will pass through your arms and be blessed. There is still a work for you to do. You will not leave this earth until your work is complete.' God, I've made a lot of mistakes, but I haven't held those children yet or completed the work You sent me to do. Please don't let me have lived through all that just to end up dying from cancer. So here's the deal. I refuse to depend on a doctor to determine the outcome of my life. I'm in Your hands. Forgive me for the times I failed and disappointed You, and please tell Mama I love her but it will be a while before I see her again. I love you, Jesus. Amen."

As I sat reeling from the uncertainty and terrified about the future, I thought about Bob. After all these years, we finally had a second chance at love. How in the world was I going to tell him I have cancer? My thoughts became desperate as I prayed once again a prayer forever etched in my memory. "One more thing, God. Why would you allow Bob back in my life when I am once again facing a serious illness and possibly who knows what? I broke up with him years ago because of sickness. Is it fair to put him through this again? By the way, why is it every time we have an opportunity to be together, my life bites? Sorry, God, but I might as well say it; You already know what I'm thinking. Forgive me, but I'd really like to know the answer to this one."

Thunder and lightning did not come out of the sky and zap me, so I figured God wasn't too mad about my outburst. Although I did not have any answers, I knew what I had to do first: tell Dad. Second on my list: tell Bob.

Taking a deep breath, I gathered my thoughts and went inside.

Daddy was lying down, so I sat on the bed and asked him if he felt like talking for a minute. He sat up and said, "Sure, baby."

Usually I could tell Dad anything without hesitation, but not this. I began with, "Daddy, I went to the doctor today …" and then I said the word we hated, "cancer." He looked away in shock and disbelief as tears rolled down his face. Trying to be positive and upbeat, I reminded him about God sending an angel years earlier and the promise it gave me. Unfortunately, I don't think he heard anything after the dreaded word, *cancer*. We sat in silence as Dad wrapped his arms around me and cried.

Next on my list … Bob. Not wanting to repeat the same mistakes I made seventeen years earlier, I decided not to push him away this time. I would let him choose to stay or go. Bob remained true to his nature and rock solid. He stayed, assuring me we would get through this together.

The next day, I awoke focused and determined to beat this ugly, cruel thing called *cancer*. Dad wanted me to call Mom's cancer specialist. He was a wonderful Christian man, not to mention an amazing doctor. I called his office, and he rearranged his schedule to see us that afternoon. Looking over the surgeon's report, he appeared stunned and confused. Our family had been through so much, and he couldn't believe what he was reading. After processing his thoughts, he arranged for us to go directly to the office of an ear, nose, and throat specialist. We tearfully hugged goodbye and thanked him.

The specialist wasted no time. Further tests confirmed the diagnosis of a rare fibrosarcoma, a soft tissue sarcoma in the third stages of cancer. He wanted to do some research and meet with colleagues before proceeding with any kind of treatment plan.

Within a few days, we were back in his office. With pen and notebook in hand, I prepared to write down everything he said. He began the conversation by reading from a medical journal. In summary, he stated, "There is only about one case per million reported each year of this type of sarcoma, and it does not respond to chemotherapy. Radical surgery will be necessary to remove the tumor, surrounding muscles, and anything I feel may possibly be affected. It is a reoccurring cancer, and there are no guarantees. Case reports show surgery with radiation are our only options and may prolong a reoccurrence, but I cannot say how soon before another one. The surgery is our first priority and will most likely leave you disfigured with extensive scarring; then I recommend radiation therapy. Our goal is to stop it from spreading, and we don't have much time."

We thanked him, scheduled surgery, and left. Driving home, I once again reminded Dad of everything I'd overcome and how God always brought me through. I tried to encourage him by saying, "Don't worry, Daddy; this will be a piece of cake." He smiled but wasn't buying my optimism.

I desperately needed the Lord's help in a big way, but how do you ask God for healing with the shame of divorce and past mistakes hanging over your head? Unable to grasp the concept of God's forgiveness, Bob and I both suffered with so much condemnation. To be honest, many within the church felt we deserved a life of pain and hopelessness. Regardless of people's opinions and the heaviness of shame, we found the courage to go for it anyway and ask God for help. So often, that is all God is waiting for, a truly repentant heart willing to call on Him in spite of our messy lives and shortcomings.

Although Bob and I talked for hours on the phone and saw each other as often as possible, we were not officially dating. Due to our history and recent divorces, we felt awkward being seen in public. Living in a small community can be difficult. Just about everyone who knew us knew our history together. The destructive rumor mill and wagging tongues were already on an accelerated high. Bob's daughter (only eleven at the time) was much too young to understand how to process the hurtful gossip. It didn't matter that we lived in different states for many years with no contact. Our history proved too fascinating and coincidental to overlook.

To be honest, we walked around looking guilty because we felt extreme shame for still loving one another. I'm sure that added a bit of spice and curiosity to onlookers. When you have secretly never stopped loving someone and then—*surprise, surprise*—they're back in your life ... well, you get the picture. For years, Bob was carefully tucked away in a private corner of my heart, with no hope or thought we would ever be together. He was part of my painful past, and the thought of a future with him honestly felt like an impossibility. Years earlier, we went our separate ways, and that was that. Little did we know what was going to happen when I moved back to Florida.

Falling into Faith

One thing was certain, we were not looking forward to facing the fallout or putting Traci through any unnecessary pain. With surgery right around the corner, we decided to wait until it was over before going out on an official, public date. At least I had something to look forward to.

The day of surgery arrived. Doctors removed everything they felt the tumor affected, including muscles and nerves. Even though the procedure proved quite extensive and half my neck and chest had been cut open, I did not have the degree of disfiguration they prepared us for, just heavy scarring. My doctor did an amazing job.

Following surgery, radiation therapy was recommended to delay a rapid developing reoccurrence. I decided to place total trust in God and refused further treatment. After losing Mother, I knew Dad couldn't handle any additional stress, so I kept my decision quiet and private between Bob, myself, and the doctor. For the first time in my entire life, it felt wonderful to have the final say about what anyone did to me.

My refusal of further treatment did not go unchallenged. The doctors strongly and vehemently disagreed. Most of them had known me for many years, so I understood where they were coming from, but it was my decision. After researching the effects of the radiation therapy they wanted to pursue, and the downside of not having a spleen and sufficient immune system to fight off infection caused by radiation, side effects from the treatment could be devastating if not fatal. Although they tried, the doctors could not refute my findings, so my decision stood firm. No radiation. Bob prayerfully stayed by my side and supported my decision.

Every day, I asked God to look past my faults and heal me. Little did I know His plans were so much bigger than we dared to dream or imagine. He knew something important; the little girl who grew up trusting Him with her whole heart would soon come out of hiding. She was finally on a new and exciting journey, learning how to fall into a life-changing trust relationship with her heavenly Father. You see, in spite of all my failures, God still had a good plan for my future.

The majority of my life had been spent dependent on doctors and medicine, only to end up in worse shape with lots of ugly scars. Although I did not know what to do, I continued to pray, and God filled me with an unexplainable peace. He surrounded me with an unconditional love and strategically protected me from feelings of hopelessness and despair.

My goals were quite simple: trust God (even though I knew I did not deserve His mercy and favor), stay positive and happy, and hold on tight to Bob.

After a few days of recuperating, Bob and I went on our first official date. A huge bandage adorned my neck like a hideous necklace, but I felt blessed and excited to be alive. Many obstacles lay ahead, but we planned to face them together.

When the doctor removed the bandages from my neck and chest area, I looked like the bride of Frankenstein. As the months progressed and to the doctors' amazement, I continued showing no reoccurring signs of cancer. This didn't stop them from voicing their disapproval over my decision to decline further treatment, as they constantly reminded me of the statistics. On the upside, the scar is shaped like a large heart etched on my neck.

For the sake of clarity, the treatment was in no way a cure. Studies showed it only delayed a reoccurrence; however, documented cases revealed a rapid reoccurrence even with radiation. Without treatment, the tumors grew and advanced in an aggressive manner, penetrating your muscles and soft tissue and quickly moving into your bloodstream. It is an extremely fast-moving cancer. Mercifully, God faithfully and mysteriously did what doctors and medicine couldn't do.

During that same year, our family dealt with many challenges and changes. Dad suffered another stroke, heart attack, a triple bypass and corrective bypass surgery. God's mercy prevailed, and he made a full recovery. My biggest concern was Dad's mental state. He was lonely and missed Mom. Some longtime friends realized Dad needed someone to love, so they played matchmaker and set him up with Polly Cameron from Mississippi. When Dad and Mom pastored in Hattiesburg, they were friends with Polly and her husband. Now, they were both widowed and in need of companionship. Dad and Polly dated a brief time and decided life's too short to wait. They got married and embarked on a new journey together. God gave me an amazing gift through their marriage, a wonderful new family. The Cameron's embraced me with so much love and acceptance. I am truly grateful.

Dad's marriage to Polly also gave Bob and me time to focus on each other and develop a stronger, more mature relationship, but we faced a huge obstacle from our past. When we first began dating, I was only a teenager and very dependent on Dad. I ran to him for everything. Bob served in the military and was twenty-one years old. Regardless of my youth and immaturity during those first years together, Bob needed reassurance I had grown up in this area of my life. Determined not to lose him again, I prayed for God to show me what to do, and He did. Wisdom is a beautiful thing.

The first time we met, Bob pursued me; now the roles were reversed. With unashamed determination, I set out on a mission to prove my love and devotion. I honestly think he enjoyed this turn of events. Being pursued can be fun when it is someone you are passionately in love with.

I want to close this chapter with a message for those who are facing cancer. I understand and appreciate the difficulty of your situation and the decisions weighing heavily on your heart. Your doctors may have recommended chemotherapy or radiation. It is your life; the decision is yours. Seek God for wisdom and do your own research. A doctor's job is to present the facts and determine the best possible treatment. You have the final say. Give it all to God and know whatever you choose, God is able and willing to carry you through to victory.

If you choose treatment, go forward with great determination. Do not allow the facts to destroy your faith in God's power and ability to do the impossible. He promises to never leave or forsake us, and He also promises another beautiful thing, "The Lord will fulfill His purpose for me" (Psalm 138:8 NIV).

Grab hold of His promises and with a bulldog mentality take a bite, hold on, and do not let go. No matter how long it takes, never lose sight of who God is. He is the Great Physician, and He is an on-time God. His promises are for you, and they are "Yes and amen ... So be it." Your very life depends on your decision to believe, receive, and stand on this truth.

Don't allow anyone to sow seeds of doubt regarding treatment. Pleases know this: receiving treatment *absolutely does not and will not* hinder God from redeeming your life from the pit of despair and healing every area of your mind, soul, and body.

Practice the praise principle. Praise Him in the dark hours, not just when everything is full of sunshine and peace. God longs to accomplish great things through all of us, but praise is essential toward the fulfillment of His beautiful plans.

> For no matter how many promises God has made, they are *"yes"* in Christ. And so through Him the *"amen"* is spoken by us to the glory of God. Now it is God who makes both us and you stand firm in Christ. He anointed us, set His seal of ownership on us, and put His Spirit in our hearts as a deposit, guaranteeing what is to come. (2 Corinthians 1:20–22 NIV; emphasis added)

God used cancer to teach me the importance of getting His Word from my head to my heart, and the absolute power that comes from speaking it forth in faith. His glory revealed itself in ways I never dreamed possible. A few years down the road, you will see how the Lord opened doors for my healing testimony to be shared around the world.

I've never experienced a joy as wonderful as spreading the good news of my wonderful Father, Savior, Redeemer, Healer, and Friend. He has been so faithful and oh so merciful. Like the old hymn says, great is Thy faithfulness.

Thomas Chisholm wrote "Great Is Thy Faithfulness" in 1925. It is one of my favorite hymns and beautifully testifies of God's mercy, abiding love, and faithfulness.

CHAPTER 17

LEARNING WHAT IT MEANS TO BE FORGIVEN

From the moment we officially began dating, I asked Bob to marry me. This is not exactly proper etiquette, but I'm not one to waste time. It is not every day a second chance like this comes along.

We did not feel comfortable getting married in our hometown. Wearing the divorce label created quite a little scandal in our church community, especially with our history together. A select few envisioned us going around in sackcloth and ashes for the rest of our lives. Some even felt cancer was God's punishment for divorce, and the thought of asking Him to heal me seemed quite brazen and beyond their comprehension.

It is a terrible thing to go through life with such an angry image of God. He is not a tyrant waiting to slap us into hades every time we mess up. The only way to get a glimpse of His loving character is to spend time in the Word and walk in a committed relationship with Him. I can spend hours talking about God's love, goodness, and compassion, but each person has to experience and receive their own revelation of His all-consuming, unexplainable love. Once it happens, you are never the same.

Feeling a little wild and crazy, we made plans to fly off to Las Vegas and elope. Dad and Polly were happy and gave us their blessing. Polly and I went shopping, and she bought me a beautiful wedding dress. It was simple yet elegant. I felt like a princess. In fact, I remember telling Polly, "Cinderella finally found her prince."

Trying to appear and feel a bit more mature for Bob, I dyed my hair brunette. Bob said he liked it but made it clear he loved me just the way I am, regardless of my hair color. Here is some advice: ladies, embrace who you are and learn to enjoy being the real, authentic person God created you to be. Life is too short to be something you are not.

The morning we boarded the plane, Bob finally officially proposed. The poor guy needed a chance to make it legit. When I see television shows with romantic and extravagant proposals, I laugh. My man didn't have an opportunity to surprise me, because he was in love with a crazy woman who asked him repeatedly, "Okay, baby, when are we getting married?" Playing hard to get wasn't a game I dared to risk. Years earlier, I put Bob through schizophrenic and manic torture. He needed to see stability and unwavering commitment.

Bob made all the arrangements and did an outstanding job. In true fairy-tale fashion, a limousine arrived and whisked us off to the Little Chapel of Flowers. Just in case you are wondering, Elvis did not perform the ceremony; however, we did enjoy some comical moments. Our driver talked with a heavy New York accent and proved to be very multitalented. He took our wedding photos, stood up as our witness, and escorted us all over Vegas in the limo.

Before proceeding with our honeymoon plans, we felt compelled to pray together as man and wife. Hand in hand, we knelt down and repented of our past. We prayed for Bob's precious daughter and asked God to give her peace. Children of divorce face many challenges, and Bob's heart had been broken over the situation for a long time. We also prayed for wisdom on how to help her during this transition. Giving our future and lives completely over to God, we gave Him permission to do whatever He wanted with us. As the burden of sin and condemnation lifted, we were broken and humbled by God's mercy.

Something new and beautiful began at that very moment—forgiveness. Feeling deep humility and gratefulness to God, we planned on living life to the fullest, jointly agreeing to keep each other encouraged and refusing to dwell on cancer, along with all the unknowns that go with it. It felt as though God blew a new, fresh breath of life in both of us. His strength would carry us through whatever the future held. True repentance and the Father's powerful forgiveness are amazing energizing forces to the mind, body, and spirit.

When the blood of Jesus is applied to sin, a miraculous transformation happens. You can physically feel the burden and weight of sin lift. Our sins are not only forgiven, but they are thrown into "the depths of the sea." Never to be held against us again.

> You will again have compassion on us; You will tread our sins underfoot and hurl all our iniquities into the depths of the sea. (Micah 7:19 NIV)

An overcoming and blessed future depended on our willingness to receive this awesome gift of forgiveness. Yes, there are consequences for our choices; however, God never intended for His children to be held prisoners by their past. Choosing to embrace this gift meant we were free from the burden of condemnation and guilt. We could walk in the anticipation and excitement of God's blessings, His liberty, and freedom.

Truly embracing this truth took time. Overcoming the past, along with all the shame and condemnation is not always immediate. It is a process, full of teaching moments and growing pains. Often, you find a certain few who want to dredge up the past and remind you of your shortcomings; but it is important to understand, this is not your concern or within your control. Learn to reject condemnation and remind yourself of the forgiveness Jesus lovingly extended when you repented. What others tend to hold onto has to do with their own choices and heart issues. Pray for them and leave it in God's hands.

In time, I became outspoken enough to tell those who liked to remind me of my many sins, "I have given that to God, and He forgave me. When I bring up a past sin, He simply responds, 'Donna, what sin?' In the future, please take your concerns to God. He is the one with all the answers. I am just the one He forgave." As we say in the South, this response pretty much nipped things in the bud!

For any of you who are struggling in this area, let me share an illustration that might be helpful. If a couple engages in premarital sex, they can ask God to forgive them, and He will. That sin will be thrown into "the depths of the sea" and never be held against them again; however, what if they become pregnant? Is God punishing them? No. We reap what we sow, and this is simply a result of sex. When the baby arrives, they have an important choice to make. Embrace God's forgiveness and raise their child in the joy and fear of the Lord, or live in shame and see this precious life as punishment instead of a blessing.

Their child can be a reminder of God's forgiveness as they teach by example how to enjoy and appreciate a loving relationship with their Creator. When the child grows up and makes his or her own mistakes, they will remember the example set before them by their parents. Instead of living in bondage and shame, they can walk in freedom with a heart's desire to serve God in humility, gratitude, and joy. All parents should want this for their children.

When Bob and I knelt down and prayed for the first time as husband and wife, our hearts felt consumed with condemnation and shame, but we rose to our feet forgiven and full of hope. We longed to get on with our lives without the heaviness from our past, and that is exactly what we did. It is a scriptural and wonderful way to begin the healing process.

> Therefore, if anyone is in Christ, he is a new creation; old things have passed away; behold, all things have become new. (2 Corinthians 5:17 NKJV)

Next on the agenda ... sightseeing. Anxious to get out of the big city of Vegas, we rented a car and set out to explore the countryside. Our first stop, the Hoover Dam and then off to the Grand Canyon. What a beautiful sight. Everyone should see the Grand Canyon at least once in their lifetime. The world is full of magnificent portraits God has painted for us to enjoy, as a reminder of how great and powerful He truly is.

Heading home, we felt anxious and excited about the future. Little did we know the cleansing, purging, pruning, and molding that lay ahead. Entering this covenant with our Redeemer meant our lives belonged entirely to Him. Going through the motions of being a Christian and serving God was no longer an option. The time had come to grow up, get serious, and learn how to die to the things of flesh that destroy and bring pain. Just as Paul wrote, flesh has to die so that Christ may be exalted and live. "For to me, to live is Christ and to die is gain" (Philippians 1:22 NIV).

There is a reason the Bible refers to our Christian walk as a "narrow road." The path is not easy, causing many to give up and quit before even getting started. It is a humbling experience filled with growing pains. We often question, "What will it cost? What do I have to give up? Will I really be happy? Is it worth it?" We must decide for ourselves; no one can do it for us.

Sometimes our attempts to serve God have ulterior motives, such as pleasing others, or we want God to do something for us. For some, the motivating factor is simply the fear of not going to heaven. In these instances, we are often left wondering why we lack fulfillment and feel like a failure. Only when we fall in love with Jesus Christ and get sick and tired of complacency, mediocrities, and limited blessings can we realize the wonderful benefits of walking the "straight and narrow," with pleasing the Father as our only motive. The question is, Will flesh or Spirit rule our lives?

God does not make bad things; therefore, flesh is not bad. However, when we allow our desires and impulses to dictate our thoughts and actions, the results can be dangerous and destructive. This is why the subject of flesh versus Spirit is so important.

Striving to satisfy flesh with no self-control or balance is a recipe for pain and suffering. Let's look at an example. Flesh would like to abandon all restraints and eat ice cream (or chocolate) every day, watch television, avoid work, and play nonstop. This is not God's best. Because of the law of sowing and reaping, a lifestyle committed to satisfying our flesh regardless of the cost will yield a troublesome harvest. We will reap many things when flesh rules: obesity, health problems, relationship issues, debt, depression, loneliness, and the list goes on and on. If we strive to obey God and walk in wisdom the benefits will be great, and blessings will flow forth.

When we choose to walk with Christ, dying to flesh is no easy task. We need the help of the Holy Spirit and the Word of God active and alive inside our hearts. It is important to learn how to encourage ourselves in the Lord, just as King David learned to do. "But David strengthened himself in the LORD his God" (1 Samuel 30:6 NASB).

Above all, do not despair or allow yourself to take the easy way out by doing just enough to get by. Anyone who has fallen into this trap knows how miserable life becomes.

As you continue to cast down and deny flesh, your spirit person grows stronger and more dominant. The key is to submit to God and resist temptation. With consistent and purposeful determination, you will be greatly rewarded for your obedience.

> Submit yourselves, then, to God. Resist the devil, and he will flee from you. Come near to God, and He will come near to you. (James 4:7–8 NIV)

When someone says *I love you*, there is an expectation, and rightfully so. You anticipate spending time with that person and being a priority in his or her life. If this does not happen, you begin doubting their words. In fact, insecurities and feelings of hurt will surface. If the issues are not resolved, it will destroy the relationship and damage your own self-esteem. Too often, the root of the problem is a destructive, selfish spirit.

For many years, this is how I treated God. In desperate and lonely moments, I cried out for help. Mercifully, He came to my rescue as He patiently waited to have a genuine and intimate relationship with me. Somewhere along the way, I lost my *first love* and no longer knew what pleased the heart of God. It breaks my heart to admit it, but I didn't know because I didn't care enough to find out. Facing the ugly truth was the first step to repentance and beginning a new and exciting love walk with the Lord.

God is a loving, patient, yet jealous Father who longs for His children to desire intimacy with Him. Unfortunately, we often find every excuse to place God at the bottom of our to-do list until desperate times hit. He alone is the one true God, and He deserves to be our top priority.

"You shall not bow down to them or serve them, for I the Lord your God am a jealous God" (Exodus 20:5 NIV). This passage of scripture refers to worshiping idols. For the sake of relevance, many things in today's world have become idols we put before God: money, status, power, relationships, and so on. God doesn't play second fiddle to anything. What does this mean? To reap the benefits of the Lord's favor and blessings, we must choose to put Him first. Spending time in prayer, reading His Word, and obedience to His commands becomes a priority, not an option. Just like eating and breathing, a blessed and happy life depends upon time spent with God. He alone is our lifeline and hope.

When we are passionate about something, nothing can stop our pursuit. God knew one day I would go after Him with the same zeal and determination I used to pursue Bob. Just the thought of this must have pleased His heart tremendously. For the first time in many years, my words and actions lined up. With unashamed abandon, I earnestly meant it when I said, "Jesus, I love and appreciate You. With every breath I take, I desire nothing more than to please You."

Now is a good time to examine your own life. Too often, our lips say we love the Lord and want to serve Him, but our actions reveal the truth. Allow the Holy Spirit to speak into your life. With an open heart, draw near to God and find the path to a loving, healthy, and growing relationship with your Father, the Creator of the universe.

Jesus Christ is the only reason I'm alive and breathing today. I am a living example that no life is too messed up or has drifted too far away from His hand of grace and mercy. Instead, it is an awesome opportunity for God to powerfully transform your life. The best psychiatrist, therapist, or psychologist in the world cannot do what God can.

Right now as you read these words, express your love and gratitude for His unmerited grace and mercy. Refuse to allow your circumstances to dictate or define your relationship with the Father. Rejoice in Him and keep a thankful heart of praise. This will open wide the door to miracles in your life.

Today can be a brand-new beginning. Come before the Lord with a repentant heart and desire to please the Father. Once you have done this, let go of the past and begin anew. With determination and zeal, draw near to God and be assured He will draw near to you. The things of this world are temporary, but the things of God are eternal. Seek Him today and don't delay.

> Forget the former things; do not dwell on the past. See, I am doing a new thing. Now it springs up; do you not perceive it? I am making a way in the desert and streams in the wasteland. (Isaiah 43:18–19 NIV)

Open your Bible to Deuteronomy, chapter 28. Carefully read and study both the blessings and curses. As you meditate on the scriptures, a greater desire to walk in obedience and reap the benefits of His blessings will surely take root within your spirit. It is important to remember that God is just. Although we cannot fully comprehend this truth, His Word teaches us about His amazing character. The Lord is full of love and mercy, and He is *not* a God of favoritism. In other words, Romans 2:11 assures us He does not pick and choose favorites among His children, and He does not show favoritism.

> For God does not show favoritism. (Romans 2:11 NIV)

> For the Lord your God is the God of gods and Lord of lords. He is the great God, the mighty and awesome God, who shows no partiality and cannot be bribed. (Deuteronomy 10:17 NLT)

As Christians, we are instructed to be imitators of God; therefore, we must also avoid showing favoritism in our relationships with others. This is not always easy, but through Christ and His strength, we can do it. In the book of James, chapter 2, we are told showing favoritism is a sin. God is very clear about being merciful and impartial.

> But if you favor some people over others, *you are committing a sin.* You are guilty of breaking the law. For the person who keeps all of the laws except one is as guilty as a person who has broken all of God's laws. For the same God who said, "You must not commit adultery," also said, "You must not murder." So if you murder someone but do not commit adultery, you have still broken the law. So whatever you say or whatever you do, remember that you will be judged by the law that sets you free. *There will be no mercy for those who have not shown mercy to others. But if you have been merciful, God will be merciful when he judges you.*" (James 2:9–13 NLT; emphasis added)

Falling into Faith

What He has done for me He will do for you. Receiving God's blessings comes with one important requirement: you must choose faith. By faith, choose to believe, expect, and receive. The scriptures reveal an awesome truth: those of us who are flawed and struggling, who step out in faith with knees knocking and teeth chattering, will beautifully and powerfully receive God's blessings. Even though you may feel scared and unsure, take a step of faith. Choose to believe God's Word is true, and He will do what He promises. Then patiently wait. God's blessings are on the way.

Make the scriptures personal. Write your name in them and boldly speak it forth in faith. For example, the scripture below says, "The Lord will make you the head, not the tail, if you pay attention to the commands of the Lord your God that I give you this day and carefully follow them." Now, read it again and replace the word "you" with your name. For example, *the Lord will make Donna the head, not the tail, if Donna pays attention to the commands of the Lord her (Donna's) God.*

Please understand, this is not in any way adding to or taking away from God's Word. Where He says "you," He means us, His children. Putting our name in the scriptures simply acknowledges and establishes our commitment to accept and believe God's Word is meant for us (individually and corporately) to receive, obey, and honor. Next step: walk it out with your life, and in grateful anticipation, expect a miracle.

> The Lord will open the heavens, the storehouse of His bounty, to send rain on your land in season and to bless all the work of your hands. You will lend to many nations but will borrow from none. The Lord will make you the head, not the tail, if you pay attention to the commands of the Lord your God that I give you this day and carefully follow them, you will always be at the top, never at the bottom. (Deuteronomy 28:12–13 NIV)

> Yet the Lord longs to be gracious to you; He rises to show you compassion. For the Lord is a God of justice. Blessed are all who wait for Him. (Isaiah 30:18 NIV)

> And I pray, that you being rooted and established in love, may have power, together with all the saints, to grasp how wide and long and high and deep is the love of Christ, and to know this love that surpasses knowledge, that you may be filled to the measure of all the fullness of God. Now to Him who is able to do immeasurably more than all we ask or imagine, according to His power that is at work within us, to Him be glory in the church and in Christ Jesus throughout all generations, forever and ever. Amen. (Ephesians 3:17–21 NIV)

Bob and I were on a brand-new journey of falling into a strong and healthy faith-filled relationship with God. Abundant blessings and more miracles were in store for our growing family. And trust me, our family was growing exponentially!

CHAPTER 18

MARRIAGE ACCORDING TO GOD ... POLITICALLY INCORRECT

There are many books on marriage telling us how to or how not to love our spouse and conduct our household. The best book you will ever read for guidance is the Bible. If both parties walk according to the Word of God, your home will be filled with His blessings, peace, and joy; even if you have an extended family due to divorce or loss of a spouse. In today's society, there are many blended combinations, but God's Word will work in every home when we apply it in love and wisdom.

I am not suggesting you won't have struggles; you will. The good news is we have a Father who hears and answers prayer. We also have the Bible as our guide and the Holy Spirit to instruct and direct us in the wisdom needed to bring harmony and peace within our relationships and family structure.

Wise instructions for daily living and loving one another can be found in 1 Corinthians, chapter 13. We discussed this in an earlier chapter, but it is a critical component for overall healthy relationships. If you find yourself struggling and arguing with your loved one, ask yourself, "Am I being rude, boastful, or proud?" or "Am I demanding my own way, easily angered, or bringing up things from the past we resolved and forgave?"

> Love is patient and kind. Love is not jealous or boastful or proud or rude. It does not demand its own way. It is

not irritable, and it keeps no record of being wronged. It does not rejoice about injustice but rejoices whenever the truth wins out. Love never gives up, never loses faith, is always hopeful, and endures *through every circumstance.* Prophecy and speaking in unknown languages and special knowledge will become useless. But love will last forever. (1 Corinthians 13:4–8 NLT; emphasis added)

As a counselor and chaplain, the most common complaints I hear from couples are the issues of money or constantly bringing up past mistakes. So many times, we hold a past indiscretion over our loved one's head like a hostage. These actions are anything but Christlike or how love is to be lived out and demonstrated.

Allow me to clarify something important; if someone is repeating the same unloving and painful behaviors, they are not repentant and choosing to act selfishly. In these situations, there is a problem, and I recommend seeking counsel from your pastor or a Christian therapist. Repetitive behaviors of this manner will destroy a relationship.

If we put the scriptures from 1 Corinthians, chapter 13 into practice, our relationships will not be torn apart due to a lack of respect for one another and selfishness. A Christian's home should be an example to the world.

It is painful to hear and witness someone who belittles, ridicules, and disrespects his or her loved ones in public. It also should not be happening in private. We must choose to behave like men and women of God in public and in private. The world is in desperate need of Christian examples actively demonstrating love and respect toward each other. I grew up hearing, "Your life is the only Bible some people read," and guess what? It's true. By treating others according to scripture, people will want what we have instead of running the other direction, trying to avoid us or anything related to God.

When faced with difficult family situations, it is always best to pray before reacting. The Holy Spirit will give us wisdom, but we have a responsibility to act in love. Doing the right thing is not always the easiest or most popular. It is also not politically correct according to the world's standards. For a Christian, it is the only way. When we choose to disregard and not uphold the Word of God in our homes, we open the door to confusion, pain, chaos, division, and destruction.

> Live in peace with each other. And we urge you, brothers, warn those who are idle, encourage the timid, help the weak, be patient with everyone. Make sure that nobody pays back wrong for wrong, but always try to be kind to each other and to everyone else. Be joyful always, pray continually; give thanks in all circumstances, for this is God's will for you in Christ Jesus. (1 Thessalonians 5:13–18 NIV)

Bob and I longed for a healthy and God-centered marriage. Together we promised to live according to scripture and strive for peace with everyone. Family issues and critical spirits did not always make this an easy task. There were those who did not understand how we could get on with our lives as though divorce never happened. We were painfully aware of the negative effects of a broken home; however, staying in a pit of guilt and condemnation only keeps you beat down and prevents you from being fruitful. According to scripture, this is not God's best, or His will and purpose. Once He has forgiven you, get up and get on with your life. Remember to keep your tongue from evil, walk in love toward others, pray for those who persecute you, and refuse to allow bitterness to grow within your heart. Finally, leave the results to God.

You cannot talk about marriage without discussing the subject of money. Some people feel an overwhelming desire to control the finances in their home as a symbol of power. I have two words for you: *stop it*. This is not scriptural, and participating in such behavior is destructive and unloving.

We must also be careful not to make money an idol. The Bible tells us, "The love of money is a root of all kinds of evil" (1 Timothy 6:10 NIV). This scripture is frequently quoted incorrectly and stated this way, "Money is the root of all kinds of evil." The Bible clearly says it is "The love of money." Making money and doing well in life is not a sin or by any means wrong, unless it becomes an idol and source of pride.

According to statistics, the almighty dollar is one of the main reasons marriages end in divorce. Christian homes were not exempt from this study. In fact, the final analysis showed just as many Christian homes were destroyed due to money issues. This is a sad testimony and hinders the world from seeing how abundantly God longs to bless His people when they walk in total obedience. For this very reason, financial control issues are not only dangerous but foolish. As Christians, we must pray for wisdom when dealing with money matters. Couples who work together concerning finances will enjoy harmony and unity, not division and animosity.

What about the issue of tithing; is it something we have to do? The answer is no. We are not forced by God to do anything. We have been given *free will* to make our own choices. If your choices line up with God's infallible Word, you will be blessed. Tithes and offerings are scriptural and full of blessings. In our home, tithing is a must. There is no other option. We have seen and experienced God's blessings through our giving.

The subject of tithes and offerings are very dear to our family's heart. We have experienced firsthand how beautifully giving works. There are too many Christian families needlessly struggling financially. Every Christian home can enjoy God's blessings, not just a few. It is all about stepping out in faith and choosing obedience over selfishness and fear.

When we pay tithes and offerings with an obedient and cheerful heart, God gives us a promise in Malachi, "Test me in this, says the Lord Almighty, and see if I will not throw open the floodgates of heaven and pour out so much blessing that you will not have room enough for it" (Malachi 3:10 NIV). This promise comes with a responsibility on our part to give, along with an urging from God, "Test me in this, says the Lord Almighty."

Many times Christians allow fear to overtake their mind when it comes to giving. They struggle with overwhelming doubts about how they can pay tithes and make sure all the monthly bills are paid. Christians are called to live by faith. When fear enters our mind, it is imperative to replace it with faith. If we don't, it will weave its way into our heart and interfere with our ability to make healthy and wise decisions. God's promise is clear and He is a faithful Father. We can trust Jehovah Jireh, our Provider.

> Will a man rob God? Yet you rob Me. But you ask, how do we rob You? In tithes and offerings. You are under a curse, the whole nation of you, because you are robbing Me. Bring the whole tithe into the storehouse, that there may be food in My house. Test me in this, says the Lord Almighty, and see if I will not throw open the floodgates of heaven and pour out so much blessing that you will not have room enough for it. I will prevent pest from devouring your crops, and the vines in your field will not casts their fruit, says the Lord Almighty. (Malachi 3:8–11 NIV)

When we rob God of His portion, we choose to live under a curse that is absent of the Father's blessings. We are instructed to be good stewards of all He has blessed us with. Having a greedy and selfish mentality is an attitude we cannot afford to walk in if we want to reap the benefits from the floodgates of heaven.

When God said, "Test me in this," it is not meant as a dare. The Lord had already commanded the principle of tithing. By saying, "Test me in this," He actually puts Himself under observation and examination. You see, there is something very special about giving. God is letting us know we will see His powerful hand at work when we choose a lifestyle of selfless giving. It goes back to God's law of sowing and reaping.

> Remember this: Whoever sows sparingly will also reap sparingly, and whoever sows generously will also reap generously. Each of you should give what you have decided in your heart to give, not reluctantly or under compulsion, for God loves a cheerful giver. (2 Corinthians 9:6–7 NIV)

Some argue tithing was abolished with the law (the Old Testament). I've heard people claim it isn't even mentioned in the New Testament. Read your Bible! Matthew, chapter 23 and Luke chapter 11, offers insight concerning this matter as Jesus issues a strong rebuke.

> Woe to you, teachers of the law and Pharisees, you hypocrites. You give a tenth of your spices, mint, dill, and cumin. But you have neglected the more important matters of the law, justice, mercy, and faithfulness. *You should have practiced the latter, without neglecting the former.* (Matthew 23:23 NIV; emphasis added)

> Woe to you Pharisees, because you give God a tenth of your mint, rue and all other kinds of garden herbs, but you neglect justice and the love of God. *You should have practiced the latter without leaving the former undone.* (Luke 11:42 NIV; emphasis added)

Jesus is not criticizing the observance of the law, but He opposes the hypocrisy involved; "You should have practiced the latter, without neglecting the former." They gave their portion (tithe) so they could boast about it. But like any seasoned hypocrite, they pompously chose what commandments and laws they wanted to obey. In doing so, they neglected something dear to the heart of Jesus: justice, mercy, faithfulness, and the love of God. Because of their selfishness, arrogance, hypocrisy, and neglect, He gave them quite a tongue lashing.

God can and will do amazing things with a budget when we walk in obedience. It does not matter if it is one hundred or one thousand dollars a week. When we tithe and give generously, God miraculously protects our finances and meets our needs.

> I am young and now I am old, yet I have never seen the righteous forsaken or their children begging bread. They are always generous and lend freely; their children will be blessed. (Psalm 37:25–26 NIV)

Scripture also tells us to be cheerful givers. In other words, we should not have a bratty or selfish attitude. Growing up in the church, I heard people say some crazy things, such as, "I've paid tithes for years, and God better come through for me," or, "I paid tithes this week so that God will bless me with …" You can fill in the blank. We often have an "I'll

Falling into Faith

scratch your back, you scratch mine" mentality. How foolish and selfish we must look to the Father when we act like a spoiled, demanding child. If our hearts are right toward the things of God, our attitudes will reflect a life of praise and cheerful giving. A faithful, Christ-centered heart will not pick or choose what, where, or when to be obedient. Our goal and purpose in life will be focused on obedience in every area, including finances.

If there is a problem with money in your marriage, talk to your spouse. Spend time in prayer and fasting (yes fasting) and ask the Holy Spirit for wisdom. Do what is right and obedient, and you will be blessed. God's Word will not fail. "Test Me in this, says the Lord Almighty ..."

If you are married and your spouse is not a Christian, explain the importance of faithfulness in committing to God what is His. Be prepared; have scripture ready and a gentle spirit. Ask the Holy Spirit to help you choose your words wisely. Do not argue, accuse, or raise your voice. Keep the following scriptures in mind, and although it says "wives," when applied, it works for men as well. Over the years, I've heard many testimonies of men and women coming to the Lord because of their spouse's loving spirit.

> Wives, in the same way be submissive to your husbands so that, if any of them do not believe the Word, they may be won over without words by the behavior of their wives, when they see the purity and reverence of your lives. (1 Peter 3:1–2 NIV)

If you are single, begin today committing your finances to God. When seeking a mate, make sure they understand your convictions. In fact, study the scriptures together. This matter should be settled before entering the covenant of marriage. How someone reacts when it comes to money offers valuable insights into their heart. Single people ... pay attention!

The first book of Peter, chapter 3, encourages us to do what is right, even when it hurts. I know what you're probably thinking, *Ouch ... how can this be a good thing?* Not to worry. Once you begin applying these wise principles in your home and every relationship in your life, you will never want to lose the peace and blessings it brings. Even when someone hurts you or the situation is not fair, continue walking in these principles and trust God to be faithful and true.

> For, whoever would love life and see good days must keep his tongue from evil and his lips from deceitful speech. He must turn from evil and do good; He must seek peace and pursue it. *For the eyes of the Lord are on the righteous and His ears are attentive to their prayer, but the face of the Lord is against those who do evil.* Who is going to harm you if you are eager to do good? *But even if you should suffer for what is right, you are blessed.* Do not fear what they fear; do not be frightened, but in your hearts set apart Christ as Lord. *Always be prepared to give an answer to everyone who asks you to give a reason for the hope that you have.* But do this with a gentleness and respect, *keeping a clear conscience, so that those who speak maliciously against your good behavior in Christ may be ashamed of their slander.* It is better, if it is God's will, to suffer for doing good than for doing evil. *For Christ died for sins once for all, the righteous for the unrighteous, to bring you to God.* (1 Peter 3:10–18 NIV; emphasis added)

Finally, I want to focus on submission and what it means. Get ready, ladies, and take some deep breaths. This is scriptural but not politically correct (PC) in today's society. However, it does not mean we are less than or subservient to men.

For absolute clarity, we will look at Ephesians, chapter 5. Take a moment and ask the Holy Spirit to open your mind to receive the truth from God's infallible Word. Be prepared for Him to speak to your heart.

> And *give thanks for everything to God the Father in the name of our Lord Jesus Christ. And further, submit to one another out of reverence for Christ. For wives, this means submit to your husbands as to the Lord. For a husband is the head of his wife as Christ is the head of the church.* He

is the Savior of his body, the church. As the church submits to Christ, so you wives should submit to your husbands in everything. For husbands, this means love your wives, just as Christ loved the church. He gave up his life for her to make her holy and clean, washed by the cleansing of God's word. He did this to present her to himself as a glorious church without a spot or wrinkle or any other blemish. Instead, she will be holy and without fault. In the same way, husbands ought to love their wives as they love their own bodies. For a man who loves his wife actually shows love for himself. No one hates his own body but feeds and cares for it, just as Christ cares for the church. And we are members of his body. As the Scriptures say, "A man leaves his father and mother and is joined to his wife, and the two are united into one." This is a great mystery, but it is an illustration of the way Christ and the church are one. So again I say, each man must love his wife as he loves himself and the wife must respect her husband. (Ephesians 5:20–33 NLT; emphasis added)

Over the past thirty years, the women's movement and its belief in total equality (regardless of our obvious differences) have changed the way people think about their roles in marriage and life. What surprises me most is the fact we (Christians) have allowed this to filter in and flow over into our churches and homes. Did we decide at some point we are wiser than God and have a better handle on how to conduct ourselves in relationships? It appears in many of our churches and homes the answer to this question is sadly, "Yes."

As Christians, we accept the Bible as the authoritative Word of God. Today's standards twist and manipulates biblical truths. Women want to juggle career and family, along with gender equality in all things. Women's movement and liberal views state they want *all* gender-based distinctions eliminated in every area of their existence. For years, many women have felt like second-rate citizens and a doormat to men. This has created a spirit of anger and bitterness, and they've come out swinging. In an effort to stop the oppression, this movement has made the word "submission" mean something ugly and degrading. To be fair, humans have certainly fueled the fire by their unloving actions.

There is nothing wrong with a woman having a career and family. We are wonderfully created by God with specific callings and many things to accomplish while on this earth. Every human being possesses gifts and abilities God longs to use for His glory. One thing is certain, absolutely no one should ever feel like a doormat, especially from someone who claims to love them. This kind of spirit should not be an issue in any home, particularly a Christian-based, Christ-centered home. If it is, there is a prideful and controlling spirit present that lacks understanding concerning God's Word, what submission means, and who we are submitting to.

A man who truly loves his wife as Christ loves the church will create an atmosphere where his wife feels loved, supported, and precious to him. If a wife feels beat down in any way or is having to compromise her spiritual beliefs and biblical truths, yet her husband claims to be a Christian, something is spiritually wrong. Seek God's help and Christian counsel.

How the world wants to live is their choice, but Christians should proactively live out what God commands. The world we live in is fueled by rebellion. Let's not forget Satan's original sin. He resisted God's authority in an effort to make himself equal. "I will climb to the highest heavens and be like the Most High" (Isaiah 14:14 NIV). We apparently haven't learned very much over the years.

According to the standards of this world, to be under any authority is to strip a person of their rights as a human being. It is a sad commentary of our society. Therefore, a Christian home should stand out in a positive light and in no way resemble what we are seeing in society as a whole.

To put things in perspective, we will examine the scriptures on Spirit-guided relationships. "Submit to one another out of reverence for Christ" (Ephesians 5:21 NIV). From the very beginning, we are told to submit to one another. This command is not gender specific in any way, and it goes out to every living, breathing human being who has decided to become a follower of Christ. By not obeying this command, we have made a choice. Our actions prove we are refusing to walk in the fear of the Lord, thus participating in rebellion toward Jesus Christ our Lord and Savior. Pure and simple, disobedience is rebellion. The Bible gives us a strong message concerning rebellion in 1 Samuel, chapter 15, by comparing it to witchcraft.

> Rebellion is as sinful as witchcraft, and stubbornness as bad as worshiping idols. So because you have rejected the command of the LORD, he has rejected you as king."
> (1 Samuel 15:23 NLT)

Submitting to one another doesn't mean leadership is not present. It simply means we have servant-led hearts with actions validating our claims. Within the union of marriage, when we make a conscious decision to follow the godly principles of putting our spouse above our own agendas (or desires), God's blessings and favor will envelop our marriage and family.

Now that we have read what the Bible states are our respective roles as husbands' and wives' we must understand another important fact: it is not a husband's responsibility to *force or demand* submission from his wife. A husband is to love his wife as Christ loves the church. Pray for your wife and allow God to move in her heart. The Bible never once *demands* the husband to be the head of his household; however, it states it as a fact in discussing the husband's role. It is the wife's responsibility to obey God's Word regarding her role and vice versus.

What does submission look like? First of all, lets address what it doesn't look like. A submissive person isn't fighting for his or her rights and demanding equality. With submission, there is no fight. A submissive person makes a purposeful decision to trust God to meet his or her needs, knowing he or she is acting in obedience to His Word. A driving force to prove a point and hold fast to your rights as a person is not present. It is settled in your mind.

Submission can best be described like this: a person of peace, anchored, hopeful, confident, and resolute. You see, it takes a strong and confident person to understand the benefits and blessings that comes from true submission to God and His commands. Women, it boils down to a very important fact: *when we submit, it is God we are obeying.* We have confused the issue of submission by thinking we are obeying humans.

A husband who is loving and attentive to his wife will not force her to do anything against God's will and His holy Word. He will not assert his authority to get his own way. If a husband is wise and walking in submission to God's commands, he will carefully seek his wife's opinions and insights. God's peace will reign in the home, and the respect demonstrated to his wife will open the door to mutual agreement and trust. First and foremost, a loving husband seeks godly wisdom, and his wife's overall well-being is a priority.

There have been times Bob and I did not fully agree on an issue but a decision needed to be made. In those moments, I gave it back to Bob to pray about and seek God for direction. Have I always been happy about the final decision? No. However, by relinquishing control and trusting Bob to pray, I knew God would give us wisdom and peace. He is a good Father and loves His children. The end result of those situations showed God's faithfulness. Even in the hard times, we have been truly blessed.

When a husband finds he must assert himself and exercise authority over his wife's opinion, he should display a gentle spirit, and walk in humility and reverence. As the spiritual leader of the home, God will hold him accountable for those decisions. It is a heavy responsibility.

Wives, when you find yourself at odds with your husband concerning a situation, carefully consider your words by keeping your tongue in check, and your heart clean before God. With a Christlike spirit, we are to respect and encourage one another, not tear down and wound.

I have sought God's forgiveness about my attitude more times than I care to recount. When you are an opinionated, strong-willed woman who comes from a long line of stubbornness on your mom's and dad's sides of the family, life is often interesting and challenging.

In closing, it is important to understand what wise and loving *spiritual leadership* truly is, and the *fruit of good leadership*. A leader brings out the best in those around them. Everyone has their own style and personality, and a leader learns to use those God-given qualities to promote a productive and positive impact within their home team.

A leader in a Christian home reflects a godly character and exemplifies the characteristics of the fruits of the Spirit. A good leader communicates and builds the family up through an open, authentic, and positive influence. Active and compassionate listening is part of his or her daily life, along with courage and confidence to pursue and engage the family in the things of God.

Last but not least, a leader strives for excellence and is the first to seek forgiveness when his or her actions hurt or wound others. With humility, a true leader will seek peace and reconciliation. Even when he or she does not understand why something is offensive and hurtful, they will swallow their pride and seek forgiveness.. This kind of leadership reaps trust and respect within the divinely instituted covenant of marriage and family.

We all face struggles every day within our homes and families. It is easy to fall into bad habits when dealing with the challenges of living with another person, running a household, and raising children. Circumstances and differing personalities can be difficult, creating many obstacles as we persevere and push through life's ups and downs, but circumstances do not define us. What we do and how we choose to respond to them become the defining moments that shape our character and determines our outcome. It also teaches those watching what we are made of and who we truly are.

What do you want your leadership to look like? What outcome do you desire? At the end of the day, what do you want to flow out of your home and life? What is your marriage and family's testimony right now? As you ponder the answer to these questions, keep in mind it's not too late to change and seek God for wisdom.

CHAPTER 19

GUARD AND PROTECT YOUR MIND

God's plans for Bob and me involved healing, restoration, and the fulfillment of a call to ministry. We were clueless about how things were about to unfold, but the Lord lovingly prepared the way for the journey ahead.

First, God led us to a small church that accepted and welcomed us into their congregation after a probationary period. Yes, a probationary period. But we humbled ourselves and submitted, knowing God's forgiveness for divorce in our lives prevailed.

Bob is a gifted soundman, and I am a musician and speaker. Although our talents should be used for God's glory, sometimes He says, "Be still," in an effort to bring much-needed healing and a time of refreshing. This period of quiet fellowship with the Lord proved to be a blessing because we were about to become very busy. The pastor and his wife needed help, and once we received their approval, I began playing the piano and leading worship while Bob went to work in the sound room.

Prior to getting married, I accepted a job with a cellular company. Within one year, I received a promotion, and my salary doubled. Bob owned a heating, air, and electrical company that God continued to grow and bless. In every area of our lives, we saw the Lord's favor, blessings, and benefits.

My overall health improved tremendously. I continued to suffer with occasional urinary, bladder, and kidney problems, but when I felt the onset of an infection, Bob and I prayed together and held tight to the healing scriptures. Along with God's medicine, I increased my water intake, which was a considerable improvement. With each attack, God wonderfully came through.

The one troubling struggle I dealt with daily was a constant pain in my neck and chest area where they removed the tumor. I refused prescription pain medication due to family history and my own personal battle with addiction from previous years with the blood disease. Every day, we sought God for wisdom and prayed healing scriptures over my body. Unfortunately, I secretly knew why our prayers were not answered. I lived with a fear and increasing anxiety that cancer still lurked somewhere inside me. I could hear the doctor's words running through my brain like a steam roller. Desperate for confirmation no cancer remained, I decided to make a doctor's appointment.

Because of my refusal for further treatment and the *cancer facts* doctors stressed at nauseam, I dreaded the appointment, but we felt it was the wise thing to do. After the examination, he stated the pain could be a result of scar tissue or reoccurring cancer. The only way to know for sure meant another surgery to remove and test the tissue. Fear and panic immediately took ahold of my heart. Things were going so good I quietly wondered if the hammer was about to come crashing down. You see, the root of my fear came from another issue altogether, and I desperately needed God's healing touch along with a renewed mind.

Fear is a stronghold Satan uses to torment God's children. It is important to understand *faith exits* when we open the door to fear and allow it to remain. They will not keep company and room together because faith is light, and fear is darkness. The Bible tells us light has *nothing* to do with darkness.

Job usually comes to our minds when we think about suffering because of what he endured. In spite of all he went through, he proved to be a righteous, God-fearing, and faithful servant of the Most High God; however, the scriptures enlighten us about something important, "What I feared has come upon me; what I dreaded has happened to me. I have no peace, no quietness; I have no rest, but only turmoil" (Job 3:25–26 NIV).

What Job feared came upon him. Think about this for a moment. Doubts and fears will enter our minds, but we must learn to immediately speak truth and cast out those fears. The following scripture instructs us to do something very important: "We demolish arguments and every pretension that sets itself up against the knowledge of God, and we take captive every thought to make it obedient to Christ" (2 Corinthians 10:5 NIV). The New International Version brings such clarity to what I must do by using the words "take captive" and "demolish." To demolish means "to completely and utterly destroy."

For the sake of understanding so that application can occur, I want to focus on how "to take captive every thought." We have the ability to control and redirect our thoughts. Exercising control over our thoughts is not only possible but is a proven scientific fact. Making the necessary changes in our thought life means we must discipline our minds and take responsibility for what we allow to take root and grow.

Avoid reacting to negativity; instead, think things through and refrain from disabling, destructive thoughts. It is easy to literally think yourself into a pit of despair or become embattled between the two worlds of positive versus negative. Turn those thoughts over to God and allow Him to transform your thinking. God is able to powerfully renew our minds and thought life; however, we must feed and fill our minds with His Word, then accept His redirection and correction.

> Do not conform to the pattern of this world, *but be transformed by the renewing of your mind.* Then you will be able to test and approve what God's will is-His good, pleasing and perfect will. (Romans 12:2 NIV; emphasis added)

Our bodies physically react and change in response to the thoughts running through our minds every minute of every day. The good news is, as God's children, we have authority in Jesus's name to refuse any negative report or thought about our lives that is contrary to the Bible. We can cast it down and speak life while waiting with expectancy for Jesus to come through. "Do not be overcome by evil, but overcome evil with good" (Romans 12:21 NIV).

Just thinking about something causes your brain to release neurotransmitters. They are chemical messengers communicating with parts of itself as well as your nervous system. Neurotransmitters control virtually all of your body's functions. Studies have proven thoughts alone can improve vision, fitness, and strength. These communications improve your overall cognitive functions, reduce anxiety, and increase awareness, or they can lower your immune system, cause depression, and render a number of additional negative effects. Positive input equals positive output. Negative input equals negative output.

A thought is an electrochemical event taking place in your nerve cells, producing a rapid flow of physiological changes. What does this mean? If you allow negative and damaging thoughts to invade your mind and body and begin dwelling on them, you lessen the number of receptors able to receive positive and healthy thoughts. The end result is you are more inclined to negative thoughts and behaviors, which will also affect your overall health as well as your reactions and decisions.

What flows through your mind engraves and carves into your brain, some temporary and some lasting. Epigenetics is proving your perceptions and thoughts control your biology. This means you have the ability to influence and shape your own genetic output by changing your thought patterns.

I remember studying in psychology how your thoughts activate your genes. To further prove this, studies show about 5 percent of gene mutations are thought to be a direct cause of health issues, leaving 95 percent of genes linked to disorders acting as influencing agents. For instance, stress and our emotional state are directly dependent on our thoughts. Developing healthy stress-management tools in our lives is important to overall healthy mental and physical well-being.

Let's focus on the issue of stress for a moment. Due to my work as a hospice chaplain and counselor in a large metropolitan city, it feels as though I live in my car. Knowing how many patients I need to see and the serious nature of their situation, I don't have time to waste; therefore, driving is a huge stressor for me. There are times I can feel my blood pressure rise when traffic slows below the speed limit and there is no visible rhyme or reason. The further down the road I go, people seem to be drifting along in their own little world and paying no attention to anything around them. Then you have those who are glued to their phones when they should be paying attention to the road.

Because of the anxiety I often experience while driving, I have stress

Falling into Faith

balls in my car and squeeze them like crazy as I maneuver the roads. One day I squeezed the stress ball so hard it exploded. Fine white powder floated all around and covered my entire body, as well as the once-beautiful brown outfit I chose to wear that day. For the sake of brevity, I won't go into all the details, but let's just say I got to know a policeman really well, and I'm thankful for his kind and gracious attitude toward the situation. I'm also thankful he quickly realized it wasn't cocaine floating around in my car. Our brief encounter became quite amusing. He even visited my office a few weeks later and dropped off some new stress balls he purchased for me. What a great example of "to protect and serve."

With everything life throws at us, it is no wonder scripture says, "Watch over your heart with all diligence, for from it flow the springs of life" (Proverbs 4:23 AMP). Diligently protecting our hearts and minds is so important to God because he created us to accomplish amazing things. The very fact we can control our thought life, means we can redirect and reprogram those pessimistic and negative thoughts we often entertain and nurture.

One way to begin is to adopt a habit of positive, optimistic, and God-focused thoughts by simply being grateful. Studies show when people consciously practice gratitude, they get a surge of rewarding transmitters; for instance, dopamine. Their minds become generally alert and bright. Dopamine is a neurotransmitter that helps control the brain's reward and pleasure centers. It also helps regulate movement and emotional responses, enabling us to not only see rewards but take action to move toward them. Basically, it's those feel-good endorphins we all enjoy the benefits of when released.

In order to guard and protect our minds, it is critical to speak and think on God's truth as we combat lies, assumptions, and misconceptions regularly invading our thoughts. Only then can we ensure what is flowing in and out is healthy to our overall well-being.

Let me give you an example of speaking truth to a lie. If you have been told nothing good can ever come of your life, this is an absolute lie. Your Creator and Redeemer says when you repent of your sins, He is faithful to forgive, restore, and bless your life. Find scriptures that apply to your situation; speak them out in faith and refuse to allow the lies of the enemy to cause lingering doubts or fears. They simply do not belong in your God-given brain. If you secretly harbor unbelief and fear, repent and continue speaking forth *truth,* regardless of the circumstances or how you feel. God responds to faith, not feelings.

As tests and trials come, we must remember whatever happens in our lives has gone through the Father filter. Other words, He has allowed it for a reason. It is up to us to seek His face and trust Him. If we allow Him to work in our lives, these difficulties will bring us into a closer relationship with God, as He works out all things for the good.

God allowed Job to be tested, and he withstood the test. Because of this, the Father rewarded his faithfulness. In fact, he received double for his trouble. "After Job had prayed for his friends, the Lord made him prosperous again and gave him twice as much as he had before" (Job 42:10 NIV). Pay close attention to what the scripture says: *twice as much.* What God did for Job He will do for all who faithfully believe and stand firm.

> For God hath not given us the spirit of fear; but of power, and of love, and of a sound mind. (2 Timothy 1:7 KJV).

> There is no fear in love. But perfect love drives out fear, because fear has to do with punishment. The one who fears is not made perfect in love. (1 John 4:18 NIV)

The day of surgery came, and Bob stayed faithfully by my side in constant prayer. A praying spouse is a powerful and wonderful thing. The scar tissue was removed and tested. No cancer found; praise God for victory.

The doctor advised us to give it a few weeks, and the pain should be gone. Three, four, then twelve weeks passed; instead of the pain leaving, it intensified. In fact, it was actually worse. Panicked, I hit my knees. "What is going on, God? There is no cancer, and they got the scar tissue, so why am I having this pain?"

Desperation can be a wonderful blessing. It causes us to take giant steps toward God, with a willingness to learn. Which is probably why He allows certain obstacles to come our way. He knows what is necessary to get our complete and undivided attention.

Falling into Faith

In the midst of the struggle, we felt the Lord leading us to pray and fast about not only the pain but also our faith walk. Daily Bible reading and meditating had become a priority, but we found ourselves longing for a more intimate relationship with the Lord. As our hunger grew, just attending regular church services no longer satisfied our desire for more of God. We decided to find additional teaching and add it to our weekly devotion time. We began listening to a minister on television who taught a series on prayer and fasting. Scanning the channels, we found a few other teachers and preachers we enjoyed as well. A new strength and confidence began to emerge and grow.

One thing became very clear early on: we had to stop tolerating things in our lives that did not line up with an overcoming life. It is quite liberating when you decide to stop putting up with the enemy's lies and attacks; however, once you make this commitment, be prepared for spiritual warfare. Satan does not take kindly to losing his edge. The fear I once secretly tucked away began dismantling. Piece by piece, faith replaced fear as Bob and I fell further into God's hands and depended on His strength. We became a powerful force because there is strength in numbers. The Lord continued teaching us the importance and benefits of coming into complete, unwavering agreement with Him.

Halfway through the fast, I quickly noticed an entire day passed without pain. The next day came and went, still no pain. The enemy tried to tell me the relief was only temporary. Every time those thoughts entered my mind, I completely and utterly destroyed them by singing praises and speaking healing scriptures with authority in the name of Jesus. The fourth and fifth day passed, still no pain—it was gone.

The evening of the fifth day, I finally told Bob. I explained how fear tried to creep in, causing me to wait before saying anything. After a year of constant pain and suffering, I was healed. We sat crying and praising God for answered prayer. We realized once we stood in unity with God, and made sure our hearts, mouths, and actions lined up with biblical truth, the miraculous manifested.

From the very beginning, God desired to heal me completely. Unfortunately, I allowed circumstances and pain to cause me to veer off track. Without realizing it, my faith hinged on the doctor's assurance cancer no longer existed. God allowed confirmation through surgery in order to get to the heart of the matter—fear, feeling unworthy of healing, and a lack of trust.

We are thankful for this experience because it gave us an understanding on how powerful the Word of God is when you truly come into agreement with Him. The anointing that breaks yokes and delivers miracles gloriously manifested as we spoke truth in faith and applied the Word to our lives.

Before complete healing and deliverance manifested, pain and fear persisted; however, I went into fight mode and faithfully read and meditated on healing scriptures throughout each day. I also refused to allow negative thoughts to stay, and personalized the scriptures by putting my name in them, "By His stripes, I (Donna Grant Wilcox) am healed." God did not ignore my persistence. It became a vital key to receiving a miracle and also revealed areas lacking faith and in need of spiritual growth.

If you are doing this already and still have not received an answer, ask the Holy Spirit to reveal any areas of unforgiveness, fear, doubt, or sin. After you have done all you know to do, *stand firm*. Nurture a heart of praise and expect a miracle. See yourself healed and whole with the eyes of the Spirit. Do not allow circumstances and flesh to create a spiritually blurred vision. God works in the spirit realm first, the supernatural. Your miracle is already complete in the spirit realm; with a heart of praise and anticipation, wait on the Father to manifest it in the natural. Above all, guard and protect your mind and heart. Humankind's impossibilities are God's possibilities. "Jesus looked at them and said, with man this is impossible, *but with God all things are possible*" (Matthew 19:26 NIV; emphasis added).

The miracle of my healing has touched many lives, and we give God all the praise and glory. I make it a point to share my testimony every opportunity I get. It thrills me when people see the scars and are willing to ask, "Did you have a car accident or something?" Sharing the miracle-working power of God is such a privilege.

The lessons we learned and the long road to recovery continues to serve a tremendous purpose in our lives, as it helps and encourages other to fall into a lifelong trust relationship with the Father. Through it all, we've learned to humble ourselves, hold on in faith, never give up, and not put God in some theological box. For that matter, don't put Him in any kind of box. His Word is true and trustworthy.

> Praise the Lord, O my soul; all my inmost being, praise His holy name. Praise the Lord, O my soul, and forget not all His benefits—who forgives all your sins and heals all your disease, who redeems your life from the pit and crowns you with love and compassion, who satisfies your desires with good things so that your youth is renewed like the eagles. (Psalm 103:1–5 NIV)

God not only healed me of cancer and constant pain, He healed the self-esteem issues I wrestled with and thoughts of never being worthy of God's mercy. This was the root cause of my fear. You will soon read how He managed to finally get through to my heart regarding my low self-esteem issues.

No human being on earth, regardless of how many wonderful things you do for others (and this world), makes you worthy of God's mercy. The only hope we have is in Christ and His precious blood. It covers our past and every sin, allowing us to stand clean before Him. The blood of the Lamb puts us in direct communication with our heavenly Father. "Let us then approach God's throne of grace with confidence, so that we may receive mercy and find grace to help us in our time of need" (Hebrews 4:16 NIV).

Before Mother went home to heaven, she prophesied that God planned to do this very thing. One night while we sat talking and laughing, she looked at me and stated, "Donna, you spent your entire young life in pain, and the Lord is going to restore those years. You will be youthful and full of life. You are going to do all the things you never got to do when you were growing up without pain." God answered Mom's prayers, and He restored my youth just like the scripture in Psalm 103 (NIV) promises, "Who satisfies your desires with good things so that your youth is renewed like the eagles."

I cannot help but feel a little sorry for Bob; he often says he married a teenager who only knows one speed ... *full blast*. The beauty of that statement is the fact Bob knows my past and how the enemy robbed me of so much. Hallelujah and pass the cornbread ... I'm making up for it now!

Bob expanded my horizons in many fun and exciting ways. He taught me how to snow ski and go four-wheeling, but more importantly, we share Jesus together with everyone God brings our way. I have energy and enjoy life to its fullest, without fear of sickness, disease, or constant pain. Life is good, and it is all because of Jesus.

The Lord continued to work His supernatural magic as He orchestrated the next move. The youth pastor at our church resigned, and only a handful still attended class. The pastor's wife asked us to step in, and we hesitantly said yes, even though we quietly prayed for a way out. Seeing so much rebellion in young people caused us to pull back and avoid working with them. The fact is we did something awful and prejudged those precious lives. God soon convicted us of our rush to judgment, and we asked for forgiveness. As we stepped out in obedience, His blessings poured down.

Jesus spent His life serving. He left us a beautiful example of compassionate servanthood that we are to continue today. Too often, we are full of excuses as to why we cannot help others. It is time to wake up and realize God should not have to speak in an audible voice before we are willing to contribute our time and talents. If we expect the Father to be faithful, shouldn't we be faithful too? A servant-driven and compassionate heart must be a huge part of who we are if we wear the Christian label. "I tell you the truth, whatever you did for one of the least of these brothers of mine, you did for me" (Matthew 25:40 NIV).

Please do not misunderstand. Volunteering for everything under the sun will cause us to lose balance and harmony in our own lives, creating disorder and neglect. We must take care of what God has already entrusted us with, such as our family. Sometimes *no* is the right answer. When saying no is necessary, it usually paves the way for someone else to rise up and reap blessings from their obedience.

Bob and I sought God for wisdom in dealing with the youth group, and something interesting happened. One of the new girls with a limited knowledge of church or the Bible began asking questions. Her inquisitive nature became contagious, and the kids who were raised in church started asking questions as well. We were surprised at how little they knew about the Bible. It only took a few questions to realize just how ignorant we were too.

Falling into Faith

Don't you just love it when you look stupid in front of a bunch of teenagers? We should have known the answers to their questions, but we didn't.

These kids were hungry and needed spiritual food. We knew healing and faith scriptures to the point of memorization, but that was not enough. Feeling a strong conviction and burden for the youth group, a deeper desire to grow more radical in serving the Lord in spirit and truth burned within our hearts. This could very well mean the difference in where they spent eternity, and we were accountable to them and God.

As our relationship with the young people flourished, we made a discovery—the ones who had been raised in church with parents in active ministry were not seeing God's Word put into practice in their own homes. This made us take serious inventory of our lives with a determination to change. Some of them continued to refuse to accept Jesus as their Savior because they did not believe anyone truly lived a Christian life. They did not want what the church offered. As far as they were concerned, we were all a bunch of hypocrites. You know what? Sadly, they weren't too far off base.

Committing the youth group and their spiritual situation to prayer, we came up with a simple answer: "Don't just talk it, but live it. Avoid being just another social hangout. Teach them the Word of God without a lot of fluff or pretense and love them unconditionally." In our heart of hearts, we knew if these young people fell in love with Jesus, they would quit looking at everyone else and start getting their own lives right. With prayer and fasting, we put our plan in motion.

We began teaching salvation and the very basics of Christianity, then slowly moved into more of God's Word. As they soaked it in, the atmosphere changed. We were having the time of our lives, and you could feel the very presence of the Holy Spirit. They continued to ask questions, and we all grew and learned together.

Some of these young people were going through difficult situations at home and came to live with us. We became parents spiritually and in every way. God began fulfilling His promise to bring children into my life. They learned to trust us and realized living a Christian life is possible inside and outside the church. We felt like proud and protective parents, constantly thanking God for our growing family.

Through this experience, the Father gloriously fulfilled a void in my heart. It allowed me the privilege of loving, mothering, and pampering these kids, both in the youth group and the ones who shared our home. He did not just give us a couple of children; little did we know this was the beginning of forty-nine God-given gifts who would come into our lives and call us Mama Donna and Papa Bob. Isn't that just like God to give us more than we ever dared to dream or imagine!

Our heavenly Father also knew Bob and I needed growth in every area of our walk, not just in faith and healing matters. To accomplish this task, He made us accountable to a bunch of young people who were not afraid to ask the hard questions and expect answers. His ways are mysterious and wonderful.

God moved mightily within our youth group. Young people were literally coming in off the streets and receiving Jesus as their Savior during our services. The kids were so on fire for God, we even set aside an additional night just for prayer. Our dreams and desires for them were manifesting right before our very eyes. Just when things were going great, the enemy reared his ugly head and launched an attack.

One Sunday morning as I played the piano, the entire youth group came up to the choir singing and worshiping the Lord. Suddenly they moved out into the congregation and began praying for people. This had been a dream of ours—to see the youth worshiping like this in our regular services and reaching out to others in prayer. Crying so hard I could hardly play, I glanced back at Bob in the sound room and saw tears streaming down his face. A moment later, I looked back at him, and there was a strange look on his face. I didn't give it much thought, figuring he just felt overwhelmed with how God answered our prayers.

When we got in the car to go home, he looked at me and said, "Sweetheart, God spoke to my heart during worship." Excited and sure it was something good, his expression said otherwise. He then took my hand and stated, "God said our time here is done."

In disbelief, I began to cry, "What do you mean, done? These are our kids, and we love them. We can't leave them now that they are just beginning to fall in love with Jesus." I knew how much Bob loved them too. He tried to comfort me, but the Word of the Lord had been very clear to him. I also knew he never said things like, "God spoke to my heart" unless He truly did.

Within days, our congregation began suddenly unraveling. The enemy attacked without mercy, using church people to bring about destruction and chaos. He tried to destroy all the good God was doing in our youth group. Many people were uncomfortable with "unchurched" street kids wandering into the congregation. We could not believe our eyes and ears—weren't we commanded to win the lost to Christ? The Lord quickly reminded us of what He spoke to Bob just a week earlier. We were obedient with everything He asked us to do, and now it was out of our hands.

The young people were devastated as they watched things unfold. When we told them the Lord said our time there was done, their hearts were broken. We had become a very special family. We prayed for God to protect their hearts and minds and bring people into their lives who would continue sowing truth and love.

Scriptures tell us there will be persecution and trouble, but God will deliver us from them all. I truly do not believe our hearts could have taken any more pain and heartache. In prayer, we committed the situation and those precious lives back to Him.

It may be eternity before we see the fruit of our labor, but God will complete it and bring glory to His kingdom. Whatever you are doing for the Lord, remember this scripture, "Let us not become weary in doing good, for at the proper time we will reap a harvest if we do not give up" (Galatians 6:9 NIV). Give it to the Lord and stay obedient. Leave the results to God.

Some of the young people God brought into our homes and hearts strayed away from serving the Lord because of what transpired. Without a doubt, we knew God's Word had been planted deep in their souls, and they knew how to get back on track. This knowledge continues to bring us comfort and peace.

Conflict is never easy, but it can be a great teacher. The entire situation proved to be a valuable stepping-stone, preparing the way for a life in missions and ministry. Through it, we learned the importance of how Christ learned obedience through His suffering.

> "Even though Jesus was God's Son, he learned obedience from the things he suffered" (Hebrews 5:8 NLT).
>
> The straight and narrow may not be an easy road, but it is well worth it, and we were pressing forward.

CHAPTER 20

LESSONS FROM FURNITURE

Before proceeding with my story, I want to dedicate this chapter to those of us who have suffered with self-esteem and rejection issues, those overwhelming feelings we are never going to be good enough. Those of us who have struggled to seek God's mercy, healing, and forgiveness due to feelings of failure and utter shame.

I have ministered and counseled with so many over the years who do not understand how God can truly forgive their past or erase the negative things spoken over their lives. Some even wonder if God really cares about them at all. People have hurt and rejected you. Their words have penetrated your very soul so deeply you can't see anything of value. You are not alone; I was one of those people.

I pray this chapter brings insight and assurance about how much Jesus Christ loves each of us and longs to show His mercy in amazing and life-changing ways. God is always faithful. "What if some did not have faith? Will their lack of faith nullify God's faithfulness? Not at all. Let God be true, and every man a liar" (Romans 3:3–4 NIV).

> *This righteousness from God comes through faith in Jesus Christ to all who believe. There is no difference, for all have sinned and fall short of the glory of God, and are justified freely by His grace through the redemption that came by Christ Jesus. God presented Him as a sacrifice of atonement, through faith in His blood.* (Romans 3:22–25a NIV; emphasis added)

> But He was pierced for our transgressions, He was crushed for our iniquities; the punishment that brought us peace was upon Him, *and by His stripes we are healed.* (Isaiah 53:5 NIV; emphasis added)

God can speak to us in many different ways. As I have stated numerous times, it is not wise to put Him in a box and limit His ability to speak however He pleases. I love the story in Numbers 22, where God spoke through a donkey. Below are a few interesting and intriguing scriptures. Hopefully it will ignite a desire to study in depth God's ability to speak to us in mysterious and powerful ways.

> When the donkey saw the angel of the LORD, it pressed close to the wall, crushing Balaam's foot against it. So he beat the donkey again. Then the angel of the LORD moved on ahead and stood in a narrow place where there was no room to turn, either to the right or to the left. When the donkey saw the angel of the LORD, it lay down under Balaam, and he was angry and beat it with his staff. Then the LORD opened the donkey's mouth, and it said to Balaam, "What have I done to you to make you beat me these three times?" Balaam answered the donkey, "You have made a fool of me. If only I had a sword in my hand, I would kill you right now." The donkey said to Balaam, "Am I not your own donkey, which you have always ridden, to this day? Have I been in the habit of doing this to you?" "No," he said. Then the LORD opened Balaam's eyes, and he saw the angel of the LORD standing in the road with his sword drawn. So he bowed low and fell facedown. The angel of the LORD asked him, "Why have you beaten your donkey these three times? I have come here to oppose you because your path is a reckless one before me. The donkey saw me and turned away from me these three times. If it had not turned away, I would certainly have killed you by now, but I would have spared it." Balaam

said to the angel of the LORD, "I have sinned. I did not realize you were standing in the road to oppose me. Now if you are displeased, I will go back." The angel of the LORD said to Balaam, "Go with the men, but speak only what I tell you." So Balaam went with Balak's officials. (Numbers 22:25–35 NIV)

This story is so rich in food for our lives. So often God is trying to get our attention, and we keep pressing forward without doing something important, *practicing the prayerful pause*. Take a deep breath, pray, and pause in the struggle. Ask God to open your eyes to see and ears to hear what He is trying to reveal. If you wait patiently, He will speak.

He often uses His holy scriptures to speak to our hearts, but sometimes He uses strange ways or things to reach us. God is our Creator, and He knows the perfect way to get our attention.

In my particular situation, He used dreams about furniture to teach me valuable lessons on healing and standing as the righteousness of Christ. By sharing these lessons with you, I pray they shed important biblical truths on the mercy and unconditional love our Father has for all His children. In spite of our shortcomings and failures, He truly longs to show Himself merciful.

Throughout my book, I've detailed many obstacles and challenges I faced due to sickness and "stinkin' thinkin'." Thankfully, there is a "but" in my story; but, because of God's grace and mercy, I miraculously and victoriously overcame. Although the scars remain, I'm thankful for them. They are a constant reminder of God's healing power, tender mercies, and desire to fulfill His promises in and through me—His daughter.

After being diagnosed with cancer and all that followed, I found myself in a state of desperation. A growing hunger grew not only for healing but also a deeper and more intimate relationship with the Lord. As Bob and I faced the giants and sought God's help, something revealed itself. My prayers were hindered because of major insecurities and rejection issues. You see, I did not feel worthy to receive healing. The idea of standing as the righteousness of Christ without the shame of my past and all its failures constantly lurking in the shadows felt impossible and prideful.

God knew this, and He understood the importance of getting the truth of His love and mercy inside my heart and mind. This is where furniture comes into the story. Allow me to back up in time for just a moment and explain why furniture probably consumed my thoughts during this season of life.

Not long after Bob and I got married, we purchased our first living room suite together. A few months later, we bought new bedroom furniture. Both times, I enjoyed the best shopping experiences of my life. What made them so enjoyable? We paid cash and could actually afford to purchase exactly what we wanted. It felt great. No monthly bills, no added interest to pay, and no eating peanut butter and jelly for months on end because of debt. I felt rich. God knows everything about us, and He knew the lasting and positive impact these experiences etched upon my heart and mind.

After my diagnosis, a typical day consisted of reading scriptures and begging God for mercy and healing. At the end of each day, I fell into bed desperate for sleep to take over because it was the only thing separating me from another day of once again begging God for undeserved mercy.

As I lay sleeping one night, I began to dream. In my dream, Bob and I walked into a huge furniture store. We found everything we wanted, and Bob pulled out his wallet and gave the man cash. The clerk gave us a receipt, and we left the store. Hand in hand, we strolled to the car, excited about our new purchases. The next thing I saw, we were pulling in our driveway and going inside the house. As I entered the front door, I heard God speak to me in a clear and powerful voice. He asked a question, "Donna, is the furniture you just bought yours?"

I quickly replied, "Yes, it's all ours, Lord."

Then God asked something else. "Why do you say it is yours? It is not in your house; it is still in the store."

Without hesitation, I responded, "We gave the man cash. It's paid in full, and we have the receipt. We are just waiting for delivery."

When I heard myself utter those words, I awoke to hear the voice of God say, "Donna, healing is already yours; it has been paid for by the blood of Jesus. Just like the furniture in your dream, you are simply waiting for it to be delivered. Not all of My miracles are instantaneous." Waking up from something like this is quite incredible. I lay there

Falling into Faith

weeping as the love of God ran through every cell of my being. Bob woke up, and I began sharing the details of my dream and the words God spoke to me. Excited and consumed with an intense passion, I confessed and acknowledged healing was mine and paid in full by Jesus on the cross. Just because it did not happen the very moment I prayed did not mean God said no or that I wasn't going to receive it.

Bob held me in his arms as tears of joy flowed down my face. Together we praised God for His message of love and mercy. It is amazing how simple the revelation of healing became to me in that moment. All the confusion and overwhelming compulsion to repeatedly beg God for undeserved mercy just disappeared. I could never deserve this amazing gift, but He did it for me anyway.

His gifts are for each and every one of us. God's beautiful act of unconditional love has been paid in full. The gift of healing is part of the salvation plan and is free to all who believe and by faith *calls things that are not as though they were*. What a loving, generous, and powerful Savior.

> As it is written: "I have made you a father of many nations." He is our father in the sight of God, in whom he believed—*the God who gives life to the dead and calls things that are not as though they were*. (Romans 4:17 NIV; emphasis added)

The pain Jesus bore and the blood He shed on the cross is all-encompassing. It covers everything and everyone. During my studies of the Bible in Hebrew and Greek, I was overcome with gratitude to discover the very word *salvation* includes everything we could ever need or want in life. The truth of God's Word is liberating and exciting.

This dream and revelation turned out to be just the beginning of several lessons I learned from furniture. You see, I still struggled with another problem that continued to have an impact on my prayer life. I felt so beat down and unworthy of God's blessings. In fact, when good things happened, my thoughts went something like this, *I know I don't deserve this; something bad will probably happen soon. I just don't see how God can look past all my mess-ups and still want to bless my life. I'll just enjoy these blessings while I can and pray for strength when the hammer comes down.*

To embrace these kinds of thoughts meant my mind possessed an inaccurate image of Father God's loving character. I desperately needed a new and accurate revelation of His love and mercy. Truth soon arrived in the form of another dream—about furniture.

A little more than a month passed, and every day I felt a spirit of confirmation concerning God's power and desire to completely heal my body. Physically things were quickly improving, yet I continued to struggle with insecurities and feelings of worthlessness. In fact, it became a daily (sometimes hourly) struggle. The enemy did not want me to accept healing, and he targeted my weakest area—my mind.

God knows everything, and He knew my struggle with insecurities and mistakes from the past, including the hurtful things spoke into my life that needed to be dealt with once and for all. I felt incapable of shaking them off and feeling any sense of value. He came to my rescue and waited for me to get completely quiet and sound asleep. Then He visited my dreams once again in a magnificent way.

I truly feel God has to speak to a lot of us in our sleep. It is probably the only time He can get us to shut up and listen. At least that seems to be the case with me.

Sound asleep, I once again dreamt about furniture. It began with my dad coming to see me with a wonderful surprise. Keeping every aspect of my personality in mind, he bought the most exquisite bedroom suite I had ever seen. It was painstakingly and intricately designed down to every precise detail, made just for me—his daughter. The mattress had been strategically created so that I'd awake every day feeling rested and refreshed. The inside of each dresser drawer was lined with the fragrance of my favorite perfume. I could not believe my father's generosity and the time he invested in making sure it was perfect down to the smallest detail. Giving him a great big hug, I expressed how much I did not deserve this lavish gift. He beamed with excitement and proclaimed, "I want you to have it to show you how much I love you." He gave me another hug and left, leaving behind this beautiful reminder of his love for me—his daughter.

As the dream continued, it fast-forwarded to several days later. Hearing a knock on the door, I opened it and saw my sweet dad standing there smiling from ear to ear. He anxiously stepped inside and began walking toward the bedroom. Excited and full of joy, he asked, "How does the bed sleep? Do your clothes smell like your favorite perfume every morning?" Opening the bedroom door, he noticed something strange. My clothes were in a box on the floor, not in the beautifully lined and scented drawers he so meticulously picked out for me. To make matters worse, the bed with the perfect mattress looked as if I never slept in it. Stunned and confused, he turned to me and asked, "Why?" I hung my head in shame not knowing what to say, but I knew he deserved an explanation.

Finally, with tears streaming down my face, I looked up and said, "Daddy, it is just too beautiful, and I don't deserve it. I cannot bring myself to sleep in that wonderful bed or put my clothes in those perfect drawers. Please forgive me, but I am just not worthy to receive such a gift."

Broken and sad, he turned around and said, "Baby, I did all this just for you. I did not ask you to be worthy; you are my daughter. I just wanted to express the depths of my love." As his eyes filled with tears, he walked out the door.

Once again, I awoke to a powerful, booming voice saying something incomprehensible inside my very soul: "Donna, when I see you, I see red, the blood of Jesus. I see My daughter, one that I love. Take this gift and learn to stand as the righteousness of Christ. Do not live in shame or disgrace because of the past. I have forgiven you and put a new song of joy in your heart. Receive this gift so others will see My love and realize I long for them to walk in freedom too. Be a light of truth in the midst of the darkness."

In my dream, I could not bring myself to enjoy this awesome gift of love. Because of my insecurities and unwillingness to receive, Dad walked away sad and hurt. He just wanted to express his love for me. Not because I did anything special or deserved it, and not because I never made mistakes. He simply wanted to say, "Daughter, I love you."

God used this dream to show me just how much He loves His children and demonstrated that love by sending His Son as a sacrifice for our sins. When Jesus died and rose again, He purchased forgiveness, healing, and the ability to stand clean before Him through the cleansing power of His blood. When He sees His precious ones, He truly sees the blood of the Lamb. Not our shortcomings or failures.

No one is worthy of such an act of love, but He did it for us anyway.

How could I continue to hurt His heart and not receive this gift? As I lay there in a puddle of tears, the all-consuming love of God covered me like a blanket. My heart overflowed with joy and a deep humility. I once again woke Bob up to share this new revelation of God's love.

The moment I began sharing my dream with Bob, something happened I didn't expect—a holy boldness. I have never felt such determination to shake off the past. No longer would I allow my vision to be blinded and unable to see God's love and mercy. I felt free, loved, and so thankful to be a daughter of the Most High God. This new revelation sent me down a brand-new path of freedom and liberty with my Savior. By catching a glimpse into a love I will never fully understand or deserve, I began learning how to walk in the light of His truth without bondage and condemnation. This all-consuming love allowed me the freedom to grow in my relationship with Christ and live every day full of praise and gratitude to be a recipient of its life-changing power.

It is one thing to possess book knowledge but something altogether different to receive an understanding or revelation about what you are reading and studying. Having been a student of God's Word since childhood, I knew the scripture clearly states, "And all our righteous acts are like filthy rags" (Isaiah 64:6 NIV). The option to work our way into heaven is nonexistent. Truly understanding what this means and getting it from our head to our heart makes an incredible difference.

There is absolutely nothing any of us can ever do or accomplish that will make us a more worthy or acceptable recipient of God's love and mercy. This brings true equality and justice to the gift of salvation for everyone. God's requirement for receiving this precious gift is to acknowledge Jesus Christ is the Son of God, with repentant hearts seek forgiveness for our sins, and make Jesus the Lord and Savior of our lives. Once we are saved, by faith we begin the process of working out our salvation in fear and trembling.

> So then, my beloved, just as you have always obeyed, not as in my presence only, but now much more in my absence, work out your salvation with fear and trembling; for it is God who is at work in you, both to will and to work for His good pleasure. (Philippians 2:12–13 NASB)

Falling into Faith

> *Know that a man is not justified by observing the law, but by faith in Jesus Christ.* So we, too, have put our faith in Christ Jesus that we may be justified by faith in Christ and not by observing the law, because by observing the law no one will be justified. (Galatians 2:16 NIV; emphasis added)

What does it mean to work out our salvation in fear and trembling? When people hear the word "fear," they usually think in negative terms, such as being afraid, anxiety, alarm, or dread. Our heavenly Father does not operate on the principles of fear; therefore, it is important to understand what the word "fear" means in this text.

Our heavenly Father is a God of faith. When we accept Jesus Christ as our Savior, we are to walk in the fear of the Lord. Below is a definition Bob and I learned during our days in missionary school. It truly spoke to our hearts, as it brought clarity and understanding to the phrase "the fear of the Lord."

> **Strong's Dictionary:** *The Fear of the Lord* is a "Reverential fear of God, as a controlling motive of life, in matters spiritual and moral, *not a mere fear of His power and righteous retribution, but a wholesome dread of displeasing Him.* A fear which banishes the terror that shrinks from His presence."

When we walk in *the fear of the Lord*, we will work out our salvation in a reverential fear and wholesome dread of displeasing our loving and wonderful Savior. We will be inspired to seek wisdom about the choices we make in life and desire to walk in love toward God and our fellow human beings.

The Bible often compares our relationship with Christ to marriage. Isaiah 62:5 tells us the Lord rejoices over us as a bridegroom rejoices over his bride. When I think about this comparison, it causes me to reflect on my wedding day. I cannot ever remember feeling so many emotions at one time. It was incredibly scary yet wonderful. When Bob and I left for the chapel, my nerves went into overdrive. I literally shook so hard I felt like one of those big jackhammers.

You may ask, "Why?" Was I terrified of Bob, and did I dread the idea of marrying him? *No.* I trembled with excitement from the love I felt and all the expectations about our future. I also felt the weight of responsibility and sensed the importance of what was taking place. With every fiber of my being, I longed to be a blessing to Bob. I desired to be a good wife, lover, and friend. I can only imagine how Bob felt. He was about to marry a woman diagnosed with a rare cancer, and without a miracle, the future did not look too promising.

For just a moment, think about how much Jesus must love each and every one of us to suffer the shame and agony of the cross. Reflect back to the day you made a commitment to let Him into your heart. Something wonderful and frightening happened in that moment—a change, a glorious change. The day you welcomed Him into your life, He became your beloved Redeemer.

> I delight greatly in the LORD; my soul rejoices in my God. For he has clothed me with garments of salvation and arrayed me in a robe of righteousness, as a bridegroom adorns his head like a priest, and as a bride adorns herself with her jewels. (Isaiah 61:10 NIV)

> As a young man marries a maiden, so will your sons marry you; as a bridegroom rejoices over his bride, so will your God rejoice over you. (Isaiah 62:5 NIV)

> Let us rejoice and be glad and give him glory. For the wedding of the Lamb has come, and his bride has made herself ready. (Revelation 19:7 NIV)

When we walk in the fear of the Lord, it builds a powerful and miraculous relationship between us and our Creator. As Children of God, we have the right to boldly approach the throne of grace and make our petitions known to our heavenly Father. In turn, our lives will produce a harvest of blessings and become a testimony for all to see.

Becoming a Christian does not mean we will never make mistakes or we can somehow work hard enough to deserve what Christ did for

Falling into Faith

us on the cross. We will never be good or saintly enough to merit His beautiful gift of unconditional love and mercy. It also does not mean we can sloppily live our lives in a destructive way, expecting God's mercy and grace to come to our rescue and cover our sins when we are not truly repentant to begin with.

Yes, if with a repentant heart we ask for forgiveness, God will forgive. However, true repentance means to turn from the path of disobedience and walk the straight and narrow. In other words, *walk in the fear of the Lord*. The precious blood of Jesus is not a free ticket for us to continue sinning and expect blessings and favor to overtake us. The following scriptures bring clarity and truth concerning the attitudes and actions of a true believer.

> No one who is born of God will continue to sin, because God's seed remains in him; he cannot go on sinning, because he has been born of God. *This is how we know who the Children of God are and who the children of the devil are: Anyone who does not do what is right is not a Child of God; nor is anyone who does not love his brother.* (1 John 3:9–10 NIV; emphasis added)

I pray these lessons from furniture have given you a glimpse into the mercy and love God has for us, along with the blessings that come from being His child. It is hard to imagine a love this pure and unconditional, but it is real, and it is for all who are willing to believe and receive.

I've been cancer-free for over twenty years, and it truly is a miracle. As a hospice chaplain and cognitive behavioral therapist, I have seen suffering and experienced many things I cannot explain or understand. At the end of the day, I have to make a decision to give it to God and trust Him with these mysteries. I'm called to bring comfort while speaking words of truth, love, and peace over my patients. The end results belong to God.

Starting today, speak God's truth over your life. Stop allowing the enemy to consume your mind with guilt and condemnation over your past or anything else. You are a child of God, and the precious blood of the Lamb covers your sins. You are gloriously and amazingly forgiven.

There is no place in your God-given brain and heart for issues of rejection and low self-esteem. These are lies of the enemy and traps to keep you beat down and prevent God from accomplishing everything He longs to do in and through you.

In closing, I want to leave you with a few Greek definitions of three words: atonement, righteousness, and justification. Take time to read Romans, chapters 3 and 4. As you read and study, keep these definitions in mind and meditate on the scriptures. Some of our kids have a saying when they are describing something amazing: "This will rock your world." Trust me, it most definitely will.

1. **Atonement:** Our wrath taker; hilasterion—meaning; an overflowing, overwhelming, out-of-control love.
2. **Righteousness:** Perfectly measured up to God's standard or right standing with God.
3. **Justification:** A declaration that a person is righteous.

"The fear of the LORD is the beginning of knowledge,
But fools despise wisdom and instruction" (Proverbs 1:7 NKJV).

CHAPTER 21

IT'S TIME TO GET YOUR PRAISE ON

Over the next year, we witnessed God's restoration power and many changes. A new corporation bought out the cellular company I worked for, which resulted in a huge pay cut. No worries. God's good plans for our lives continued manifesting. A major corporation in town offered me a position in one of their call centers, with double the salary plus commission. There is truly no way to out-give God.

My new job opened many doors of opportunity to testify about Jesus's power to heal the sick and restore the broken. I also met other Christians in the workplace, and together we became a powerful army, claiming the call center as our mission field. God's amazing grace sprang into action as we witnessed salvation and miracles, right there in corporate America. I'm so grateful for the friends God blessed me with during that time. Over the years, they have continued to be a blessing and encouragement in our lives.

Financially, things were booming. We purchased property with plans to build a house. God blessed Bob with many talents, especially in the area of construction. With very little help, he built our home, and within nine months, we moved in.

Before putting up the Sheetrock, I wrote scriptures of healing and blessings on the walls, floors, and above the doors. Around our pool, I wrote scriptures of protection and joy. God's promises literally surrounded us in every room of the house and throughout the entire property. People often commented on how peaceful our home felt.

Along with the excitement of a beautiful home and new beginning, came a strength and ever-present attitude of praise and worship. We were learning the abundant joy and amazing rest that comes from placing complete trust in Christ.

> And hope does not disappoint us, because God has poured out His love into our hearts by the Holy Spirit, whom He has given us." (Romans 5:5 NIV)

During this transition period, God directed us to "The Harbor" in Holley, Florida. The pastor and his family were longtime friends. In fact, they produced the album I recorded years earlier when I turned eighteen. The entire family's musical talents and abilities are known around the country, and they have recorded albums for numerous Christian artists. Pastor Greg's motto was "Our mission is fishing." We truly appreciated his faithful support, and his heart for the lost was an inspiration to us. Through the years, our friendship grew in love and admiration.

Once again, the Lord positioned us in a place of quiet and rest as He prepared to move us up to another level in our Christian walk. One of my heart's desires was to be healed of hand tremors and blood pressure problems without taking pills every day, but several physicians advised me I would suffer a chemical imbalance and other physical complications without the medication. Doctors and medicines are not sinful or wrong; however, over the years, it proved easier at times to rely on their abilities instead of God's power to heal. After facing cancer and seeing God move so powerfully, I knew in my heart the Lord wanted to increase my faith walk in a greater way concerning this issue. Some strongholds take longer to break free from than others. This victory was going to cost my flesh something, but if I held on to God's Word and trusted the Lord, the benefits would outweigh the sacrifice.

Unfortunately, flesh ruled my life for a very long time in this area; therefore, bringing it under total submission to the spirit of the living God who dwelled within me would not be easy. Regardless of the difficulties, I purposed in my heart not to give up or cave in under the pressure.

The enemy quickly attacked by replaying the many years I spent in a fog of confusion with constant tremors and severe headaches. Tired of his annoying attempts to dampen my faith, I decided to show him a

Falling into Faith

thing or two. I went off the medication cold turkey. I made the mistake of presuming since God healed me of cancer, everything else would be a piece of cake. Once again, I fell into the old pattern of presumption instead of prayerful wisdom and patiently waiting on God.

It wasn't long before my head began pounding and my mind felt like it short-circuited. I sat in my glider rocking back and forth, yelling out healing scriptures like a crazy woman. Thank heavens no one came lurking around peering through the window at that moment. I'm sure they would have called 911 and reported a deranged woman. Bob soon arrived home and came to my rescue. As I sat incessantly rocking and explaining to him what was going on, Bob made a very wise suggestion, "Baby, maybe your faith is not big enough just yet to go cold turkey. It needs to grow. Why don't you take half now and, as your faith grows, steadily decrease the medication." Wow! What an awesome revelation. I just needed to take some baby steps and keep growing my faith.

This lesson continues to ring true today. We must never stop growing in the Word and faith, regardless of everything we have overcome by God's grace and mercy. Yesterday's victories will not sustain us. It is vital to keep the soil fed and regularly watered. We are all given a measure of faith, but God didn't intend for it to remain the same, day after day and year after year.

Listening to Bob's wise counsel, I cut the dosage in half and set out on a new and deeper faith-growing adventure. Within a month, I was off the medication altogether with no negative side effects. Victory at last. A few weeks later, I came home with a blinding headache. I knew I had been delivered, but the pain would not go away. Bob suggested I go upstairs and get alone with God. He encouraged me to begin praising Him for any and everything I could think of. I immediately knew in my heart this was the right thing to do, so I sprang upstairs and got my praise on.

Lying across the bed in one of our guest rooms, I starting singing praises and worshipping God. I thanked Him for everything I could think of, rejoicing in His power of restoration and blessings in our lives. In the midst of praying, God gave me a vision of a broken television. In bold letters on the front was the name of the manufacturer. In one of the most humbling moments of my life, I heard these words, "Donna, if you tried everything and could not fix this TV, what would you do?"

I immediately responded, "I would call the company that made the television."

After my response, I heard the Lord speak this deep within my soul, as it seemed to penetrate every cell of my being, "I created you, I will fix you, but will you trust Me?"

Sensing the very presence of the living God, without hesitation I quickly replied, "Yes, Lord, I trust You."

Although the pain continued for a while, a spirit of joy burst forth like a fountain as I enjoyed a sweet and glorious time of fellowship with the Father. Before long, the pain disappeared. These lessons in praise and trust have become a treasured gift. My prayer is for others to discover the power that comes when we place our complete trust in God, and practice this praise principle.

When the battle is raging all around us, praise is one of the greatest weapons we have at our disposal. With authority in Jesus Christ, we should boldly speak forth God's truth as we offer praise and gratitude for His love and mercy. Even if we have to speak it in fear, trembling, and pain. In our weakness, God will be our strength. A minister I often listen to made a statement I love, "Instead of telling God how big your problems are, tell your problems how big your God is." In the middle of the storm, remembering to do this delivers victory.

God continued to teach us the importance of a growing faith. Every time I grew anxious and thought about what the doctor said would happen if I stopped taking the medication, I gave it to the Lord. One day I came across a scripture in Isaiah that put everything in perspective, "Stop trusting in mere humans, who have but a breath in their nostrils. Why hold them in esteem?" (Isaiah 2:22 NIV). The doctors are mere humans. I appreciate their wisdom, but God delivers the final say. He is the Great Physician.

Miraculous victories manifest when we are tested, tried, and matured. Only then will we develop the kind of faith Mary exemplified when she said, "Be it unto me according to Thy Word" (Luke 1:38 KJV). A faith that continually praises God in thanksgiving as it waits and rests in His ability and power, regardless of the circumstances.

> You dear children are from God and have overcome them, because the One who is in you is greater than the one who is in the world. (1 John 4:4 NIV)

> Consider it pure joy, my brothers, whenever you face trials of many kinds, because you know that the testing of your faith develops perseverance. Perseverance must finish its work so that you may be mature and complete, *Not lacking anything.* (James 1:2–4 NIV; emphasis added)

Feeling victorious and a little wiser, I decided to go into battle again. This time I sought God for deliverance from monthly hormone shots. The pills did not absorb properly in my system, so for years I had been receiving injections. Concerned about the dangerous side effects, I prayed for another miracle.

If you suffer with power surges (commonly referred to as hot flashes), you appreciate the benefits of hormone therapy. Like any good drug, there are downsides and often serious side effects. Science has found a direct link to cancer caused by these drugs, and I believe I'm a prime example of this very fact. When I lived in New York, my doctor discovered over a ten-year period I was given 40 milligrams of Delestrogen shots once a month because my hormones were so out of balance. He was shocked, stating it should have never been more than 10 milligrams.

Every time I received an injection, it threw me into a sick headache with nausea and vomiting that lasted three days. I complained but continued to be told it was the result of receiving the hormone by shot and nothing could be done except control the symptoms with pain and nausea medications. After being diagnosed with such a rare cancer, doctors speculated this might have played a big part in the disease.

It is vitally important to educate yourselves and seek wisdom about anything we allow in our temple, because the Bible says our bodies are the temple of the Lord. Saying yes to everything that is prescribed is not wisdom. Pray, research, get a second medical opinion, and educate yourself, then you can make a wise decision.

Under the supervision of a holistic medical doctor, I stopped taking the shots and began experimenting with natural herbs and vitamins that balance mood swings, reduce hot flashes, and build up the immune system. Exercise and a good diet also became a daily part of my life (not just occasionally). I consistently began treating my body in a way pleasing to God, and His blessings enveloped me in wonderful, life-changing ways.

Any victory in this life will cost us something. If we dig in and answer the call to move up higher in God, it will be worth it. Throughout my book, you have heard me say, "Father God does not show favoritism." This statement is scriptural and true. Jesus Christ will do the same for you as He did for me or anyone else in the Bible who received a miracle. He longs to bring healing and deliverance to all who seek Him in faith and refuse to waver in doubt and unbelief. In and through Him, the weak are made strong, the poor are made rich, and the sick are made well. I pray this truth gets deeply rooted in your mind and spirit.

There is a story in the Bible the Lord brought to my attention regarding King David. In 1 Chronicles 21:1, Satan incited David to take a census of Israel. David ordered Joab and his army commanders to take a military census of all his fighting men. His actions perhaps were a source of pride, turning David's focus on humankind's ability and away from the Lord's mighty power. God wanted David to *count on and boast in His strengths and abilities alone*, not in the strength of his fighting men.

> David was conscience-stricken after he had counted the fighting men, and he said to the Lord, I have sinned greatly in what I have done. Now, O Lord, I beg You, take away the guilt of Your servant. I have done a very foolish thing. (2 Samuel 24:10 NIV)

The Lord spoke to David through Gad, the prophet. He gave him three options and told David to choose one to be carried out against him. The options were three years of famine, three months of fleeing his enemies while they pursued him, or three days of plague in the land. David thought it over and made his decision.

> David said to Gad, "I am in deep distress. *Let us fall into the hands of the Lord, for His mercy is great*; but do not let me fall into the hands of men." (2 Samuel 24:14 NIV; emphasis added)

The Lord sent a plague on Israel for the designated time. David cried out to God to spare his people and only punish him and his family. The Bible says the angel stretched out his hand to destroy Jerusalem, and the Lord was grieved. He told the angel, "Enough. Withdraw your hand" (2 Samuel 24:16 NIV). Pay close attention to God's response toward a truly repentant heart.

When the angel withdrew, it was at the threshing floor of Araunah the Jebusite. Gad told David to build an altar to the Lord on the threshing floor of Araunah, so David went up as he was commanded. When Araunah saw him coming, he went out, bowed to him, and asked King David why he was coming to see him. David advised Araunah he came to buy the threshing floor to build an altar to the Lord so the plague on the people would cease. Araunah wanted to give it to David without charge.

Meditate on the following scripture and allow what David said to penetrate your spirit with insight and wisdom. "But the king replied to Araunah, "No, I insist on paying you for it, *I will not sacrifice to the Lord my God burnt offerings that cost me nothing*" (2 Samuel 2:24 NIV; emphasis added).

There are numerous lessons to be learned from this story, but take a moment and focus on two important things David said:

1. He requested to fall into God's hands of mercy, not the hands of men.
2. David realized that God is worthy of our sacrifices and it should cost us something.

Whether we are being tested or growing our faith, the choice to fall into a trust relationship with God and allow Him to mold us into His image and likeness will cost us something. However, we can rest in the fact He is merciful, just, and full of goodness.

Donna Grant Wilcox, MTH, CBT, PhD

As Bob and I continued to be tested, we stood in awe of the blessings and benefits reaped from our obedience and desire to see more of God's power demonstrated in our lives. We purposed to stay armed and ready for whatever came our way but had no idea the many rewards from staying the course our journey would render.

CHAPTER 22

HOW BAD DO YOU WANT IT?

Jesus Christ can break the generational curses in our lives when we commit our will to Him and determine to pursue obedience, regardless of circumstances or what we perceive it will cost. It boils down to one question: how bad do you want it?

I continued to deal with occasional bladder and kidney infections, causing frustration and a lot of discomfort. God always came through, but I grew weary from the attacks. Deciding to add this to my list of things I no longer wanted to tolerate, the next request was complete deliverance and healing from these infections.

Experiencing victories like this requires sacrifice and soul searching, so we took the matter before the Lord and prayed for a total internal makeover. The road ahead turned into a path of self-awareness and positive changes. In case you are wondering, it was also painfully hard at times.

First, we looked at the medical facts: 1) a small urethra, 2) bladder and kidney problems passed down through generations on Mother's side, and 3) scarring on my left kidney caused by the diseased spleen. Giving these facts to God, we prayed for wisdom on how to proceed.

> Trust in the Lord with all your heart and lean not on your own understanding; In all your ways acknowledge Him, and He will make your paths straight. Do not be wise in your own eyes; fear the Lord and shun evil. *This*

will bring health to your body and nourishment to your bones. (Proverbs 3:5–8 NIV; emphasis added)

The next step in the process was looking at our lives through a spiritual microscope. No matter how insignificant, we searched for anything standing in the way of our prayers being answered. Within just a few days, Bob made an unwanted observation and brought it to my attention in a loving but firm way.

Every morning before leaving for work, I grabbed a Coca-Cola as I headed out the door. In fact, I kept a Coke nearby all the time, and anyone with kidney or bladder problems knows sodas are frowned upon. When Bob pointed this out, without missing a beat, I presented my argument. "Baby, I only drink a few sips, and usually the same Coke I leave with in the morning stays in my car, and at the end of the day I pour out what remains."

While this statement held fragments of the truth, I failed to fess up to everything. As we say in the South, "My man ain't no dummy." He knew I usually drank several Cokes throughout the day. Sad to say, but anyone around me for very long knew several things: Donna doesn't go anywhere without perfume and makeup, she fiercely loves God and family…and she loves her Coca-Cola.

As I continued sounding off my defense, Bob looked me in the eyes and asked a simple but powerful question, "Baby, how bad do you want it?" An alarm went off in my brain. Why did I become so defensive over something as ridiculous as Coca-Cola?

Quickly realizing I needed deliverance from this crutch and addiction, I decided to go on a fast from my beloved soft drink. Doing without food was not difficult for me, but giving up Coke meant serious business.

To some, this may seem small and ludicrous, but it is the seemingly small things in life that often become the disabling and destructive strongholds. "Catch for us the foxes, the little foxes that ruin the vineyards" (Song of Songs 2:15 NIV).

Growing up, I remember typing sermon notes for Dad on "The Little Foxes." I never fully understood or appreciated his message until God began revealing the little foxes in my own life. When we give the Lord permission to prune and cut away things that hinder or hurt growth (spiritually, emotionally, or physically), He shines a spotlight on every area preventing us from becoming and accomplishing every good thing He has prepared. He longs for His sons and daughters to be fully equipped, powerful, and "lacking no good thing." Throughout the process, we have the choice to take heed and obey or ignore His instructions and suffer the consequences. Our decisions and actions determine and reveal an important fact—how bad we really want it.

You may wonder why I didn't stop drinking Coke years earlier. Short and simple, my flesh ruled. Before you pass judgment, allow me to point out a few little foxes that may be spoiling your vine. Ask yourself the following questions and keep in mind God already knows the answers. We must admit the truth before healing and change can begin.

1. What consumes your life to the point you refuse to do without it, regardless of what it costs your spirit, health, family, church, friends, finances, or emotional stability?
2. Are you praying for God's help in an area of your life yet are unwilling to help yourself due to a lack of self-control, discipline, or slothfulness (laziness)?
3. Do you say you want to pray and read your Bible more but cannot find time, yet you always have time for your favorite sports or television shows? Ouch!
4. Could you turn your television off for a week or even a day and use that time to fellowship with God and your family with a Christlike and joyful attitude?
5. What would you have to give up in order to set aside thirty minutes (or an hour) each day in prayer, Bible reading, and communing with God? Just as important, are you willing to do it?
6. Do you pray for God's help with a weakness or addiction yet continue to hang out with old friends or acquaintances who participate in those same activities?
7. Are you defensive about why you do what you do, using excuses and tolerating negative things in your life that are clearly not God's best for you and contrary to the truth in His Word?

Here are some examples of popular excuses we often use:

- God made me this way; surely He does not expect me to change.
- So and so hurt me, and it was not my fault. Because of them, I am a victim and will have to live like one for the rest of my life. It is my cross to bear.
- I am just like my mother/father; everyone knows you can't fight heredity.

These are all lies and traps of Satan. They are devised to destroy and quench the spirit of the living God from breathing life and truth into our situation.

Take inventory today. As you meditate on these things, ask the Holy Spirit to reveal the little foxes in your life and stop allowing the enemy's lies to hinder your prayers. Although it is painful, give the Holy Spirit permission to prune these destructive branches away. When Satan tries to bring them back, resist and draw near to God. You will be amazed at the fruit just waiting to burst forth. Your life will never be the same; it will be worth it all.

As each day passed with no Cokes, my spirit felt stronger. I determined to change and do whatever it took to walk in divine health. Before long, the issue no longer held me captive, and I learned the importance of moderation. It is a beautiful thing. My beverage of choice today is Dr. Pepper; however, wisdom must be adhered to or trouble will surely follow.

Our bodies are the temple of the Lord, and we control what enters them. My bladder and kidneys simply responded to the law of sowing and reaping and produced infections. Although Coke was not the only culprit, it held the strongest grip on me.

Through this experience and willingness to become obedient in all things, the Holy Spirit began revealing other hindrances in the healing process, and I made the necessary changes. I purposed to use wisdom in all matters pertaining to my spiritual, emotional, and physical well-being. Am I always successful? No. However, I no longer tolerate and allow negative and damaging things to take up residence as I once did.

"Everything is permissible—but not everything is beneficial. Everything is permissible—but not everything is constructive" (1

Corinthians 10:23 NIV). Paul is talking about a believer's freedom in this scripture. Although we can apply it to many things in our lives, I found it particularly appropriate in reference to the Coca-Cola situation. Just because it is permissible does not make it beneficial or constructive. Many times, people scolded me about drinking soft drinks, knowing the effects it has on the bladder and kidneys. I am sure they were not the least bit surprised when I continued to have problems and my prayers were not answered.

There are varying opinions in church and society as a whole concerning other issues, such as the subject of drinking. Alcoholism in America is one of the main contributors to abuse, death, and divorce. Knowing the adverse and devastating effects of alcohol, every human being (not just Christians) should be exceptionally careful. We must love others enough to lay down our rights, even if we do not feel it is wrong. If a friend or acquaintance does not believe in drinking or refrains from it for personal reasons, do not invite them to your home and serve wine. It is just that simple.

Don't be a selfish, self-absorbed person. Consider others before yourself in these matters. Bob's father was an alcoholic; therefore, his views on the subject are from personal experience. He has seen the devastation firsthand substance abuse and addiction brings. Bob has wonderful memories of his father, but there is also a great deal of pain associated with many of his memories.

Being raised in a minister's home, I recall countless times Dad trekked out all hours of the night to deal with a situation involving alcohol-related incidents. It is truly heartbreaking. As believers, we must be keenly aware of the impact our Christian walk has on those around us. Knowing this, Paul goes on and instructs us to be careful not to judge one another by what is right or wrong according to our conscience and admonishes us not to cause anyone to stumble by what we say or do. The Bible does not always state "such and such" is a sin; however, if it is bringing harm to your temple or creating a stumbling block for anyone, we obviously shouldn't do it.

Food is another area of concern. Statistics show obesity is at an all-time high in America. We should practice moderation and balance in all things, including what we eat. Exercise must also be a part of our lives.

I often hear people complain about how hard they try to lose weight, but nothing happens. The fact of the matter is many do not exercise or change their eating habits, instead, they think a diet pill will fix the problem. Then you have those who spend a day binging because they were good for a week. This kind of behavior reminds me of a famous saying, "The definition of insanity is doing the same thing over and over and expecting different results" (Benjamin Franklin). Think about it for a moment. It goes back to a nagging but critical question: how bad do you want it?

It is hard not to smile and break out laughing uncontrollably when I think about exercise. My idea of exercise used to be buying my niece and me matching outfits for the gym. On the way to work out, I stopped and purchased magazines. When we arrived, I'd pull up a chair by the machine she was exercising on. Loud and proud, I read interesting articles to her while my sweet, beautiful niece sweated her cute tuchas off. My entire goal consisted of several important things: under no circumstance, sweat; hang out with my girl; and make sure my hair and makeup stayed intact ... Ha!

There are times I long for those days. Turning forty changed everything, requiring me to begin a love/hate relationship with exercise. "Gravity and age, why are you so cruel?" As you can see, God has His hands full with me. Not to worry; He doesn't give up on His children. Even the crazy, prissy, hardheaded ones.

After a time of walking in wisdom and making the necessary changes, infections grew fewer but did not cease. We were dealing with more than Coke; we had to break the bondage of a generational curse and stronghold. This required prayer, fasting, and a determination to hang on until the miraculous manifested.

The Bible talks about blessings and curses handed down from generation to generation. As far back as anyone could remember, kidney and bladder problems prevailed on Mother's side of the family. I intended to destroy this curse once and for all with the bondage-breaking power of Jesus Christ.

There are difficult situations in our lives requiring intercessory prayer. Someone willing to stand in the gap and pray; someone tenacious and unrelenting who refuses to give up until victory arrives. Bob interceded

Falling into Faith

on my behalf, and I'm forever grateful. When I felt weak in spirit, physically tired, and emotionally drained, he persevered.

There is a wonderful illustration of intercession in the book of Exodus. The Amalekites attacked the Israelites while they were at Rephidim. Moses instructed Joshua to choose some men and go to war. Through intercession, they won the battle.

> As long as Moses help up his hands the Israelites were winning, but whenever he lowered his hands, the Amalekites were winning. When Moses hands grew tired, they took a stone and put it under him and he sat on it. *Aaron and Hur held his hands up—one on one side, one on the other—so that his hands remained steady till sunset. Joshua overcame the Amalekites army with sword.* (Exodus 17:11–13 NIV; emphasis added)

God moves in mighty and mysterious ways when we allow ourselves to be an Aaron or Hur. I personally desire the spirit of intercession more in my life, a prayer warrior willing to stand in the gap for others. I pray you have this same desire.

Go before God with a willing spirit and open mind, but be prepared; prayer and intercession often leads to some kind of necessary action on our part. Not to worry, God is with us. "Have I not commanded you? Be strong and courageous. Do not be terrified; do not be discouraged, for the Lord your God will be with you wherever you go" (Joshua 1:9 NIV).

> The righteous cry out, and the Lord hears them; He delivers them from ALL their troubles. The Lord is close to the broken hearted and saves those who are crushed in spirit. *A righteous man may have many troubles, but the Lord delivers him from them all.* (Psalm 34:17–19 NIV; emphasis added)

CHAPTER 23

BALANCE, BOLDNESS, AND DISCOVERY

After one year of enjoying great health, I developed a serious kidney infection. Feeling confident in the steps I had taken toward walking in wisdom and taking care of my temple, I concluded doctors were no longer necessary in my life. After all the miracles God performed in my body, surely I didn't need anyone or anything else, including my holistic medical doctor. If you haven't figured it out by now, I tend to go all-in, and to the extreme at times. Doing anything halfway is usually not a thought or option.

Just thinking about ever going to the doctor again brought feelings of failure and condemnation. This should have been a big red flag. "Therefore, there is now no condemnation to those who are in Christ Jesus" (Romans 8:1 NIV). When we are burdened with condemnation, it is important to examine our heart and ask the Holy Spirit for clarity and wisdom as we seek God's truth. Remember, falling into the trap of condemnation is believing a lie, and creates unhealthy thinking.

With stubborn resistance and a rising temperature, I walked around the house every day with intense pain. Determined to overcome this, I spent hours praising God and quoting healing scriptures. I knew a kidney infection was nothing for the Almighty Physician to heal. I told Bob, "God's ways are not our ways, and I am certain He does not want me to put my body in the hands of mere humans!" Bob knew all too well the pain I endured throughout my life, due in part by trusting doctors who misdiagnosed my illness. He also knew how stubborn I was because of it. He said he wouldn't force me to go, so he believed for a miracle and continued praying and fasting. We both knew nothing is impossible with God.

In my estimation, I just needed to toughen up and hang on. After all, God does not lie, His Word is true, and He is required to do what He says. Right? The answer to that question is *yes*, if put in proper context and applied in humility. God will always be faithful to His Word; however, we must humbly seek Him for direction and not use the Bible as a tool to demand our own way and tell God what He is required to do for us.

At this point, between the pain and fever, I lost all rational perspective. The Lord was my physician, and mere humans had no right to touch me. Somehow, I envisioned every doctor who crossed my path was cleverly sent by Satan. In my mind's eye, I imagined the enemy at work in these unsuspecting men and women, causing them to lose all sense of good judgment when they encountered me in their exam rooms. Their goal consisted of diagnosing and prescribing things to bring about destruction and death. I realize this sounds a bit paranoid, but because of my past history with so many doctors, the enemy did not need any help getting me to arrive at this misguided conclusion.

I want to be clear; going to the doctor does not stop the Lord from performing miracles. When we can do something for ourselves, such as seek medical help, it is not wrong to do so. Unfortunately, at this point, no person on earth could have convinced me of that fact. Only God Himself possessed the ability to straighten out my thinking and bring a balance to my mind and life. Little did I know, there was a very important reason for this battle.

After a week, things deteriorated drastically as I struggled to stand up and the simple act of breathing caused excruciating pain. In desperation and feeling defeated, I finally turned to Bob and asked him to take me to the emergency room. He immediately jumped into action and carried me to the car.

By the time we arrived, my white cell count showed an astonishing thirty thousand. Normal is approximately five to seven thousand. After a stern reprimand from the doctor for allowing my condition to become so serious before seeking medical help, she began an intravenous antibiotic treatment and admitted me to the hospital.

A few days passed, and my kidneys were not responding to treatment.

Falling into Faith

The doctor advised Bob the prognosis did not look good and she needed to change the antibiotic. Everyone continued in prayer; even people from work called to say they were praying for me. They sent cards and letters thanking me for all the times I prayed for them, stating they were happy to return the favor. Their response blessed me beyond words. Many of them were not believers but witnessed God's favor and power through prayer in my life. I felt blessed to call them *friend*.

Knowing our faith firmly rested in the healing power of God, I questioned why I ended up in the hospital. How could God receive any glory from this situation? Why was my life once again dependent upon humans? There simply had to be a reason, but what? Although I did not understand, I trusted God to work things out for the good in spite of my obvious failure. If only I knew where I went wrong.

The Lord does not bring sickness or disease upon us; it is contrary to His character and His Word. However, He allows things to happen for a reason. Sometimes it is simply the law of sowing and reaping, and other times it may be a Job situation. Regardless of the why, as God's children, our responsibility is to trust Him, even if it means trusting without understanding. The key to victory is a spirit of unwavering faith, refusing to move away from the truth of God's Word, and a purposeful decision to fall into His merciful hands.

Days passed, and the doctor told Bob if my body did not start responding to the medication within twenty-four hours, things would take a devastating turn. Everyone waited and prayed. Approximately twenty-three hours later, my body finally began responding to the new antibiotic. God's sense of timing is quite interesting.

The doctor ordered a CAT scan and series of x-rays to determine how much damage my kidneys suffered. The test came back and miraculously showed a perfect set of kidneys. Wait just a minute. Where was the scarring on my left kidney caused by the spleen? It strangely disappeared, but that is not possible. "Jesus looked at them and said, *with man this is impossible, but with God all things are possible*" (Matthew 19:26 NIV; emphasis added).

Praise the Lord, we serve an awesome God. Sometimes we just need to wait for the "but God" to show up. He knew I avoided doctors like a plague (except for my friends who were doctors), and would never agree to a CAT scan or x-rays, although they pleaded with me to have follow-up tests after the cancer. For my good, He allowed this trial as a tool to expose the truth. When He healed me of cancer, He also healed my kidney.

Having this knowledge meant I could stop professing I had a scarred and damaged kidney. What we speak is vital in every area of our lives, and the Father found a way to get the information to my mind and heart, taking away all deception, lies, and double-mindedness. This added an additional testimony to my long list of praises filled with God's powerful blessings and miracles. The Father knows I am not shy when it comes to testifying, so getting the information to me was of utmost importance.

What Satan meant for harm God used to bring glory to His name, right thinking, and balance back into my life. I no longer believe all doctors are under the enemy's control and out to destroy me. I appreciate their contribution and pray for more of them to personally know and believe in the Lord. I also pray they seek godly wisdom as part of their protocol when diagnosing and treating patients.

Today, because of my profession, I'm surrounded by the world of psychology and medicine. Many of my closest friends are medical professionals. God truly has an interesting sense of humor and beautifully knows how to keep our mind and heart humbly in check.

Let this be a lesson to you who are stubborn, on the extreme side, and slightly wacky at times. There is hope. God knows just how to get our attention. I am thankful for His steadfast determination to mold me into a vessel capable of doing mighty things for Him. I can offer hope and encouragement to those who are struggling with sickness, pain, and confusion; teaching them about the life-changing power of the living God, along with the importance of keeping a balance.

Through every phase of our journey, Bob and I continued yearning and praying for a manifestation of the "greater works" Christ talked about in John, chapter 14, "I tell you the truth, anyone who believes in me will do the same works I have done, and even greater works, because I am going to be with the Father" (John 14:12 NIV). We longed for the greater works actively displayed more in our own lives and within the entire body of Christ. Our hearts desired to see the gifts of the Spirit at work in a powerful way, producing lasting fruit for the kingdom of God.

Blessed beyond our wildest dreams and living the good life, we were no longer satisfied. Our desires changed with each new victory. We wanted more of God and less of what money can buy, with a longing to go into all the world reaching the lost with the good news of Jesus.

Some people go through their entire Christian walk as bottle babies or toddlers. Once the Lord blesses them with "things" (friends, a good job, position in church or community, etc.), they are fully satisfied to stay right there. There is nothing wrong with material blessings and working faithfully in your church and community; however, we must continue yielding kingdom fruit and resist complacency.

Growing in the Lord and winning souls is an essential part of our daily walk with Christ. A good test to see how we are progressing in our relationship with the Lord is to examine our fruit on a regular basis. Below are a few questions to meditate on during this process.

1. When is the last time I led someone to the Lord or shared His goodness in my life?
2. Have I prayed for someone other than myself lately?
3. Have I walked close enough to God to hear His voice and feel the Holy Spirit urging me to intercede and fast for the lost, sick, or discouraged souls within my church, community, or neighborhood?
4. When the opportunity arises, am I willing to speak up and step out of my comfort zone to obey God?
5. Am I daily praying, reading the Word of God, and applying what I have learned?
6. Do I live a life of integrity and excellence in everything I put my hands to, willing to stand up for what is right according to the Bible, regardless of the cost?
7. Do I continually seek the Holy Spirit to reveal areas in my life that are not pleasing to God as I strive for a closer walk with the Father?

Meditate on these questions and allow the Holy Spirit to speak to your heart. We all fall short, but that should be the exception, not the habitual norm. Making steady progress and growing in wisdom and maturity in Christ should be our daily goal.

You may feel called to teach a Sunday school class or work with children's church. Regardless of what it is, ask the Holy Spirit to place those students on your heart. With any calling, a desire to pray for the ones God has entrusted into your hands usually follows. When those moments happen, it will be a joy, not a burden. Buckle up and get ready. You may be awakened in the middle of the night, with no rest in sight until you hit your knees in prayer for the ones you are sowing into. As you go about your daily chores, one of those precious faces may come to your mind. Don't dismiss it; stop and intercede on their behalf. In doing so, a fruitful and powerful ministry begins developing. You will no longer just be "filling a slot."

Bob and I felt a shift in our spirits. We sensed an expectancy as God opened doors of opportunity in our new church. Once again, Bob worked as a soundman, and I directed the choir. Forgive me for boasting, but our choir was anointed and filled with hearts seeking hard after God, not to mention beautifully gifted voices. People came throughout our community just to hear them sing. They blessed me more than I ever dreamed possible. Miracles and blessings came about as we lifted our voices in praise and spent time interceding for one another.

A call to full-time ministry grew heavy on our hearts. Bob felt directed of the Lord to take the next two years and get all of our affairs in order. This meant selling the business and deciding what to do with our home, property, and "stuff." We trusted the Lord to reveal His plans for us within those two years as we continued to stay the course. "Let integrity and uprightness preserve me; for I wait on Thee" (Psalm 25:21 KJV).

> Be still and know that I am God; I will be exalted among the nations, I will be exalted in the earth. The Lord Almighty is with us; the God of Jacob is our fortress. Selah. (Psalm 46:10–11 NIV)

In the midst of the waiting, the Holy Spirit spoke to me about writing my life's story. Filled with questions, I pondered on where and how to begin such an undertaking. I thought, *How do I put into words all God has done for me? Will people feel His love and presence as they read the pages of my life? Will they be encouraged or judge me for all the mistakes I've made? Could my life ever truly convey God's unstoppable desire and ability to forgive our sins and restore our lives to something of beauty, all for His glory?*

The Lord quickly reminded me of the question He asked a year earlier, "Donna, will you trust me?" I've never regretted saying *yes*, as His blessings and miracles literally began overtaking our lives. How could I do anything different now? Although terribly nervous about writing a book, I promised to be obedient. This meant writing the good, the messed up, and the not so pretty. Through it all, my desire is for healing and encouragement to flow through the pages for all who read it.

I prayed for courage and peace about telling Bob, but how do you tell your husband, "Hey, baby, I think the Lord wants me to write my story"? A week passed, and I still had not said anything. One afternoon, Bob came by the office and took me to lunch. As we sat talking in the truck, Bob said something odd. "You know, baby, we need to find some new books to read on faith." Tears ran down my face, and I began spilling everything. I shared with him what I felt the Lord directing me to do, and he quickly responded with assurance, encouraging me to be obedient and start writing. Feeling so relieved to have his approval, I thanked him for loving me and being so supportive. When I arrived home from work that day, a laptop computer and Bible disk were sitting on the kitchen counter.

Nothing is more important to a woman than the man she loves displaying faith and encouragement in the gifts and call God has on her life. A woman's gift to the man she loves is to show respect and trust in his abilities and leadership. Add on a heaping, helping portion of generosity and support, and you have the amazing.

God blesses our path with peace when we choose obedience. Regardless of our past or the obstacles ahead, His purposes will be accomplished, and His Word does not return void. His plans for us are good and full of blessings, even when we walk through pain and heartbreak. Our job is to proceed ahead in faith, refusing to give in to doubt, shame, fear, or disgrace.

As I conclude this chapter, I want to address a question we all ask at some point, "Who am I?" Through the years of falling into a faith relationships with God, I began understanding who I am and what God created me to be. Years ago, I wrote a poem in response to this question as I reflected on my own personal journey.

Donna Grant Wilcox, MTH, CBT, PhD

THIS IS WHO I AM

I am a little girl who hates being sick.
God, please heal me.
I am a teenager struggling to understand why sickness plagues my life.
Why am I alive?
I am a Christian who believes in the gifts of salvation and healing.
God, where are you?
I am only nineteen years old and will never have children of my own.
I am sad.
Why am I here?
I am a confused young woman in my twenties. All I feel is pain.
Am I being punished?
I am in my early thirties, divorced and full of shame.
Can I ever be forgiven?
I am a woman with a past: broken promises, poor choices, and painful memories.
God, please don't forsake me.
I am only thirty-five, scared and facing cancer.
I want to live.
I am a joyful woman approaching forty who was not forsaken.
Thank you, God.
I am a sinner saved by grace.
I am alive.
In Christ, I am healed and strong.
In Christ, I am happy and free.
In Christ, I am blessed and highly favored.
Because of Christ, I am restored.
I am a wife, missionary, mother, and grandmother to many.
Father God, You are so faithful.
Because of Christ, I have a testimony that I shall never cease to tell.
Who am I? Oh, I know full well.
I am the King of king's daughter.
I am loved beyond measure and accepted just as I am.
Because of the blood of Jesus, I am the righteousness of God in Christ.
This is who I am.
With all my shortcomings and imperfections, *this is who I am!*

Falling into Faith

It took many years to finally start discovering who I am in Christ. As believers, it is a process we all must go through. My journey of discovery continues, and every day God surprises me with a new revelation of His love for me—His daughter.

Oh, how desperately we strive to instill these truths into the lives of the precious ones God has brought our way. I pray they never stop searching and asking questions. To continuously seek God's truth and what His Word says about our lives is as important as food and water is to the body.

Parenting and working with young people has many rewards; however, it also delivers numerous challenges. The most common issues seem to center on the search for answers to some age-old questions, such as "Who am I? What purpose do I have? Why am I here?" The answers can be hard to find. Especially if you spend your life looking in all the wrong places.

Dietrich Bonhöeffer was a young theologian born of great promise on February 4, 1906. He was condemned to death on April 8, 1945, and executed by hanging in the concentration camp at Flossenbürg on April 9, 1945. He was one of four members of his immediate family to die at the hands of the Nazi regime for their participation in the small Protestant Resistance Movement. It has been said of Bonhoeffer, "The integrity of his Christian faith and life, and the international appeal of his writings, have led to a broad consensus that he is the one theologian of his time to lead future generations of Christians into the new millennium."

Bonhoeffer was a spiritual writer, a musician, and an author of fiction and poetry. His writings and his life have greatly influenced people. As I researched information about this man, I became intrigued and amazed. From a very young age, he seemed to grasp God's purpose for his life. While in prison, he wrote a poem titled, "Who Am I," and it is written with such honesty, yet one cannot help but feel a sense of vulnerability. The last line of his poem says, "Whoever I am, Thou knowest, O God, I am Thine." This is such a profound and powerful statement, because he realized no matter what, he belonged to God. If you research information on Dietrich Bonhöeffer's life and read his prison poems, they will truly bless and inspire you.

Bob and I desire for all the young people God has placed in our lives to know they are God's children and He is their Father (and a very good Father). The greatest gift we can give these precious jewels is to simply point them toward the truth of God's infallible Word. This is where they will find the answers to life's questions, especially when they are seeking the Lord's will and purpose.

When it comes to seeking direction for our lives and our true purpose, opinions do not really matter. Submitting our will and desires to Jesus Christ makes the difference between success and failure. Does this mean our desires and dreams are not important to God? No. He created us with certain desires, gifts, and talents for a reason. We are here to be God's instruments and walk in His blessings. In turn, we will experience joy and fulfillment. Our lives will overflow with the blessings of God and impact everyone we meet. In other words, we are blessed to be a blessing.

It is up to each individual to seek the Lord for wisdom and direction. No one can or should do it for us. When we are focused on Christ, we can walk in the confidence and determination needed to face the obstacles and challenges life throws our way while successfully pursuing and fulfilling our mission on earth.

Below are a few important scriptures in your search for the answers to the questions that often consume our thoughts and life. If you take heed, this information will change your thinking and point you to the truth. Taking a *trust fall* into the powerful hands of God allows us to fulfill absolutely everything we were created to do. The true meaning of happiness and success can be found in the following scriptures.

- I am God's child, John 1:12
- I have been redeemed and forgiven, Colossians 1:14
- I have been justified, Romans 5:1
- I am Christ's friend, John 15:15
- I am bought with a price, 1 Corinthians 6:19–20
- I am a personal witness of Christ, Acts 1:8
- I am the salt and light of the earth, Matthew 5:13–14
- I am a member of the body of Christ, 1 Corinthians 12:27
- I am free forever from condemnation, Romans 8:1–2
- I am a citizen of heaven, and I am significant, Philippians 3:20

Falling into Faith

- I am free from any charge against me, Romans 8:31–34
- I am a minister of reconciliation for Christ, 2 Corinthians 5:17–21
- I have access to God through the Holy Spirit, Ephesians 2:18
- I am seated with Christ in the heavenly realms, Ephesians 2:6
- I cannot be separated from the love of God, Romans 8:35–39
- I am established, anointed, and sealed by God, 2 Corinthians 1:21–22
- I am assured all things work together for good, Romans 8:28
- I have been chosen and appointed to bear fruit, John 15:16
- I may approach God with freedom and confidence, Ephesians 3:12
- I can do all things through Christ who strengthens me, Philippians 4:13
- I am the branch of the true vine, a channel of His life, John 15:1–5
- I am God's temple, 1 Corinthians 3:16
- I am complete in Christ, Colossians 2:10
- I am hidden with Christ in God, Colossians 3:3
- I am God's coworker, 1 Corinthians 3:9; 2 Corinthians 6:1
- I am God's workmanship, Ephesians 2:10
- The good works God has instilled in me will come to pass, Philippians 1:5–6
- I have been adopted as God's child, Ephesians 1:5; Romans 8:16–17

As you spend time in prayer and meditation, ask Jesus for a revelation of who you are in Him. Boldly state, "I am complete in Christ, and I will fulfill my purpose on this earth for the glory of God. Everything I have need of or will ever need is in Jesus Christ my Lord and Savior. In and through Him, I can do all things. Amen. So be it."

> For I know the plans I have for you, declares the Lord, plans to prosper you and not to harm you, plans to give you hope and a future. Then you will call upon Me and come and pray to Me, and I will listen to you. You

will seek Me and find Me when you seek Me with all your heart. I will be found by you, declares the Lord. (Jeremiah 29:11–14 NIV)

So is My Word that goes out from My mouth; *it will not return to Me empty; but will accomplish what I desire and achieve the purpose for which I sent it.* You will go out in joy and be led forth in peace; the mountains and hills will burst into song before you, and all the trees of the field will clap their hands. Instead of the thorn bush will grow the pine tree, and instead of briers the myrtle will grow. This will be for the Lord's renown, for an everlasting sign, which will not be destroyed. (Isaiah 55:11–13 NIV; emphasis added)

Do not be afraid; you will not suffer shame. Do not fear disgrace; you will not be humiliated. *You will forget the shame of your youth* and remember no more the reproach of your widowhood. For your Maker is your Husband-the Lord Almighty is His name-the Holy One of Israel is your Redeemer; He is called the God of all the earth. The Lord will call you back as if you were a wife deserted and distressed in spirit-a wife, who married young, only to be rejected, says your God. (Isaiah 54:4–6 NIV; emphasis added)

He settles the childless woman in her home as a happy mother of children. Praise the LORD. (Psalm 113:9 NIV)

CHAPTER 24

WATCH OUT, WORLD ... HERE WE COME

> Trust in the LORD and do good; dwell in the land and enjoy safe pasture. Take delight in the LORD, and he will give you the desires of your heart. Commit your way to the LORD; trust in him and he will do this: He will make your righteous reward shine like the dawn, your vindication like the noonday sun. Be still before the LORD and wait patiently for him; do not fret when people succeed in their ways, when they carry out their wicked schemes. (Psalm 37:3–7 NIV)

I love the outline God gives us in these scriptures to victoriously live out our dreams. He emphasizes some important things we must do as we wait and grow in Him: *trust*, dwell, delight, commit, *trust*, be still, wait patiently for Him, and do not fret. Notice *trust* is mentioned twice. After the second *trust*, it states, "and He will do this; He will make your righteous reward shine like the dawn, your vindication like the noonday sun."

What does this mean? God will make our restoration and testimony be as visible to people as the sun shining on their face in the middle of the day. What a glorious promise, and all because we choose to fall into a trust relationship with the Lord God, our Father.

As Bob and I applied these principles, the next chapter of our lives took us completely out of our comfort zone and into a new dimension of faith. Within the two years God gave us to get things in order, Bob sold his business, and the call center I worked in unexpectedly closed. Full-time ministry was on its way to becoming a reality. We sent applications to global ministries and mission organizations and soon received a phone call stating we were accepted in Youth With a Mission (YWAM).

We met with our pastor and asked for his blessing as we stepped out in faith and began preparation for our new adventure. We longed for the opportunity to sow into young people and encourage them in their purpose and call in the kingdom of God while spreading the good news to the world of Christ and His healing power.

During our meeting, our pastor shared a word he received from the Lord as he prayed for us. He did not know it at the time, but he said the same words the angel spoke in my hospital room when I was nineteen years old and doctors prepared my parents to say goodbye to their daughter. With tears in his eyes, the pastor looked at me and said, "Many children will pass through your arms and be blessed. God will not allow you to leave this world until you fulfill His will and purpose for your life." Then looking at both of us, he went on to say. "God has been preparing you both for such a time as this." Overcome with emotion and unable to utter a word, Bob and I sat hand in hand, crying.

Even with these confirmations, we were not without challenges. Before leaving, Polly (my stepmom) suffered diabetic complications and passed away. Heaven gained another jewel. Dad seemed to be handling it well but needed our support. He had a large five-bedroom home with a swimming pool, too much house for just one person.

My niece, her husband, and two children were experiencing some major changes in their lives, so they decided to leave Indiana and move in with Dad. They felt called to the mission field, so this enabled them to itinerate, raise support, and spend quality time with Papa while waiting on the Lord to open the right doors. Amanda absolutely adored her Papa, and loved the sunshine and Florida beaches. Papa loved his grandbaby and great-grandbabies. It was perfect timing. Knowing he would be surrounded by so much love and support gave us a comforting peace about leaving for missionary school.

God continued to beautifully orchestrate His plans, and everything fell into place. Traci graduated from high school with honors and was accepted in the nursing program at Auburn University in Alabama. This

Falling into Faith

gave Bob peace about leaving his little girl, who was a beautiful young lady about to set out on a new adult adventure of her own.

Two weeks prior to leaving, I suddenly came down with a bladder infection. I did not want to go to the doctor, but if the symptoms persisted, it was inevitable. In our hearts, we knew this was a test.

Going into missions often means living in communities where hospitals are unsanitary and doctors are not always reliable. The right medications can be hard to come by, and it is a huge step of faith for someone who has experienced serious health issues. The enemy desperately tried to knock me down and keep me there in an effort to get our eyes focused on the good and comfortable life. He is cunning and deliberate in his attempts to stop the love of Christ from being shared to a hurting world. Wanting us to shrink back and change our minds, I couldn't help but say out loud, "Have you forgotten who my Father is?" Venting can be very therapeutic when properly executed.

His plans failed miserably; instead, they created an unrelenting determination in our hearts to walk the path of obedience and trust God. One morning, Bob looked at me and said, "Baby, maybe we should try something different and go on the offense. Tell the devil to bring on the symptoms. As he tries to afflict you, purpose to go out and talk to anyone you meet about Jesus. Tell them about all the healings and miracles God has done for you. We will get him where it hurts." Then Bob reminded me of an important scripture in Revelation, "They triumphed over him by the blood of the Lamb and by the word of their testimony; they did not love their lives so much as to shrink from death" (Revelation 12:11 NIV).

Wow! I cannot explain it, but my spirit jumped and caused me to spring into immediate action. Fearing past health issues no longer held me captive. At that moment, I realized if I died on the mission field while telling others about Jesus, at least I would leave this earth giving something in return for all the Lord had done (and continues to do) for me. God brought me this far; He would victoriously take me all the way.

With that in mind, I got on the phone and called three of my dearest friends who were faithful and committed to the Lord. I began the conversation like this, "If illness ever interferes with my ability to minister, Bob or I will get in touch with you." Then I asked each of them a question, "Will you intercede on my behalf and hit the streets telling others how Jesus miraculously healed me of cancer and any other testimony you want to share, until I am able to continue the work God called me to do?" Without hesitation, they all said *yes*. After hanging up the phone, I expressed loudly and with authority in Jesus's name, "Devil, the battle lines are drawn. Go ahead and bring it on but you will be sorry. Not only will I boldly testify for Jesus with every pain and symptom, but my friends are also prepared to go for me!" Numbers are powerful in the spirit realm.

We went to bed that night full of hope, but I awoke the next morning feeling worse. This just instilled a stronger sense of stubborn determination. I dressed, kissed my husband, and headed out the door, exclaiming, "I'm off to witness for Jesus. The devil must have thought we were kidding." Bob gave me a big hug as I got in the car and drove away. I immediately felt impressed to go to the hospital and knew it must be God, because at the time it was one of my least favorite things to do. When you spend half your life in a hospital, it isn't somewhere you want to go intentionally.

Proving God has a sense of humor, my current career means going to hospitals are part of my life, and I appreciate the opportunity to visit someone who is suffering. Hospitals no longer bother me at all. You see, God restores *all things* when you allow Him to be the Lord of your life.

Making a quick detour, I went by a Christian bookstore and bought crosses with the sinner's prayer printed on them and scripture cards filled with God's promises and blessings. Within minutes, I sat in the hospital parking lot telling the devil just how sorry he would be before the day was over.

Entering the hospital and armed with all my goodies, a nurse stopped and asked if she could help me (I apparently looked lost). I asked her if she knew of any patients who needed someone to talk with or wanted prayer. Giving a condensed version of my testimony, she quickly ushered me down the hall to a room and stated, "You can start here. Everyone on this floor could use some encouragement." Then she said, "Stay on this floor. The rules have changed, and you might get in trouble if you go anywhere else."

The Holy Spirit prepared the way as I entered each room. The

Falling into Faith

patients were kind and receptive, expressing appreciation for the gifts I left with them. Although most of them did not know Jesus as their Savior, they welcomed prayer and listened as I shared my healing testimony.

Something wonderful happened as I went from room to room praying and testifying about the goodness of the Lord. The pain, burning, and pressure in my bladder and lower back gradually subsided. By the time I finished praying for everyone on that floor, the pain left. It absolutely and completely disappeared.

I stepped outside the hospital doors completely healed and feeling victoriously refreshed. As I walked toward the car and passed the emergency room entrance, something inside my spirit said, "You aren't finished yet." I was having so much fun messing with the devil and getting points in for the good guys that I stopped, backed up, and went into the ER waiting room.

A young couple was sitting by the nurse's station, and they were quite a remarkable sight. Both of them were covered in tattoos along with numerous piercings: eyebrows, lips, nose, and Lord only knows what else. A normal person might have felt a little afraid or intimidated to strike up a conversation and boldly ask, "May I pray for you?" Not me. By this time, I felt like taking on an army.

I sat down and proceeded to share my testimony of how God healed me of cancer. Looking them in the eyes, the love I felt was palpable as I passionately explained God's power to redeem and restore lives. Before I could even finish, tears streamed down their faces, and this precious young man asked me to pray for his brother. He said something was wrong and the doctors could not figure out the problem. I immediately took their hands and began praying. Standing up to leave, I handed them a cross and scripture card, encouraging them to read the Bible and talk to God. I assured them of His ability to hear and answer prayer. They nodded in agreement, thanked me, and shook my hand. Just so we are clear … Mama Donna gives hugs, so they both received a great big one.

Looking around, I realized there were only two other people in the emergency room, a little girl and her mother. The child loudly asked, "Mom, can she pray for me?" Walking over, I told the young woman I'd be happy to pray for her daughter. She seemed a bit reluctant, but the little girl persisted. (I love children.)

I briefly went over my healing testimony again (assuming they overheard most of it already) and asked how I could pray. They were vacationing in Destin at the beach when the little girl came out of the water with red swollen whelps all over her body. There were visible, red puffy marks on her arms and legs. Probably from jellyfish stings. Taking their hands in mine, I prayed a simple prayer of faith. It just so happened I only had one cross and scripture card left. When God leads you somewhere, He always makes provision for the journey. Handing them the cross and card, I encouraged them to read the Bible and discover all the wonderful things about God and His power to heal and bless *all* who believe in Him. This sweet little girl sat mesmerized, hanging on to every word. She reached up and gave me a great big hug. God is so good.

I sat in the parking lot crying tears of joy as I called Bob on the cell phone and shared what God had accomplished in those few hours. He was ecstatic. It boosted our faith in such a real and tangible way. We grew even more excited about what the future held, knowing the Father would take good care of us regardless of what hardships lay ahead.

Even though we felt we were leaving Florida for good, we weren't sure what to do about our beautiful home. Should we rent or sell? After praying and seeking the Lord for guidance, we decided to rent it out for the time being, and we were blessed with great tenants. God's timing is always perfect. Years later, we sold our home and God's wisdom guided us through the process, along with His blessings.

With days left to go, countdown began as we sold and gave away the few earthly possessions remaining. Watching our WaveRunner and my little red Corvette leave with complete strangers left me feeling anxious and hollow; however, saying goodbye to our sweet dog, Blondie, was the most devastating task. Thankfully, she went to a loving family from our church.

The day came to leave our house for good. Bob packed every inch of our Chevy Avalanche to capacity. We were about to get in the truck and head out when a Schwan's ice-cream delivery man stopped and asked if we wanted some ice cream. I immediately began to cry and said, "We don't even have a home anymore. Where in the world are we gonna put ice cream?" It finally hit me; we were homeless for the first time in our lives.

Bob said his heart hurt for me. I began crying to the point of almost hyperventilating, but it soon turned to laughter when I recalled the look on that poor man's face. He didn't know what to say or do. As he got back in his truck and left, we glanced up at the Avalanche and realized something even funnier; we looked like the *Beverly Hillbillies*. In fact, Bob had my favorite rocking chair tied to the bed of the truck. I was Granny, and he was Jed Clampett.

Regaining my composure, God brought a scripture to mind, and we both cried and held hands as I quoted it out loud, "And everyone who has left houses or brothers or sisters or father or mother or children or fields for My sake will receive a hundred times as much and will inherit eternal life" (Matthew 19:29 NIV).

We spent a week with Dad before embarking on our new adventure far, far away. The gorgeous beaches surrounding us would soon be a distant memory. Bob dreamed of one day living in the mountains, and we were heading off to the middle of the Sangre de Cristo Mountains, located in beautiful Colorado, to begin training for a life in missions.

Mountain living has some great advantages; it is much cooler with less humidity than the South. Not to mention, we just happened to love snow skiing. The location put us close to some of our favorite places, with the added privilege of looking out at God's "purple mountain majesty" every single day.

After arriving at the mission's base, God moved miraculously on our behalf, giving us numerous confirmations concerning our move. Almost immediately, He continued fulfilling the promise He gave me years earlier by adding more children to our family from all over the world.

In the Bible, God established a new identity for Abram and Sarai. He changed Abram's name to Abraham, meaning "father of a multitude" and Sarai's name to Sarah, meaning "mother of nations." At the Youth With a Mission's base (aka The YWAM Pondo Base) and every place we've lived since, God permanently changed my name to "Mama Donna." In my heart that means "answered prayer."

Our missions work first took us to Mexico. Traveling outside of the United States opened our eyes to the poverty and pain of so many beautiful people scattered about trying to survive on the streets in barrios, slums, and villages. You truly cannot comprehend just how extravagant and spoiled we are in America until you spend time working and living among the poor and hurting from other nations.

God used Bob's talents and gifts in construction to build numerous homes and churches, a medical clinic in the poverty-stricken barrios of Juarez, and a three-story leadership school dormitory in Chapala, Mexico. Chapala Leadership School is a place for young missionaries from every nation to come together. They learn techniques and ways to go into the darkest and most unreached places of the world, sharing the hope of Christ and ministering to the needs of people on a practical level.

The clinic we built in Mexico offers medicines and medical attention to those who cannot afford it. Students and professionals from the United Sates go across the border to volunteer their time and services. The time we spent in the poor areas of Mexico prepared us for what we encountered in India.

On my dad's side of the family, we have an abundance of preachers and evangelists. And then there is David Grant. David is one of my first cousins, and he is like a brother to me. In fact, his sister Gloria and I are very close; she too is like a sister—not just first cousins. Their dad (Rev. Curtis Grant) was a minister and my father's oldest brother. He passed away a few years ago. David not only became an evangelist, but he chose the life of a missionary.

God called David to a very mysterious land—Kolkata, India (formerly called Calcutta). Some of my fondest childhood memories consisted of visits David made to our church when he came back to the States to itinerate for his missionary work. A dynamo when he preached, David never stood still. It was exciting. He shared stories about his many adventures in Kolkata and how God used him (and others) to spread the hope of Jesus to the lost and hurting. Just a little girl at the time, David's heart for India birthed a longing in me for missions. Little did I know, God planned to bring that dream full circle.

During one of David's visits to our church, my girlfriend and I knelt down in front of the pew where we were sitting and gave our hearts to the Lord; I was eight years old at the time. I always loved the Lord and felt his presence in my young life, but it was the first time I actually asked Jesus Christ to forgive my sins, come into my heart, and become

Falling into Faith

Lord of my life. As I reflect back on that moment, I still remember the overwhelming feeling of love I experienced when I prayed that day. God's unconditional love sustained me during the hard years to follow and continues to do so today.

Throughout my life, one prayer is engraved upon my heart, which I pray often, "Dear God, before I die, I want to make sure others know Jesus loves them. Help me make a difference." Never the shy one, sharing the love of Christ has always remained a priority, whether it was during one of my hospitals stays, at school, or in my community. Years later, it became a sustaining and motivating reason to live.

God performed the miraculous in my life on numerous occasions, but I can honestly say the thought of sharing and testifying of God's miracle-working power outside the United States, much less beyond the southern states, seemed improbable. For one thing, I was told many times it would take a miracle for me to see another year; yet years kept coming and going. We serve a great, big, wonderful God.

I recall thinking how brave my cousin David must be. My ever-present health issues allowed me to only daydream of doing the things he accomplished for Christ in such an impoverished, faraway land. At that time, the small amount of faith I clung to was weak and battered. Every day presented a new obstacle and challenge to overcome, but God knew a secret. He knew one day His daughter would learn how to grow a faith beckoning and believing for the impossible.

During the years Bob and I served as missionaries, God fulfilled a childhood dream and eventually led us to India. Our days in India were incredibly rewarding. Yes, the overwhelming poverty and despair we saw on a daily basis proved hard, but then life is hard regardless of geography. We walked to work every day alongside all kinds of animals—cows, pigs, donkeys, camels, and the list goes on and on. But sometimes we rode to our destination in a rickshaw.

Riding in a rickshaw was one of my favorite things to do; however, being southern, blonde, and a fair-skinned woman in India made it humorous and challenging. The drivers seemed to have a difficult time figuring out where I wanted to go. MG Road is where all the popular shops were in the city, and they could not understand why I did not want to go there.

Most Indians we encountered believe all Americans are rich and spend their days shopping. Regardless of where I asked the driver to take me, he usually smiled and said, "Ah, MG Road. I take you there." I smiled back and replied, "Nay, nay, no, no," and then proceeded to speak the name of the street slowly and clearly (okay, as clear as a southern woman can talk). When that failed, I said the name of the street really fast, hoping it might make a difference. No such luck. After a few exasperating attempts, they usually flashed another smile and once again responded with, "Ah, MG Road. I take you there." It often proved easier to walk a few miles than explain shopping wasn't my desired destination.

Our mission's work in India consisted mainly of discipleship. Bob worked with a precious Christian Indian man who is a mechanical engineer. They traveled around the city networking and building relationships with other business owners due to an export company our host missionaries started as a means to work with and among the Indians. Through this initiative, it not only provided jobs for the locals but built trust and opened many doors to share the message of Christ.

I assisted the host missionary in writing a business plan for his projects, and worked at a candle shop the family started in an effort to reach out to women. The candle shop provided jobs for widows, ex-prostitutes, women escaping a life of human trafficking, as well as those with HIV/AIDS. They learned a trade and received a salary, thus helping them provide for their families and get off the streets or escape difficult circumstances. God also used Bob's welding talents to create an amazing candle holder for dipping long taper candles. Motels purchased these for weddings and special occasions. The women were so talented and created beautiful artwork on each candle we made, very similar to the henna hand designs.

Through these business initiatives, doors were opened for discipleship and Bible studies. I spent one-on-one time with each of these precious women on a daily and weekly basis. I counseled them and shared the power Jesus Christ has to heal and restore broken and hurting lives.

Several of the women from the candle shop (and their children) came to live at the House of Hope. The House of Hope offered them a home filled with love. They received discipleship and instructions on safe, sanitary, and practical living applications. We also provided medicines for those suffering with HIV/AIDS. Some of the women who lived there did not work at the candle shop, so I set aside a time to disciple and counsel with them as well.

Sitting and talking with those beautiful women about Jesus became the thing I looked forward to the most. We saw God move in amazing and miraculous ways. Bob and I made a decision to provide each of them with a Bible in their own language. We were fortunate, because in Pune it was not difficult to find Bibles in Hindi. This is not the case for many of our missionaries serving in other countries around the world. There are times my heart literally aches for the precious people the Lord brought into our lives from the countries we served in.

We long for the day we can once again laugh and pray with them face-to-face. Until then, we will continue to intercede on their behalf, lift a prayer covering over their lives, and help send others out to the field. I'm looking forward to a beautiful reunion in heaven. I believe everyone who is physically able needs to experience at least one mission's trip in their life. And every believer should offer some kind of support to those currently on the mission field.

One thing I pray the Lord never allows me to forget are the looks on their precious faces as the women began reading God's Word in their own language for the first time. It started a fire, a passion so strong and intense inside my heart to spread the message of hope. In those moments, I realized just how desperately important it is for believers to join forces and do whatever it takes to get the Bible translated in every language and in the hands of every man, woman, and child.

It is not enough for us to tell others what God's Word says. They must have the privilege of reading the living, breathing Word of God for themselves. All the discipleship in the world can only do so much. We absolutely must be able to leave His Word in their hands so reading it becomes part of their daily lives. As missionaries, we love to lead people to Christ and disciple them in their walk with God, but then what? What happens when we leave? We may not always be there, and they need to be armed with the sword that will divide God's truth from Satan's lies.

Reading and studying the Bible creates mighty warriors for Christ who will rise up and lead others to salvation. In turn, they become missionaries, teachers, and preachers to their own people. God's Word breathes a powerful message into their hearts; they have the power in the name of Jesus to lay hands on the sick and by faith believe for healing, as well as destroy strongholds the enemy has over their people.

Remember, the Bible is not just any old book. We are giving them the Book of Life, God's living, breathing Word. The women I discipled came from a Hindu background, and this can be a tough belief to penetrate. They readily accept Jesus but usually just add Him to their long list of gods. It takes time and God's Word to disciple them in the truth. The truth of one true God and the devastation idolatry brings, for He alone is to be worshiped and adored.

I pray I never forget their beautiful faces as they read story after story of the power God displayed over idols and gods that were being worshiped throughout the pages of His Word. This bore significant meaning to these women because they live in a culture that continues to practice the same beliefs as those from the pages of the Old and New Testament.

The following scriptures spoke to their hearts and changed a generational way of thinking for the first time in their lives. Only a living, breathing God can transform a heart, mind, and life in this way.

> So, what about eating meat that has been offered to idols? Well, we all know that an idol is not really a god and that *there is only one God*. There may be so-called gods both in heaven and on earth, and some people actually worship many gods and many lords. But for us, *There is one God, the Father, by whom all things were created, and for whom we live. And there is one Lord, Jesus Christ, through whom all things were created, and through whom we live.* (1 Corinthians 8:4–6 NLT; emphasis added)

Many of these women were daily beaten and persecuted for turning away from Hinduism and accepting Jesus Christ as their Lord and Savior. Those who went home to the slums and did not live in the House of Hope shared the abuse they endured from the hands of so-called loved ones. When they entered their homes, they were required to make a sacrifice to the Hindu gods. If they refused, numerous family members began a beating ritual. Heartbroken, tears streamed down my face as they shared their stories. One of my new precious friends wiped my tears away and with boldness said something I shall forever hold dear to my heart, "Don't cry, Auntie. Thank you for telling me about the one true God. I am happier than I have ever been."

This kind of courage and strength is undeniably a miracle only God can provide. Their determination to serve Christ regardless of the cost, combined with the power of the Holy Spirit working in their lives, can turn these slums, villages, and eventually their nation toward the one true living God. They can impact their world in ways we cannot.

Saying goodbye to my newfound family and sisters in Christ proved difficult, but I knew we were leaving them with God's powerful Word. The opportunity to disciple and teach these precious souls gave us the assurance they knew how to search through the Bible and seek truth for themselves. This knowledge brought an unexplainable peace.

Oh, how my heart longs for every missionary to experience that same peace. The peace that comes from knowing those they are called to minister to will have God's Word in their hands and in their own language. I hope this story from our days on the mission field ignites a deep desire and determination in your heart to find a way of equipping missionaries with the greatest tool on earth, God's holy Word.

As believers, there is only one choice, and that is to make this a priority in our lives. I also pray it stirs a spirit of prayer and intercession on behalf of those serving in challenging and often dangerous places around the world. We have the ability to help make an eternal difference in so many lives. This side of heaven, many of us will never know the results or the amazing ways God will use our giving and times of prayer and intercession. I want to make sure I stay focused and obedient in everything God is calling me to do on this earth while there is still time. I hope this is your prayer as well.

Earlier in this chapter, I spoke about my cousin David Grant. He has spent the majority of his life as a missionary to India, along with his wife, Dr. Beth Grant, and their two beautiful daughters and son-in-law's, (Rebecca and Tyler; Jennifer and Jonathan). David and Beth are the visionaries and cofounders of Project Rescue. Project Rescue is a member of the FAAST Alliance (Faith Alliance Against Slavery and Trafficking), in Washington, DC, that enables faith-based international organizations to collaborate in fighting sexual slavery and more effectively minister to its victims. They developed a comprehensive international curriculum called Hands That Heal to train caregivers of sex-trafficking victims.

David and Beth's ministry is strategically focused on the fight to rescue and restore victims of human trafficking and share the love of Jesus Christ to the lost and hurting. Their mission and message of hope have carried them to over thirty countries around the world. I am proud of my family and their determination to stay the course and keep their hearts focused toward the things of God. If you are not supporting a mission, please check out their website: www.projectrescue.com.

Money is a blessing to missionaries and their families, but so is intercession. Intercede on behalf of our pastors, evangelists, and missionaries at home and abroad. Intercede for those who are using their gifts all over the world to offer hope and a better life for the broken and hurting. Prayer is powerful; we must purpose in our hearts to set aside time each day to tap into that power and not only talk but listen. The Creator of all things is our Father, and He still speaks to His people today.

If you attend a church that is not focused on missions or community outreach programs, talk to your pastor. Share the desire in your heart to help those spreading the hope of Christ to a lost and dying world. Start a prayer party in your church. That's right—prayer can be a party, and a fun one at that.

There are times when we may feel the need to agonize and wail before God, but prayer does not have to be that way. Open the lines of communication and make time to simply talk with God. We can do it privately as well as in a group. He loves sweet fellowship with His children.

During prayer times, be specific, especially when you are aware of certain needs or issues. Remember, the most important ingredient in prayer is faith. Always pray in faith. If you are interceding on behalf of others (whether they are missionaries or your neighbor down the street), pray for the things you know about first. Then ask the Holy Spirit to intercede on their behalf in every area of their lives. The Holy Spirit knows how to get right to the heart of the matter.

> In the same way, the Spirit helps us in our weakness. We do not know what we ought to pray for, but the Spirit himself intercedes for us with groans that words cannot express. And he who searches our hearts knows the mind of the Spirit, because the Spirit intercedes for the saints in accordance with God's will. (Romans 8:26–27 NIV)

Accept the challenge to partner with a missionary in getting God's Word translated into every language and in the hands of every tribe and nation. I also pray a missionary is added to your monthly support and prayer list. Tell your friends and ask them to do the same.

Christians have a responsibility. People are hurting, and many have not heard the good news of our wonderful Savior. They need to know there is God who loves them and longs to be their Healer, Redeemer, Father, and Friend. He is not some obscure and distant character. We are all made in His image and likeness; therefore, the Lord feels, He sees, and He longs for a growing, nurturing, and personal relationship with every one of us. As long as our motives are pure and line up with God's Word, then we can pray in faith and know the Father is faithful to hear and answer our prayers.

> Ask and it shall be given to you; seek and you will find; knock and the door will be opened to you. For everyone who asks receives; he who seeks finds; and to him who knocks, the door will be opened. (Matthew 7:7–8 NIV)

> You do not have because you do not ask God. When you ask, you do not receive, because you ask with wrong motives, that you may spend what you get on your pleasures. (James 4:2–3 NIV)

Look beyond your own comfortable and safe surroundings and do something life-changing and eternal in the lives of others. For those of you who will raise the banner high and join this mission, thank you and God bless you.

If you are reading this chapter and have practiced a lifestyle of giving along with prayer and intercession, you are my heroes. Thank you for the example of Christ you have been and continue to be. May you experience an overwhelming increase in every area of your lives.

> Then the King will say to those on his right, "Come, you who are blessed by my Father, inherit the Kingdom prepared for you from the creation of the world. For I was hungry, and you fed me. I was thirsty, and you gave me a drink. I was a stranger, and you invited me into your home. I was naked, and you gave me clothing. I was sick, and you cared for me. I was in prison, and you visited me." Then these righteous ones will reply, "Lord, when did we ever see you hungry and feed you? Or thirsty and give you something to drink? Or a stranger and show you hospitality? Or naked and give you clothing? When did we ever see you sick or in prison and visit you?" And the King will say, *"I tell you the truth, when you did it to one of the least of these my brothers and sisters, you were doing it to me."* (Matthew 25: 34–40 NIV; emphasis added)

> Commit to the Lord whatever you do, and your plans will succeed. The Lord works out everything for His own end. (Proverbs 16:3–4a NIV)

During our time in missions, I fought to overcome quite a bit of apprehension concerning my health. While in India, as well as a two-year period we traveled back and forth to Mexico for extended periods, I enjoyed exceptionally good health. In fact, I experienced fewer problems than the young missionaries who enjoyed excellent health their entire lives. However, I did eat a burrito in the barrios that didn't taste right, and I literally pulled fur from my mouth. I am happy to report I did not get sick. Even Bob faced some struggles when we resided in India, and he commented on how God seemed to have a wall of protection around me. God is faithful.

My life has felt like a roller coaster at times, but what a privilege it is to testify of the goodness of God. The dreams I thought were forever gone the Lord resurrected in a beautiful way. The next chapter offers insight on something powerful God revealed to me during the roller-coaster years and my battle to overcome cancer. It profoundly changed my thinking as I developed a healthy and productive mind-set.

In time, our mission field changed but not the mission. Being a missionary is truly never about geography. The greatest joy you will find in life is learning the value of growing where you are planted.

Above all, I pray you are encouraged to dig deeper. Take God out of the box of traditions or what you have been told ministry and missions should look like. We are all different, and our gifts can be used in amazing and nontraditional venues when we allow God to be God and let Him choose the direction.

CHAPTER 25

WHY WE STRUGGLE

Have you ever asked yourself, "Why do I struggle?" It is a great self-evaluating question. In order to overcome life's trials and grow in our walk with God, it an important question to ponder and meditate on. This chapter came about because I dared to ask that very question, and God sent me down an eye-opening road of discovery. Come along as I share a valuable life lesson that revolutionized my thinking and solidified my purpose.

Let's begin this journey examining the life of Saul of Tarsus, who after a radical conversion became Paul the apostle. He once persecuted Christians and vehemently opposed the disciples of the Lord. He was considered the worst of the worst. But wait ... God still loved him and had a glorious redemption plan for his life. Acts, chapter 9, describes Paul's conversion, and what an amazing example and glimpse into God's grace and mercy. The Lord intricately worked every detail out in Paul's life in order to redeem the hardest of hearts and get the good news of Jesus Christ spread to both the Jews and Gentiles.

In Acts, chapter 19, Paul arrives in Ephesus, and his journey is filled with many things—some bad, some incredible. Here are just a few things he encountered: daily hindrances, pain, prison, people plotting against him, miracles, kingdom fruit, and an unwavering, resolute commitment to serve Christ regardless of the cost.

To understand what Paul's journey has to do with our own struggles in life's twist and turns, we will examine his mind-set and a very important statement Paul made in verse 21. He expresses something that is on his heart. Something he must do. As you read verse 21, understand that in Greek the word "must" means something more absolute than the American definition. Greek defines the word "must" like this: *a compulsion, is a necessity (as binding), be bound by oath, be indebted.*

> Paul entered the synagogue and spoke boldly there for three months, arguing persuasively about the kingdom of God. But some of them became obstinate; they refused to believe and publicly maligned the Way. So Paul left them. He took the disciples with him and had discussions daily in the lecture hall of Tyrannus. *This went on for two years, so that all the Jews and Greeks who lived in the province of Asia heard the word of the Lord. God did extraordinary miracles through Paul*, so that even handkerchiefs and aprons that had touched him were taken to the sick, and their illnesses were cured and the evil spirits left them. (Acts 19:8–12 NIV; emphasis added)

> In this way the word of the Lord spread widely and grew in power. After all this had happened, Paul decided to go to Jerusalem, passing through Macedonia and Achaia. "After I have been there," he said, *"I must visit Rome also."* (Acts 19:20–21 NIV; emphasis added)

God moved mightily through Paul's ministry; however, it was not an easy road. He faced struggles and pain because of his boldness and determination to spread the Word of God to both the Jews and Gentiles. Although he performed many miracles in the name of Jesus, he also suffered persecution and prison. Through it all, Paul felt a compulsion, desire, and necessity to go to Rome.

What burning desire do you feel the Lord has placed in your heart about your future or present situation? Like Paul, *what must you do?* When we decide to truly trust God with our lives, it is critical to understand whatever comes our way will not keep us from our destination; instead, it is God's path and His direction toward our vision and purpose. If we continue to press into Father God and trust in His Word, then we will bring glory to His name and prepare the way for the miraculous to manifest in our lives and others.

I want to challenge you to really look at Paul's life and the obstacles he faced, all because Paul chose to walk in obedience. Then look at how he responded to those difficulties. Ask yourself a tough question: "Will I seize the moment and take every opportunity to share the love of Jesus, or waste time complaining and questioning when my path takes an unexpected and difficult turn?"

Paul felt he must to go to Rome, but how would he get there, and when? This is where things got tricky. The road God took Paul down en route to Rome was hard and filled with twists and turns, but the Father had a purpose. He strategically planned every step of the journey so that His Word would reach as many people as possible and also bring encouragement to the believers.

Scriptures tell us the spirit compelled Paul to go to Jerusalem, although he knew prison and hardships awaited him. I believe getting to Rome was never far from his mind, but being obedient to the Spirit of God consistently stayed his first priority. Read what Paul says about the journey. "And now, compelled by the Spirit, I am going to Jerusalem, not knowing what will happen to me there. I only know that in every city the Holy Spirit warns me that prison and hardships are facing me. However, I consider my life worth nothing to me, if only I may finish the race and complete the task the Lord Jesus has given me—the task of testifying to the gospel of God's grace" (Acts 20:22–24 NIV).

Paul's farewell to the Ephesian elders proved to be bittersweet. He told them they would never see him again, yet he did not waver in his determination to go. He admonished them to keep watch over themselves and all the people the Holy Spirit appointed them to oversee. He encouraged them to be shepherds of the church, which was bought by the precious blood of Christ. After a time of prayer, they wept and embraced Paul, then accompanied him to the ship waiting to take their brother far away.

The scripture tells us they were grieved the most by the thought of never seeing their beloved friend again. I can only imagine how they felt. The gospel carried a price, and they knew it all too well. On the way to Jerusalem, Paul's voyage took him to Caesarea, where he crossed paths with a prophet named Agabus. The prophet took Paul's belt, tied his own hands and feet with it, and said, "The Holy Spirit says, 'In this way the Jews of Jerusalem will bind the owner of this belt and will hand him over to the Gentiles'" (Acts 21:11 NIV).

People cried and begged Paul not to go to Jerusalem, but he responded with this: "Why are you weeping and breaking my heart? I am ready not only to be bound, but also to die in Jerusalem for the name of the Lord Jesus" (Acts 21:13 NIV). You see, Paul could not be persuaded to give up on his mission or turn away from obeying God. He may not have understood the why or how, but he knew and loved the one who called him.

The scriptures go on to tell us when Paul arrived in Jerusalem, he reported to the elders in detail the things God had done among the Gentiles through his ministry. When they heard the report, they all praised God. Paul was a chosen vessel by the Lord to carry the message of Christ to everyone, not just to the Jews. Due to his unwavering determination, this boldness eventually led to his arrest, thus fulfilling the prophecy. Let's read what happened at the time of his arrest.

> The whole city was aroused, and the people came running from all directions. Seizing Paul, they dragged him from the temple, and immediately the gates were shut. While they were trying to kill him, news reached the commander of the Roman troops that the whole city of Jerusalem was in an uproar. He at once took some officers and soldiers and ran down to the crowd. When the rioters saw the commander and his soldiers, they stopped beating Paul. The commander came up and arrested him and ordered him to be bound with two chains. Then he asked who he was and what he had done. Some in the crowd shouted one thing and some another, and since the commander could not get at the truth because of the uproar, he ordered that Paul be taken into the barracks. (Acts 21:30–34 NIV)

Falling into Faith

    Clearly, this became a very tense and volatile situation. Yet, in the midst of the chaos, Paul made a request. He asked for permission to speak, and the commander agreed. Paul began testifying and preaching, which eventually caused another uproar. Just when he was about to receive another beating, Paul said something extremely important: "Is it legal for you to flog a Roman citizen who hasn't even been found guilty?" (Acts 22:25 NIV).

    According to Roman law, Roman citizens were assured exclusion from all degrading forms of punishment. When Paul asked this question, the centurion went to the commander and reported it. The commander came back to Paul and asked him if he truly was a Roman citizen. Paul said *yes*, and then the commander became alarmed because he realized he put Paul (a Roman citizen) in chains. Not good.

    Between chapters 23 and 26, interesting and powerful things happened. Once again, let me encourage you to take time and read the adventures of Paul and the people he witnessed to everywhere he went. The Lord stayed by his side faithfully working things out, and Paul never ceased spreading the news of the resurrection of Jesus Christ.

    As you read the account of Paul's journey, I believe my point will become clear. The inner struggles we often face are due to a persistence on doing things our own way instead of trusting God and keeping our focus on our mission.

    Paul continued to be imprisoned because of preaching and testifying, but in the midst of this desperate situation, God spoke to him concerning Rome. Ah, Rome, the place Paul knew *he must go*. "The following night the Lord stood near Paul and said, 'Take courage. As you have testified about me in Jerusalem, so you must also testify in Rome'" (Acts 23:11 NIV). Notice the word "must" appears again, but this time it's the Lord confirming the very desire that had been in Paul's heart for a long time.

    Fast-forward to chapter 27. Paul requested to plead his case before Caesar. As a Roman citizen, he had a right to make this request, and it is what finally gets him to Rome. He is handed over to a centurion named Julius, who belonged to the Imperial Regiment. They boarded a ship and set out for ports along the coast of the province of Asia. Destination—Rome.

Paul found favor with Julius, and the next day they landed at Sidon. Julius allowed Paul to go and see his friends so that they could provide for his needs. They soon went back out to sea but encountered hurricane-force winds and a raging storm. The journey turned into a terrifying experience as the ship took a violent beating from the storm. They ended up throwing the cargo overboard to lighten the ship as winds raged around them. Everyone had gone a long time without food, and there seemed to be no hope of being saved or surviving. God sent an angel to Paul with a message, so he rallied everyone together and began encouraging the terrified and weary men.

> But now I urge you to keep up your courage, because not one of you will be lost; only the ship will be destroyed. Last night an angel of the God whose I am and whom I serve stood beside me and said, "Do not be afraid, Paul. You must stand trial before Caesar; and God has graciously given you the lives of all who sail with you." So keep up your courage men, for I have faith in God that it will happen just as he told me. Nevertheless, we must run aground on some island. (Acts 27:22–26 NIV)

The ship eventually struck a sandbar and ran aground. It literally fell apart, causing some to have to swim ashore while others held on to planks and pieces of the ship. But just as Paul said, everyone was saved, and no one lost their lives. Once everyone landed safely on shore, they discovered they were on the island of Malta. Scriptures tell us the islanders were unusually kind to them. They even built a fire to welcome everyone because it was raining and cold. Then something happened.

> Paul gathered a pile of brushwood and, as he put it on the fire, a viper, driven out by the heat, fastened itself on his hand. When the islanders saw the snake hanging from his hand, they said to each other, "This man must be a murderer; for though he escaped from the sea, justice has not allowed him to live." But Paul shook the snake off into the fire and suffered no ill effects. The people

Falling into Faith

> expected him to swell up or suddenly fall dead, but after waiting a long time and seeing nothing unusual happen to him, they changed their minds and said he was a god. (Acts 28:3–6 NIV)

Right before their eyes, they witnessed a deadly snake attack. These islanders knew that death was imminent for Paul, but God showed up big-time, and something shocking happened. The viper that bit Paul should have killed him; instead, it opened an incredible door of opportunity for Paul to continue his mission in a powerful way.

Next, we will read how God revealed Himself to the people on the island of Malta through a painful, deadly snakebite and His servant Paul. This story still excites my spirit and ignites my faith every time I read it.

> There was an estate nearby that belonged to Publius, the chief official of the island. He welcomed us to his home and for three days entertained us hospitably. His father was sick in bed, suffering from fever and dysentery. *Paul went in to see him and, after prayer, placed his hands on him and healed him. When this happened, the rest of the sick on the island came and were cured.* They honored us in many ways and when we were ready to sail, they furnished us with the supplies we needed. (Acts 28:7–10; NIV emphasis added)

Years earlier, Paul felt he must go to Rome, but he encountered obstacle after obstacle and numerous detours. Thanks to one of those bumps in the road, miracles were performed, and an entire island experienced Jesus in a real and powerful way. All of this happened because Paul stayed obedient and faithful to the things of God in the face of every hardship, twist, and turn.

What I love about Paul was his ability to not wrestle and struggle against the unexpected; instead, he used every opportunity to spread the hope of Christ. Even if it meant enduring beatings, imprisonment, a terrifying hurricane in the middle of the sea, and being bitten by a poisonous snake. He knew God had everything under control, so he chose to stay focused on his mission to testify about Jesus everywhere he went.

There is no way of knowing what Paul was thinking, but as we read chapter after chapter and see the obstacles he faced and how he responded, I do not think he ever lost sight of the fact God was with him. Even though he endured beatings and prison, Paul never stopped preaching and testifying, persuading and praying. That is what I call perseverance and total commitment.

What about Rome? Did he ever make it there? Yes. When he arrived, he continued preaching the gospel and persuading men to believe in Jesus. So here are a few questions to meditate on:

1. As you are traveling the road to your dreams, how do you respond to the detours, turns, and bumps along the journey?
2. Are you so intent on the end results you fail to see the opportunities the Father is giving you along the way?

This is my prayer and heart's desire, to walk this journey hand in hand with God. I do not want to waste one opportunity of spreading the love of Jesus to those who are hurting and in need due to tunnel vision. My focus cannot remain on *I*. Where *I* think *I* should be or what *I* think *I* should be doing. We must get the *I* out of the way so Jesus can fully take control of the where, when, who, and how.

May we boldly shake off the things that try to hinder and destroy, and learn not to struggle when life makes an unexpected turn. May our love walk be resolute between God and humankind—always reaching outward, not self-centeredly inward.

When I find myself struggling, I pray God lovingly reminds me to keep my eyes and heart on the calling He has placed in my life. Only then will I reach my full potential in Jesus Christ my Savior and truly rest in God without the constant inner struggle.

Next is the final chapter of *Falling into Faith: A Journey to Freedom* but not of my life. Thankfully, God still has work for me to do. Come with me as I share the new phase of our journey. Who knows? Maybe we will meet again on another book adventure.

CHAPTER 26

BABY, I WANT A MOUNTAIN

The end of 2006, Bob and I officially left Youth With a Mission (YWAM) and made Colorado Springs home for the next four years. That same year, I accepted a book contract to write my autobiography. This book is the new, revised version of the original manuscript due to the previous publisher closing in 2016. It also contains new material from the pages of my life. The opportunity WestBow Press, a division of Thomas Nelson and Zondervan, offered me is an amazing path to continue my mission and call to ministry.

While in Colorado Springs, Bob and I both ended up working for colleges in the area. Bob taught heating and air-conditioning at one college, and I worked as a high school admissions and community outreach consultant for another college. Through these positions, God used us to encourage others and share the message of hope. He also continued adding to our growing family. Our house was and is a revolving door with our many God-given kids and grandkids.

During this time, my father's health began declining. Dad was diagnosed with Parkinson's and advanced heart disease. Bob and I arranged for him to live with us during his weakest times or when any type of medical procedure proved necessary. He loved his home in the Florida Panhandle, (aka Florabama or Lower Alabama), so when he regained strength, he always wanted to return for a few months. We put a lot of miles on our cars and airfare for a number of years, but we were thankful to be there for Dad and work it out logistically on his behalf.

When he made return trips to Florida, I called every morning to hear his voice and make sure he sounded okay. Then I called again in the evening to say, "Goodnight, Daddy. I love you." When Dad went back home, I worried about him being there alone. My cousin Gloria was always willing to check on him and make sure he had everything he needed. She brought food and took on the daughter role so he could stay home as long as possible. Dad loved Colorado, but it wasn't home. My daddy was a true southern-born, southern-bred gentleman.

Work kept me busy. A usual week consisted of sixty-plus hours, but I loved it. My job put me in high schools throughout all the counties in our area. I spoke to classes and enjoyed the opportunity to share my story of survival from a blood disease and cancer, along with tidbits from our time in missions. The privilege of encouraging these young people to do something of value with their lives through education became a passion. They were very special to me. So many of them were from backgrounds filled with rejection. They felt as though adults just didn't care. These young people became my new mission field. The ones who attended our college were like my babies. You wouldn't believe how many alarm clocks I purchased just to keep these kids in school.

I developed and facilitated a program in our city for at-risk youth, and it opened doors to share my story, love on kids, and offer hope and a future to some of the toughest young people you could ever imagine. To my surprise, I received a commendation from the governor because of the program. I also volunteered time as a counselor and mentor with a women's program. These precious women suffered abuse and so much more, often finding themselves incarcerated or on probation. On top of all that, I continued to minister in churches, women's seminars, and retreats. Whew! Saying I stayed busy is an understatement.

God transformed my life in every way and He longs to do the same for all who are willing to step out in faith and dare to believe. If you truly want a blessed life and desire healing from the wounds and hurts you have experienced, it is important to understand where to begin. Start with seeking help as you process through the pain and rejection you have suffered. When we don't deal with these issues, the results can be devastating. To be whole and healthy, we must make a purposeful decision to face the hurt and seek the Lord for healing and restoration.

Admitting you need help, calling out to God for wisdom, and finding a faith-based counselor or pastor to support and direct you in the process are the first steps. If you don't, it doesn't matter how successful you become, the disease-ridden baggage still remains. Unresolved pain and rejection suffocates and destroys relationships and anything good in your life.

As Bob and I settled into our jobs and made Colorado Springs home, we once again began working with the young people at our church. Participating and contributing in their spiritual journey filled our hearts with joy. When people tell me they don't have time to volunteer or mentor, it is difficult for me to keep my tongue in check. I'm not superwoman, but if I can take care of an ailing parent, work full-time, volunteer, and mentor, along with all the God-given family we've been blessed with … you too can volunteer some time doing something for someone else.

We reap what we sow. If you are not sowing into the lives of others, your harvest will be sparse. Personally speaking, I don't want to enter heaven empty-handed or with very little to offer. Although our salvation is not based on works, living a mediocre, selfish, or complacent life is no way to say *thank you* to the Lord of lords, King of kings, Alpha and Omega, and the great I Am. After all, because of Christ, I am saved, healed, restored, forgiven, and a daughter of the Most High God.

With busy, crazy schedules, our home in Colorado Springs felt like a sanctuary. Located near Garden of the Gods, it graced a picturesque view of Pikes Peak. Our neighbors were very curious about our large, unusual family. They couldn't believe how many young people came in and out. Several of them finally asked, "Just how many kids do you have?" We always chuckled and said, "More than you can imagine or would believe." To date, we normally enjoy three Thanksgivings and three Christmases so that we can juggle all the kids. God blessed us beyond our wildest dreams and fulfilled His promise to me big-time.

Bob's daughter Traci graduated from Auburn in nursing with honors. He was one proud daddy. She met a wonderful young man named Jeremy and fell in love. They are now married and living in Mobile, Alabama.

Both of them work in the medical field. We are blessed by the amazing adults they are and continue to be. Our hearts are full.

Like the movie *What about Bob?* you may be asking, "Hey, Donna, what about Bob?" God opened an incredible door of opportunity for him. Because of his position as an instructor with a local college and his skill set, some people from the government discovered his talents and offered him a position through a government agency. After a seriously stringent hiring process, which included a background check on both of us, physical and psychological testing for Bob, (along with a few other things), he began his new career. Bob has traveled to over thirty countries using his skills in embassies and consulates. It's been a wild and wonderful but sometimes difficult ride.

Bob's job eventually moved us to the DC Metro Area in Virginia, and I accepted a position as a career counselor at a local university. We were not fans of the area, although we made many wonderful friends. We loved and missed Colorado and prayed for God to eventually get us back there. I also volunteered with a ministry in Manassas called House of Mercy. Many immigrants participated in a program through this organization, and I assisted with resumes, job-search strategies, and job interview techniques and etiquette. When you place your life in God's hands, you never know where He'll take you and the precious souls He will bring your way.

Mentoring and volunteering continues to be a passion for me. We should all have someone in our lives we are speaking into as well as someone we are accountable to. Volunteering your time weekly (or monthly) with an organization you feel a passion for is an absolute key to a positive, uplifting, and rewarding life. Feeling a strong urgency to encourage others to give of themselves with volunteering and mentoring, I developed a program for schools and churches. It was an honor to present and facilitate a women's mentoring program to our church in Fairfax, Virginia. The friendships I developed during this time remain an important part of my life.

Through the years, my parents instilled and emulated servanthood and discipleship through volunteering and mentoring in our little community. Dad bought groceries every week for people who were poor and unable to provide for their loved ones. It didn't matter if they went to our church or not. The color of their skin or their beliefs were not even considered. All that mattered to Dad was lending a helping hand and showing them the love of God. When physically able, I often accompanied him and helped deliver food. It was beautiful watching Dad in action as he served the Lord through acts of kindness.

Along with his normal pastoral duties, Dad felt drawn to young adults, particularly our military men and women. Young military couples showed up on our doorstep all hours of the night because of marital spats and some all-out fights. Sometimes the young ladies came to the house still in their robe with curlers in their hair. Mama and I sat in the bedroom together giggling like we were teenagers at a slumber party, while Daddy tried calming the raging war happening in our living room. We didn't mean any disrespect; it was just such a crazy life we lived. Those moments (and there were many) gave me quite an interesting education on marriage. Mom often shared funny stories of her and Dad's little disagreements through the years. Of course, we kids saw a few of them firsthand.

Mom also spoke into the lives of many young adults. They loved her no-nonsense approach to life. This little 4'10", ninety-pound woman was full of spunk and didn't hold back about anything; however, she didn't normally offer up an opinion unless you asked for it. Then, watch out! Coming home from church on Sundays, Daddy often said, "Mary, maybe they will let me stay here one more week." Mama would throw her head back and laugh, then inform Dad, "Edward, they asked for my opinion, and they got it." These conversations usually ended with Daddy looking over at Mama and winking.

I miss those special moments of seeing the love my parents shared. Something beautiful yet unspoken happened throughout their marriage, as we witnessed a man who loved his wife and did not try to change her. They kept one another in check but not with a condescending or ruler mentality. Even when things were tense due to disagreements, they shared an obvious admiration and respect. Through it all, they remained faithful to living a life of service. Even when Mother became so sick with her kidneys she was confined to the bed for days at a time, it wasn't unusual to come home from school or work and see someone sitting by the bed while Mom encouraged and prayed for them. And one more important thing: she always left them laughing.

I've been given a beautiful and rich heritage, which I appreciate. My role in Dad's life changed as his health continued to decline. Shortly after our move to Virginia is when we received news Dad suffered a massive heart attack. Bob and I agreed I should quit my job and head south to take care of Daddy. Although I'm a grown woman, he will always by my daddy, and Bob knew he needed me.

Upon my arrival, doctors gave us the grim news. They could not do anything more for Dad without risking his life, so they suggested hospice. At this time, I did not know a lot about hospice, but I quickly learned. I'm in hospice today because of seeing the amazing calling and dedication Dad's care team provided for him and our family.

Bob received a call from his office with orders to several different embassies due to mechanical problems needing his attention. He would be gone three weeks, return for a week, and leave again for three more weeks. Bob asked if I wanted him to stay, but things were in place with hospice, so it really wasn't necessary. The house bustled about with the hospice care team and family almost every day. My brother came and stayed often, and my sister called to check in. Her husband was very ill, and they lived in Tennessee at the time. The grandkids and great-grandkids came for visits, and Daddy could not have been happier. Many family members lived nearby, and they visited with Dad when he felt up to it.

There were days he simply did not want company and made it very clear to me: "No visitors today, baby." I honored Dad's wishes, even though many did not understand. During this time, my cousin Gloria lovingly stood by my side offering prayer and encouragement. Daddy loved Gloria like a daughter and confided in her often through the years. He also expressed his wishes to her so that there would be no confusion about what he did and didn't want when his body began its decline. He knew the family dynamics and felt Gloria would give me some much-needed support.

In the South, you drop in whenever the spirit moves, and it's just unacceptable not to appreciate this act of kindness. In this case, Dad called the shots, and I complied with his wishes. If people didn't understand, I couldn't help it. I'm truly my mother's daughter. Bob called daily and also encouraged me to stand firm and honor Daddy's wishes. After all, this was about Dad and what he wanted—good, bad, or indifferent.

Parkinson's by itself is a difficult journey; combined with end-stage heart disease, and you are dealing with many devastating complications. Daddy was a proud man and never wanted people to see him when he wasn't in his right mind or could no longer control his bodily functions. It truly horrified him. When Dad lived with us, Bob heard him instruct me many times about how he wanted the situation handled if those things happened. He repeated it often, always making me promise to honor his wishes. I assured him I would.

Stressed out and not ready to lose Dad, along with mounting family dynamics going haywire, my cousin Gloria kept me as sane as possible. Believe me, she had her hands full. She knows me all too well. Not surprising, we are very much alike.

December arrived, and Dad declined even more. Before long, he couldn't walk, but that didn't stop him from trying. Regardless of how much I begged him not to, his brain could no longer process a rational thought. Every morning when my little dog, BJ, and I went in his room to check on him (up until he could no longer communicate), he made this statement, "Well, baby, looks like I didn't get my promotion last night." I usually fussed and replied, "Daddy, you ain't going to heaven until God says its time, and I ain't ready to lose you." In return, he always gave me a crooked little smile and said, "I love you a little bit." To this day, I miss hearing those words. It was his sweet way of saying, "I love you very much."

My crazy fur baby decided to become even more neurotic during this time. BJ is a Pomapoo, a Poodle and Pomeranian mix. He looks all Pom (only a bit taller) and is a wee bit wacky. But then, he is my dog. Daddy was living with us in Colorado Springs when we rescued BJ as a puppy. As far as they were concerned, they belonged to one another. When Dad's health was better and he made his trips back to Florida, BJ missed him terribly. Every morning he raced down the stairs to Dad's room, hoping to see him. With his tail hanging low, he returned upstairs looking at me with a sad, pitiful face. He was always one happy dog when Dad returned to us. Now, we were in Florida watching Dad rapidly decline. BJ became stressed and began licking the fur off his front legs until they bled. In tears, I took him to a nearby country vet. She looked at me and with a gravelly voice asked, "What's changed in this dawg's life?" (Southerners know how to get right the point with a unique style and grammar). In a puddle of tears, I shared the latest events of Dad's health crisis. With a straight face, she firmly stated, "I hate to tell you this, but you have a neurotic, OCD breed who is grievin' and sensin' your stress. Once they start a behavior like this, it'll continue for the rest of their life. He's gonna need some medicine." I didn't want BJ drugged up, but I agreed for the time being.

When Bob called that night, in tears I told him about BJ's crazy, neurotic behavior. Keep in mind my man is a thinker and very logical. He was quiet for a moment and then he said, "Baby, I bet if you make some kind of leggings for BJ, he won't take them off, and it will protect his legs." It is good to have a voice of reason that brings wisdom into your life when things are spiraling out of control. Although BJ is crazy, he is good-natured and gentle. It was worth a try, so I went into action trying to figure out how to make leggings for my sweet fur baby.

When my brother came to help me with Dad, I headed to the Dollar Tree and bought little kid footies. By hand, I cut and sewed leggings for my dog. Even today, if I don't keep them on BJ and he gets the least bit nervous, he'll find a spot to hide away and lick. With these leggings, he just licks them but never bites the material or takes them off. Problem solved, kind of...He still licks.

Right before Daddy stopped being able to communicate with us, I walked into his room and saw absolute panic in his eyes. I ran to him, asking, "Is everything okay, Daddy?"

He pushed himself up to a sitting position, looked me in the eyes, and said, "Baby, when I say I love you a little bit, you know I'm teasing, don't you? Do you know how much I love and appreciate all you and Bob have done for me? Do you have any idea how proud I am of you?"

Reaching down, I gave Daddy a great big hug. With tears streaming down my face, I said, "Don't worry, Daddy. I've always known. And by the way, I love you a little bit too." We both smiled at one another, knowing our time together on earth was quickly fading away.

Falling into Faith

As I write this, I can't help but cry. These are the sacred moments in life that are so tender and precious. The ones you hold onto because they lovingly sustain you when grief comes in like an uninvited intruder.

Within a matter of days, Dad became verbally nonsensical and mostly nonresponsive but never stopped struggling to get out of bed. The hospice team decided to place him in an inpatient unit. In my heart, I think Dad thought if he could stand up, then he would beat this.

Parkinson's has many ripple effects, and he soon began aspirating and choking when he tried to swallow. Heartbroken, I sat by his bed in a recliner night after night, praying and crying. I watched and listened as Dad talked to Mother and others in the family who had journeyed on to heaven. Sometimes his arms went up as if he was worshiping the Lord, but he also displayed physical agitation. Every family has their issues, and I believe Dad didn't want to leave this earth until he knew all his kids were okay.

Late one morning, the nurse convinced me to go home and get some sleep in a real bed where I could stretch out. Exhausted and unable to muster up the strength to argue, I agreed. Driving back to the house, my mind raced with thoughts of Dad. I prayed God would comfort him and not let him feel alone. Arriving at the house, I barely made it to the bed, and quickly fell into a deep sleep. What felt like only moments had actually been several hours when I sat straight up in bed with a sense of extreme urgency. Calling hospice, I inquired about Dad, and the nurse said he was peaceful and resting. She told me not to worry and get some more sleep, promising to call if there was a change. Something didn't feel right. Unable to shake the uneasy feeling, I changed clothes and headed back to the hospice unit.

When I arrived, Daddy appeared peaceful, but something seemed different about his breathing. Within fifteen minutes of my arrival, Dad received his long-awaited promotion to heaven, at 3:15 p.m. on December 19, 2011. It is impossible to appropriately express the depth of gratitude I felt for the urgency in my spirit to get back to Dad. All I can say is God truly is an amazing Father. To be with my sweet daddy as he took his last breath is something I both hated and loved. At least he did not leave this world without hearing me say one more time, "I love you, Daddy. Thank you for loving me." Throughout my entire life with all the hospital stays, surgeries, and painful procedures, Mom and Dad stayed faithfully and lovingly by my side. What an honor to be there for them in their final days on this earth.

Bob was literally about to board a plane in Chile and head back to the States when Dad received his heavenly promotion. God brought Bob home safe, and on December 22, 2011, after almost sixty years of faithful ministerial service to the Lord and eighty-five years on earth, we said our goodbyes and celebrated Dad's life. My sister and I once again kept a promise and sang together for the first time since we'd said goodbye to Mama seventeen years earlier. It felt good to hear that sweet sister harmony again. Once in a while, I get a text from Robbie with these words, "I love you a little bit." It is her way of keeping Dad's memory alive for us, and I cherish it.

Dad and Mom always made Christmas very special for us growing up, and the impact of his passing felt extremely painful with Christmas only a few days away. Bob and I soon packed up and headed back to Virginia. It is the first and only time in my life I did not have a Christmas tree or decorations adorning every corner of the house. I found it difficult to simply breathe.

Life soon returned to some kind of normalcy, although we continued praying for God to open a door for us to move back to Colorado. From the day we transferred to the DC area, I told Bob, "Baby, if your job ever offers you an opportunity to get us back to Colorado, don't call to ask what I think. Just say yes." Bob always gave me a reassuring smile and nodded in agreement. He too longed to return to our beautiful Colorado.

Sure enough, within two years of living on the East Coast, Bob received an offer to cover the Latin American embassies. His home base: Denver, Colorado. When he came home and told me, I replied, "Baby, I want a mountain."

He responded, "Well, sweetheart, I guess we better go house hunting and find you a mountain." The government gave us five days to fly to Denver and find a home. We drove out on Interstate 70 West, outside of the city but not too far, and found a perfect mountain with a house almost nine thousand feet in elevation with five acres of mountain

Falling into Faith

terrain. We still call it home today and are so thankful God directed us to our little piece of heaven on earth.

Since moving to the Denver area, I pursued a career in hospice. The combination of chaplain and therapist has proven helpful in my career as a hospice chaplain, bereavement counselor, therapist, speaker, and mentor. Gaining an understanding on how our minds and emotions process and react to life's challenges provides me with invaluable wisdom in helping others.

As I mentioned in previous chapters, I specialize in various forms of counseling: marriage and family, victims of sexual abuse, at-risk youth, bereavement, music and puzzle therapy, along with cognitive behavioral therapy (specializing in seniors living with Dementia and Alzheimer's) and rational living therapy (RLT). I've also written therapeutic programs and provide support for caregivers.

If you know someone who is caring for a friend or loved one, extend a hand of love and support. It is a difficult journey, and no one should feel alone as they navigate the often cruel and difficult twist and turns the road takes them down.

God continues to open ministry opportunities for me to speak, share some comedy relief with stories from my crazy life, and provide music for many beautiful seniors and their caregivers, as they walk through the difficulty associated with Dementia and Alzheimer's. Music truly brings joy and feeds the soul. It is an honor to extend love, hope, and encouragement to others as they face life's challenges.

Life is stressful, so it is important to refresh your mind, body, and spirit. For me, it's hanging out with Bob, four-wheeling, music, spending time with friends, and enjoying our incredibly large family God has blessed us with. I also adore my four-legged, neurotic fur baby, BJ (Baby Jr).

When I ride around the mountain and see the beauty God has bestowed upon us, a calmness comes over me, and the song "It Is Well with My Soul" springs up like a cleansing rain flowing through every cell of my being.

> "See how very much our Father loves us, for He calls us
> his children, and that is what we are." (1 John 3:1 NLT)

I pray you make a choice today to fall into a trust relationship with Jesus Christ. Step out in faith and become the man or woman He longs for you to be—one who is "lacking no good thing." Always remember, nothing is impossible with Father God. He alone has the power to restore the ashes and ruins of any life, making it something of beauty, value, and worth.

CONCLUSION

If you are in need of a miracle but not sure where to begin, start by being honest and getting real with Jesus about your life. Allow Him to speak to your heart, and with purpose, begin walking in obedience according to the Word of God. Ask the Holy Spirit to search your heart for any hindrances to your prayers. Repent of any sin, doubt, or bitterness you may be harboring in your heart. Regardless of how you feel or your circumstances, speak the truth of God's Word to your situation.

Find scriptures relating to your situation and make them personal. Boldly speak them out with the authority of Jesus Christ (for example, "By His stripes, I (insert your name) am healed"). Refuse to allow condemnation to sabotage your faith and resist the enemy by drawing near to God.

Maintain a healthy balance in your life. Guard what goes into your mind, spirit, and body. Great wisdom on how to apply these principles can be found by reading and studying the book of Proverbs. Do not allow your eyes to remain focused on the circumstances. Purpose to fix your eyes on God's incredible power, infinite wisdom, and unfailing mercy.

After you have done this, wait on God. Stay the course and continue walking in obedience, with the heart of a servant. Strive for a joyful spirit and remember, "Do not grieve, for the joy of the LORD is your strength" (Nehemiah 8:10 NIV). Take a moment and meditate on the following scriptures.

> But He has said to me, "My grace is sufficient for you [My lovingkindness and My mercy are more than enough—always available—regardless of the situation]; for [My]

power is being perfected [and is completed and shows itself most effectively] in [your] weakness." Therefore, I will all the more gladly boast in my weaknesses, so that the power of Christ [may completely enfold me and] may dwell in me." (2 Corinthians 12:9 AMP)

My son, attend to My words; incline thine ear unto My sayings. Let them not Depart from thine eyes; keep them in the midst of thine heart. For they are life unto those that find them, and health to all their flesh. (Proverbs 4:20–22 KJV)

If you do not know Jesus as your personal Savior, now is the time to take a leap of faith. You won't regret it, for He truly is a powerful, loving, and merciful Father. To receive this hope and secure your place for eternity in heaven, pray the simple yet powerful sinner's prayer at the end of this chapter.

Before praying, it is important to have an understanding of what you are doing. This prayer is only effective when a person knows, understands, and believes he or she is a sinner in need of salvation. The Bible clearly tells us we are all sinners: "As it is written, 'There is none righteous, no, not one'" (Romans 3:10 KJV). Because of our sins, we deserve eternal punishment (Matthew 25:46). The sinner's prayer is a simple but profound request for mercy and grace, instead of judgment and wrath (Titus 3:5–7).

The next aspect of a sinner's prayer is to confess that Jesus Christ is the Son of God (2 Corinthians 5:21). Jesus paid the ultimate sacrifice, taking the punishment we deserved by offering Himself and dying on the cross for our sins. On the third day, He victoriously rose from the dead, conquering death. "I am the Living One; I was dead, and now look, I am alive for ever and ever. And I hold the keys of death and Hades" (Revelation 1:18 NIV). Through this sacrificial and loving act of mercy, we can receive forgiveness for our sins with the promise of eternal life in heaven.

If we receive these truths we can be saved, but it is only by grace and faith, "For it is by grace you have been saved, through faith—and this not from yourselves, it is the gift of God" (Ephesians 2:8 NIV).

Once you have prayed the prayer of salvation, life is not going to turn suddenly blissful, without difficulty and frustration; however, you are now a child of the Most High God. He is your Father. When He is your Lord and Savior and His Word is applied to your life, blessings will follow. You will enjoy the benefits of peace, joy, love, and so much more—even when the storms rage around you.

SINNER'S PRAYER OF SALVATION

Father God, I know I am a sinner. I confess with my mouth that I believe in Jesus Christ. I believe He shed His blood on the cross, and died for my sins. Forgive me and fill me with Your Holy Spirit. I accept Jesus Christ as the Lord and Savior of my life. Today, I turn my life over to You. Thank You for this gift of salvation. Help me to lead a life that is pleasing to You. In Jesus name I pray. Amen.

CONGRATULATIONS AND WELCOME TO THE FAMILY OF GOD

Your greatest weapon against the enemy is to saturate yourself with the Word of God and by faith choose to apply what you learn. As you fall into your own trust relationship with God, your life will be a testimony of His power and goodness to all who see and hear. Get ready for a thrill and enjoy the freedom that comes from the **F**
        A
        L
        L

That's all, folks ... for now.

It's time to go have some fun.

SUGGESTED READING

Praying the Scriptures
Judson Cornwall—Charisma House

God's Plan for Man
Rev. Finis Jennings Dake—Dake Bible Sales, Inc.

Beyond the Soiled Curtain
David and Beth Grant—Paperback Swap

Courageous Compassion: Confronting Social Injustice God's Way
Dr. Beth Grant—Gospel Publishing

Imprisoned in Iran
A Beautiful Way
Dan Baumann—YWAM Publishing

Tomorrow You Die
Reona Joly—YWAM Publishing

Spiritual Warfare
Dean Sherman—YWAM Publishing

Battlefield of the Mind: Winning the Battle in Your Mind
Joyce Meyer—Joyce Meyer Trade

The Power of a New Identity
Dan Sneed—Sovereign World, Ltd.

Exposing the Lie: How to Reverse the Work of the Enemy in Your Life
Dan Sneed—Chosen Books

Forever Ruined for the Ordinary
Joy Dawson—YWAM Publishing

Stick a Geranium in Your Hat and Be Happy
Splashes of Joy in the Cesspool of Life
Barbara Johnson—Thomas Nelson/W Publishing

The Tongue—A Creative Force
Charles Capps—Harrison House